The Soldier-Writer, the Expatriate, and Cold War Modernism in Taiwan

The Soldier-Writer, the Expatriate, and Cold War Modernism in Taiwan

Freedom in the Trenches

Li-Chun Hsiao

LEXINGTON BOOKS
Lanham • Boulder • New York • London

Published by Lexington Books
An imprint of The Rowman & Littlefield Publishing Group, Inc.
4501 Forbes Boulevard, Suite 200, Lanham, Maryland 20706
www.rowman.com

86-90 Paul Street, London EC2A 4NE

Copyright © 2022 by The Rowman & Littlefield Publishing Group, Inc.

All rights reserved. No part of this book may be reproduced in any form or by any electronic or mechanical means, including information storage and retrieval systems, without written permission from the publisher, except by a reviewer who may quote passages in a review.

British Library Cataloguing in Publication Information Available

Library of Congress Cataloging-in-Publication Data

Names: Hsiao, Li-Chun, author.
Title: The soldier-writer, the expatriate, and Cold War modernism in Taiwan : freedom in the trenches / Li-Chun Hsiao.
Description: Lanham : Lexington Books, [2022] | Includes bibliographical references and index.
Identifiers: LCCN 2022024601 (print) | LCCN 2022024602 (ebook) | ISBN 9781498569095 (cloth) | ISBN 9781498569118 (paper) | ISBN 9781498569101 (ebook)
Subjects: LCSH: Soldiers' writings, Chinese--Taiwan--History and criticism. | Chinese poetry--Taiwan--History and criticism. | Exiles' writings, Chinese--Taiwan--History and criticism. | Chinese poetry--20th century--History and criticism. | Chinese poetry--Taiwan--American influences. | Chinese poetry--Taiwan--Political aspects. | Cold War in literature. | LCGFT: Literary criticism.
Classification: LCC PL2278.5.S65 H75 2022 (print) | LCC PL2278.5.S65 (ebook) | DDC 895.109/95129–dc23/eng/20220629
LC record available at https://lccn.loc.gov/2022024601
LC ebook record available at https://lccn.loc.gov/2022024602

In memory of my sister, Shu-jen Hsiao

Contents

Acknowledgments	ix
Preface	xi
Introduction	1
Chapter One: "Speech after Long Silence"	17
Chapter Two: A Double-edged Sword?	39
Chapter Three: Breaking Ground in Splendid Isolation	61
Chapter Four: Two States of One Peculiar Modernism	89
Chapter Five: At Home in Exile	121
Bibliography	151
Index	169
About the Author	175

Acknowledgments

During the course of writing of this book, I have been supported financially by a grant for book writing by the Ministry of Science and Technology of Taiwan and the Special Research Project (Tokutei Kadai) grant from Waseda University, Japan.

I have been intellectually indebted, in different stages of this book project, to my colleagues and friends who knew of my project on Cold War modernism and witnessed first-hand, too, the lasting impacts of the modernist paradigm in Taiwan but who, like me, branch out or straddle other specialties and fields in their careers: Shu-mei Shih and Yu-Fang Cho in the United States; my (now former) colleagues Chia-ling Mei, Hung-chiung Li and Liang-ya Liou at National Taiwan University; and Sun-chieh Liang, Chih-ming Wang, and Chun-san Wang in other academic institutions in Taiwan. I am grateful for the interdisciplinary setup and institutional flexibility at Waseda University, especially the timely support and encouragement from my colleagues Norimasa Morita and Adrian Pinnington. Special thanks to Greg Barnhisel for the valuable exchange of ideas at an MLA conference and his impressive account of the workings of the US Cold War machine in his book *Cold War Modernists*, which crucially informs and sheds light on some main arguments of this book. Hiromi Ochi and Mayumo Inoue generously shared their works on Japan's Cold War and ongoing entanglements with the US, and have broadened my horizons on related issues. Both of their writings on this front will be indispensable for me if my work on Cold War Taiwan is to expand and engage my current site of scholarly endeavors.

Over the years, I have benefited intellectually from my interlocutions with the following scholars, though the flashes of insights therein may not register directly in my book: Oscar Campomanes, Chun-yen Chen, Kuei-fen Chiu, Hsiao-hung Chang, Chun-mei Chuang, Woo-sung Kang, Satofumi Kawamura, Alex Taek-kwang Lee, Yu-ling Li, Jiann-guang Lin, Chaoyang Liao, Hsien-hao Liao, Ping-hui Liao, Kwai Cheung Lo, Nobutaka Otobe, Hsiu-chih Tsai, and Ming-tsang Yang. I would also like to express my gratitude to the editorial team at Lexington Books, especially the kindness, persistence, and patience of Holly Buchanan, Megan White, and Linda Kessler. Many thanks to my RAs Yin-shiuan Dai and Chi-wen Cheng for their assistance, in different phases of the project, in compiling the bibliographical list and romanization, and particularly to the efficiency and hard work by Ying-jie Chen, who did the final task of indexing in addition to many bibliography entries and romanization.

Last but not least, my writing of this book couldn't have been completed, or probably would suffer indefinite delays, if not for the love and support of my family, especially given the trying circumstances of the pandemic. We have evolved and grown together the past two years, and this book is dedicated to them.

Preface

When did modernism begin? The question is surprisingly challenging to answer, if we do not content ourselves with conventional wisdom and the inevitably simplified periodization of art and literary histories. It depends in part on the question of where it began and what one means by "modernism," a loaded term that invokes a range of artistic and literary practices, examples, representative figures and movements that, despite putative similarities, have nuanced or even distinct priorities and visions not only aesthetically but also politically and socially. For, in most accounts, literary modernity often dates back to Charles Baudelaire's pivotal rendition of and reflection on the new sensations oozed out of the urban streetscape of mid-19th century Paris—which plausibly ushers in a new perception of reality made possible only with the advent of the modern. Yet the term "modernism" itself was applied and popularized earlier in the Anglo-American literary world than in continental Europe, where Mallarme, Rimbaud, and the Symbolists sprang from the watershed marked by Baudelaire, preceding and to some extent paving the way for what have often been characterized as modernism's sudden "eruptions" in early 20th century. Then there was Virginia Woolf's (in)famous claim that "on or about December 1910 human character changed," signaling and testifying to the hitherto unparalleled flux permeating modern life.[1] Although declared not via the genre of manifesto, Woolf's sweeping and self-consciously arbitrary pronouncement, incidentally, was delivered in the same year—and to arguably equal effects—as another shocking landmark declaration—the first Manifesto of Surrealism in 1924, which in turn was preceded by the outrageous, ground-breaking Dada Manifesto in 1918. Indeed, as Janet Lyon points out in her book-length study of manifestoes, "the modernist period is characterized by the production of an unprecedented number of manifestoes."[2]

What can be gleaned from the historical review above appears to be more like a series of re-starts of modernism than a certain cut-off point coinciding with the radical break the manifestoes strive to bring to the fore. This also begs the question of what we make of the proclaimed new beginnings that did not prevent similar epoch-making and field-defining declarations in their wake, problematizing the "origin" of modernism. Of course, I am not suggesting here that there is no such thing as the originality of modernism, nor that it's futile or unproductive to identify a chronologically earliest date of modernist work or practice at a specific site—provided that a certain conception of "modernist" is agreed upon. Rather, it is the nuanced utopian impulses and their concomitant subjunctive and optative (as opposed to indicative and conditional) rhetorics, the rivalling space-clearing attempts at foregrounding a slate wiped clean, and, last but not least, the necessarily *contextualized* beginnings and iterations of modernism that I seek to highlight and examine by connecting the Cold War modernism in Taiwan with the historical "precedents" enumerated above.

In light of the historical hindsight with which we are blessed nowadays, Woolf's sweeping generalization of the change of human character—given a purview so preoccupied with Western Europe—is clearly untenable. Such a universalist vision of modernity as that which is destined to emanate from the West to the rest of the world underlies the baggage of the pasts shared by almost all the manifestations of works and practices subsumed under the name "modernism": some were within the range of, or felt entitled to the right of, competing for the claim to the authentically modernist and the new, while others, having resigned themselves to being latecomers, resolved to play the catchup game. The modernist movement in Cold war Taiwan falls under the latter category on account of its pursuit of literary modernity and its avowed attempts at *modernizing* Chinese literature, but there is a "catch" about the predecessors it sought to catch up with: Even though the manifesto*es* and schools of modernist literature in Taiwan—they're plural, as in the European antecedence—invoked Baudelaire and cited and translated works by high modernists like Eliot and Woolf, their efforts were not the first instance of modernization campaigns in literature and culture. The practitioners of modernist literature in postwar Taiwan certainly were keenly aware of the May Fourth Movement that broke out in Beijing in 1919. For more recent examples and more specific to modernist literature, Ji Xian, who drafted the 1956 manifesto on modernist poetry, was involved in a modernist magazine in China in the 1930s, and some younger modernists who also relocated from China to Taiwan after 1949 had known of this earlier iteration of modernism in China. Meanwhile, a much smaller number of modernist poets born in colonial Taiwan had heard of the fledging modernist poetry in 1930s Taiwan under Japanese rule.

In the end, the Nationalist government's Cold War policies of silencing the Japanese pasts of Taiwan swiftly rendered the memories of that nascent modernism oblivious before the lifting of martial law in 1987, while the banning of the works of many writers who did not side with the Nationalists during the Chinese Civil War resulted in the arbitrary and willful elisions of some parts of those histories in pre-1949 China. Interestingly, this appears to be one of the Cold War conditions that helped to wipe the slate clean for the re-start of modernism in a drastically different context in postwar Taiwan and in a distinct form that, as I argue and elaborate in this book, can only be characterized as Cold War modernism, rather than a reincarnation of prior modernist initiatives, even if the postwar modernists aspired to do so: Initially and briefly, Ji Xian was self-consciously leveraging his involvement in the 1930s modernist literature in China to attract younger followers in his push for revitalizing modernist poetry in Taiwan, but his campaigns were waged as if it began on a clean slate. Most importantly, his manifesto had to be partly couched in the rhetorics, grammar, and keywords of the manifesto of this era—the ubiquitous slogans of the Cold War resembling the formats, if not the spirits, of historically monumental manifestoes—grafting the precepts of modernist poetry to "anticommunism" and "patriotism," presumably to circumvent potential censorship.

In addressing the "problem of belatedness" of modernism (in Euro-America) that seemingly emerged in waves of movement, Tim Armstrong raised the question: "What cultural space was there to 'make it new' *again*?"[3] In response I venture to point to the space-clearing gesture and function of manifestoes, with its utopian vision and optative rhetoric redrawing the boundaries between *what is* and *what ought to be*, legitimizing the conflation between the two, or strategically obscuring one's arbitrariness in declaring what is in the status quo in order to clear a new space or render a clean slate. The latter, when enacted in good faith, can give rise to a new perception of reality that has been celebrated in much of canonical modernism—one that, however, cannot be infinitely stretched into all other spaces and times. With restrictions on multiple fronts and at different levels, it is significant that the Cold War context in Taiwan enabled parts of the space-clearing work exemplified by the modernist manifestoes, which could not have gathered enough momentum to spearhead a modernist movement if the participants simply rode with the anti-establishment penchants implicit in their textual practices and some of the pronouncements. I argue that it's the Cold War discontinuation or truncation of certain parts of the literary genealogy, the state's imposition of policies of a monolingualism (forcing most Taiwanese who couldn't speak mandarin Chinese to learn the language and excluding Japanese and Taiwanese in public occasions) and monolithic cultural injunctions, and the promotion of decontextualized and strategically selective importation of foreign ideas and literary and artistic trends that made Cold War modernism in Taiwan "new again." In prying open layers of limitation imposed by the authoritarian Nationalist regime and concocting some seclusive garden or trenches of literary freedom, Taiwan's Cold War modernists engendered and instantiated some measure of "new perception of reality." While being filtered through a necessarily skewed worldview, as it did not and could not twist free of the splendid isolation of the Cold War structure, this new perception nonetheless epitomizes at least a glimpse of, à la Jacques Rancière, the potential re-distributions of what is perceptible in a given temporal-spatial coordinate.[4]

NOTES

1. Virginia Woolf, *Mr. Bennett and Mrs. Brown* (London: Hogarth Press, 1924), 4.
2. Janet Lyon, *Manifestoes: Provocations of the Modern* (Ithaca, NY: Cornell University Press, 1989), 40.
3. Tim Armstrong, *Modernism: A Cultural History* (Cambridge: Polity Press, 2005), 35.
4. Jacques Rancière, *The Politics of Aesthetics: The Distribution of the Sensible*, trans. Gabriel Rockhill (London: Continuum, 2004).

Introduction

The Cold War era was fraught with profound paradoxes, especially when viewed from our historical hindsight: The world was splintered into two camps that conceived of themselves as the diametrical opposite of the other, with a dividing line that couldn't have been more clearly drawn. Yet each mirrored the other in terms of arms race, mass mobilization that can hardly be duplicated henceforth, the ideology of progress underpinning and driving the maintenance of this protracted standoff of global proportion, and other uncanny similarities that blurred the presumably fundamental measures of distinction between the binary terms: the US-sponsored authoritarian regimes, such as those in Taiwan and South Korea, which touted themselves as bulwarks of "freedom and democracy," fending off the communist invasion; the communist states that boldly featured the radically redefined term "Democratic" in their formal country names; the McCarthyist Big Brother overseeing Americans' freedom of speech and the wiretapped conversations that ended up taking down the leader of the "free world"; a union in Poland that represented the working class in too real a sense for the state, which supposedly held the worker in the highest regard but cracked down on Solidarity as resolutely as would its right-wing counterpart; the volatile nuclear weaponry on both sides that accompanied periods of relative stability of the world order; the omnipresent espionage activities that are the stuff of legend and blockbuster movies, etc. The last item on the preceding list, nonetheless, is taken more seriously in recent studies than many might have thought. As Greg Barnhisel points out, reports that the Central Intelligence Agency (CIA) played a covert role in funding an overseas group which promoted experimental, modernist art as representative of pro-Western—even American—values and exemplified a crucial part of the US Cold War imperatives (carried out by both government agencies and solicited or unsolicited aids from the private sector), also bring to the fore the relationship between modernism and the Cold War.[1]

Such a relationship becomes even more complicated or somewhat tenuous, and requires further efforts in unpacking the phenomena and connecting the dots when one moves beyond the particular example of abstract expressionism in the fine arts and into the realm of literary modernism during the Cold War, as Barnhisel observes in the chapters on modernist literature in his seminal book, *Cold War Modernists* (which, however, deals mainly with the reception and dissemination of American modernism in postwar Europe). Nonetheless, outside the "iron curtain," where modernist literature did enjoy improved popularity and increasingly canonical status, one cannot help but notice the ostensible incongruity, even contradictions, between the Cold War Zeitgeist, initiatives, and policies on the one hand and, on the other, the practices as well as the ideas of modernism, especially those pertaining to the widely accepted characteristics of modernism before the World Wars: conformity vs. individuality; artistic autonomy vs. agenda from without; the postwar moralist or bourgeois mainstream vs. the antiestablishment or anti-bourgeois orientations of modernism; cultural conservatism vs. modernist celebration of experimentation and innovation; the growing prevalence of popular culture and consumerism vs. the elitist modernist abhorring the market, etc. Such incongruity and contradictions appear to be even more poignant when the vanguards of the modernist cause happened to be soldiers by profession—which was the case in the development of modernist literature in postwar Taiwan. Echoing the "profound paradoxes" of the Cold War elaborated above, the seemingly incompatible and contradictory relationship between modernist poetry in postwar Taiwan and the phenomenon of a disproportional large number of soldier-writers as its practitioners and staunch advocates, which is what initially motivated the present study, can be extended to characterize the fraught relationship between the literary modernist movement in Taiwan and the Cold War milieu.

The paradoxes may not have been evident, or even perceptible, for most people in the Cold War era, or those who are still caught up in a Cold War mentality, since loosely conceived buzzwords like "freedom" could easily explain away what has usually been rendered as the demarcations of the two sides of the Cold War order. Nevertheless, one still has to explain why modernism, rather than other artistic and literary paradigms or practices, was mobilized to represent the "free world," as opposed to the other, and could achieve a certain degree of impact or popularity. Questions of this kind have been directly or indirectly addressed in Barnhisel's, Eric Bennett's, and Roland Végső's recent book-length studies of Cold War literary culture. A handful of academic publications on postwar modernism in Taiwan by Taiwanese scholars in recent years also tackle related issues,[2] but this book will demonstrate that it nonetheless makes notable contributions to this topic and the fields involved, in addition to and apart from the existent scholarship.

Like the paradoxical hallmarks of the Cold War era, the aforementioned fraught relationship in the Taiwanese case cannot be critically understood without taking into consideration the Cold War contexts consisting of a constellation of forces that are external as well as intrinsic to the literary and the cultural. Nor can it be fully elucidated by recourse to the explanatory model based on Euro-American modernism during the Cold War years alone. How one can more adequately account for the paradoxes and explore such a relationship in more depth is the principal task of this book.

IN THE BEGINNING THERE WAS NOTHING?

In retrospect, what may strike an outsider or a reader unfamiliar with the Cold War setting as surprising or even perplexing is the phenomenon that the rise of the modernist movement in Taiwan has long been perceived and received by many in Taiwan as a brand-new beginning marked by discontinuity and groundbreaking endeavors. Such a perception and characterization of modernism has its reasons, which have often been attributed to the widely acknowledged characteristics of modernism: a drastic break with tradition, the valorization of the new, the unremitting pursuit of formal experimentation, the vanguard character of the modernist, etc. However, this image of modernism tends to eclipse the historical fact that modernist movements, in variant forms, took place in both China and Taiwan under Japanese colonial rule in the early decades of the twentieth century. I argue that, aside from the familiar mantras of modernism, the rendition and impression of a slate wiped clean wouldn't have been possible, or at least wouldn't have its long-lasting effects, if not for the radical changes in almost every facet of Taiwanese society in the first few postwar years that were brought about by the chaotic shake-ups in Taiwan's political system, economy, and demographic structure, which resulted from the following: the devastating effects of World War II itself; the civil war in China, the "retreat" of the Nationalist government to Taiwan after its defeat at the hands of the Chinese Communists; the mass migration of people (around two million) from mainland China who relocated along with the Nationalists to Taiwan; the spontaneous rioting over the rampant inflation, corruption, and administrative ineptitude after the Nationalist takeover of Taiwan; the bloody squelching of protests and the ruthless purging in its immediate aftermath; the silencing of virtually all opposition under martial law; and, last but not least, the opportunist literary establishment that tolerated and appropriated modernist discourse, astutely redirecting its narrative to align with the official ideology.

Interestingly enough, the critical or scholarly discourse on Taiwanese literary modernism had to start from scratch, as it were, even after three decades of creative outputs of modernist writings. As Sung-sheng Yvonne Chang observes in her 1993 book, *Modernism and the Nativist Resistance*, studies of Taiwanese modernist writers hitherto had been "particularly scanty" and, when available, "deeply factional."[3] Chang's book has filled a big gap in available research on Taiwanese modernism and has been instrumental for the present study, but, in my opinion, scholars today still have to begin from somewhere not far from ground zero, especially if one wishes to probe into the Cold War contexts pertaining to this modernism. Furthermore, Chang's important book also appears to follow the conventional wisdom, shared by critics in much of the nonacademic discourse, and presents the founding of the legendary literary magazine *Modern Literature* (*Xiandaiwenxue*) in 1960 as the single inaugurating event of literary modernism in Taiwan,[4] which certainly has its merit. Nevertheless, it again obscures the previous waves of modernism in Taiwan and China, seeming to examine this particular modernism in a vacuum that is concomitant with the ambience of isolation in Cold War Taiwan without critically reflecting on such isolation. Even if one momentarily disregards the prewar modernist movements, I argue that we still need to take into account an earlier moment in postwar Taiwan that laid the groundwork for the celebrated event mentioned above, and that had something to do with the soldier-writer phenomenon, as I shall illustrate in my book.

The point of departure of this book is to amend the scant critical attention (in modernism studies as well as Taiwan literature studies) paid to the peculiar emergence of two successive waves of antiestablishment literary movement in the name of modernism in postwar Taiwan, which not only became representatives of establishment literature themselves but also were enabled—at least partly—by different state-sanctioned agencies undergirding the literary establishment between the 1950s and early 1970s. To be sure, the modernist movement in question has been studied at length, mostly by scholars specializing in Taiwanese or Chinese literature, yet few highlight and critically reflect on the antiestablishment character, sentiment, and practices in the earlier phases of these movements and the subsequent co-option of many of these modernist writers by the various forms of establishment they sought to challenge or do without. Nor have there been sufficient scholarly accounts of the movement that fully engage the Cold War context(s) in which this particular modernism was deeply implicated, and to which the writers' words and deeds testified.

As Barnhisel argues, the waning of the antiestablishment image of modernist literature (and modernist art in general) in the public's perception and its eventual entry into the mainstream culture bears witness to the constellation of forces particular to the Cold War era that institutionalized, reoriented, and to some extent redefined modernism. The "rhetorical reframing that capitalized on the conjunctions of government, business, and elite cultural institutions" and undergirded what Barnhisel calls Cold War modernism had larger ramifications and broader reach, in accordance with the superpower status of the United States and Cold War geopolitical partitions, than his book investigates.[5] It is one of the major arguments of this book that the nexus of the cultural, military, political, and economic specific to the East Asian context during the early years of the Cold War gave rise to "the culture of US aids" in Taiwan (and nuanced versions of it in other US allies in the region), which in turn was appropriated, attuned, and utilized to propel the peculiar case of the local modernist movement at that juncture in history. Based on Barnhisel's work and with reference to the East Asian Cold War context, this book seeks to examine the complicated ways in which literary modernism in Taiwan in the postwar years was inflected and (re)framed by the Cold War cultural politics not only spearheaded by the United States but also reinforced—and to a limited extent, diversified—by its regional allies, such as Japan, Korea, and Taiwan. In addition to its readings of a body of representative texts by the Taiwanese creative writers associated with the aforementioned movement, this book's attentiveness to the contextual forces will also shed light on the relationship between the emergence of literary modernism and the subsequent institutionalization of the studies of American literature and culture in the academe in the ensuing years.

One of the significant contributions this book would make to the existing scholarship on related fields is its foregrounding of the "second coming" nature of this Cold War modernism in Taiwan. This does not only mean that the modernist movement in question was modeled after and partly enabled by postwar American modernism, and thus was second to and derivative of its apparent source of inspiration. More importantly, this modernist movement was not the first moment of eruption, as the Euro-American predecessors tended to claim in their relentless pursuit and branding of the new, since the first wave of modernism had occurred in colonial Taiwan as well as in China earlier in the century. I argue that what appeared to be, and was hailed to be, a "genesis" of new literature, together with the subsequent evolution of modernist movement in Taiwan, was made possible only through the "splendid isolation" within the Cold War world order. By means of digging up and sorting through a matrix of residues and traces of previous instances of modernism, my book, however, does not simply conclude with the characterization of this Cold War modernism as the reemergence or return of an earlier modernist moment. Rather, reexamining the theoretical underpinnings of modernism, I will probe into the much glorified "clean slate to begin anew" claim—the default mode of operation of this and other brands of modernism—and tease out the irreducibly hybrid character and unwittingly traditionalist undercurrent of postwar modernism in Taiwan. Although attributing its groundbreaking gesture and literary outputs to the "splendid isolation" of the Cold War contexts, I do not intend to belittle or dismiss the creativity and productivity of this particular modernism. In fact, my book proposes that its creativity is unique, unmistakable, and remarkable precisely because the Cold War modernist literature in Taiwan was indebted to such isolation and ubiquitous constraints on many fronts.

Furthermore, since this book focuses, among other topics, on the literary modernism in Cold War Taiwan, it is necessary to introduce to the readership two quintessential chapters of this modernism's institutional history that are inextricable from the history of the Department of Foreign Languages and Literatures, National Taiwan University (*Taida waiwenxi*), which for a time also reshaped, respectively, the literary scene and the discipline of *waiwenxi* in Taiwan academia: first, the founding of the influential literary magazine *Modern Literature* (*Xiandaiwenxue*) by a group of undergraduates in the department at the time who nonetheless pioneered in creating and advocating modernist literature and have now become literary luminaries themselves; second, the period of "reform" in curricula and the approaches to literary studies that were modeled upon American New Criticism, promoted by a succession of department heads, and ushered in the institutionalization of *waiwenxi* (not just the department at *Taida*) as a discipline. The introduction and reexamination of the aforementioned history of *Taida waiwenxi* would also serve as an exemplary case of negotiating a precarious local agency under the tutelage of the US "soft power" during the Cold War era, just as the Japanese experience of disseminating and institutionalizing US-brokered modernist literature and ideas in the same period can throw some light on Taiwan's past and present situations.

Last but not least, it is my hope that the historical review of modernism's rise in Taiwan and the critical reflections on the Cold War constellation of various institutional forces would help us ponder the possibility of rekindling the historically rich yet currently dormant connections between the foreign literatures studies scholarships in Taiwan and Taiwanese creative writers (including the up-and-coming ones), as well as the local literati at large. Based on such experiences and sea changes, I seek to explore the role of the United States as the Janus-faced enabler/disabler vis-à-vis the local literature and cultures of its Asian-Pacific allies by means of tapping into my vantage point of view as both an insider and outsider, my ability to access and digest the firsthand archival materials in the original language, and the historical hindsight this generation of scholars have gained over the years.

MODERNIST LITERATURE IN THE SHADOW OF WAR

Wars, along with the ensuing destruction and dislocations or relocations on massive scales, could arguably be considered the founding experience (or the founding trauma) of European modernism, the earlier modernist works prior to the two World Wars notwithstanding. As Pai Hsien-yung, another (now canonized) pioneer of modernist literature in Taiwan, claims in an interview, the war-torn era of the 1940s and the forced relocations he personally experienced can be considered a crucial conjunction through which he could relate to Western modernist literature, which he was still learning and translating when he co-founded *Modern Literature* as a junior in *Taida waiwenxi*.[6] Yet owing to multiple reasons, such as the modernist artist's/writer's emphasis on formal innovation (as opposed to the subject matter he/she treats or the content) and New Criticism's preoccupation with the supposedly self-contained universe of textuality while propagating the modernist paradigm, the context and contextualization of wars has been relatively scant in much of modernism studies scholarship in the United States; critical or philosophical reflections on the significance of wars for modernist movement and ideas have not been sufficiently explored either. This tendency was even more pronounced in the heyday of literary modernism in Taiwan, thanks in large part to the political climate at the time and a somewhat internalized Cold War ideology.

Take, for example, the best-known work of the poet Luo Fu, "Death of a Stone Cell" ("*Shishi zhi siwang*"). This poem does not shy away from the most brutal and fiercely contested site of military conflict (in fact, it foregrounds the frontline, albeit with the shield of the burrowed stony tunnels). However, the bulk of critical literature on this celebrated magnum opus of modernist poetry seems to focus on its formal elements—dense imagery, mastery of poetic language, etc.—or the reconstruction of inner spirituality out of the ruins in the material world. Given the necessity and constant pressure to respond to Cold War realities (e.g., surviving the bombing above the underground tunnels or satisfying the ideological imperative to showcase anticommunist literature), such cutting off or bracketing of real-world referents from its literary representation, as evidenced by the reception as well as the practices of modernist writings, constituted one of the hallmarks of Cold War modernism in Taiwan, which merits further critical explanations and may shed light on the theoretical discourse on modernism in general. It is due to this often downplayed context of war and its under-theorized significance that I plan to examine the soldier-writer and the expatriate in my book.

Although the term "soldier-writer" in this project refers almost exclusively to those writers who happened to be soldiers or military personnel by profession, it could occasionally be expanded to include the vanguard character as well as soldierly devotion and loyalty to the modernist cause of a writer such as Ji Xian. The disproportionally large number of soldier-writers in the postwar Taiwan literary scene was a sign of the times worthy of more critical attention, as it testified to the militarized nature of the Nationalist regime that had newly retreated to Taiwan and the US-led Cold War mobilization and division that pitted "us" against "them," offered protection on condition of one's unconditional allegiance to it, and guaranteed "freedom" that, paradoxically, could not free itself from being constantly threatened by the enemy from within and without. Bringing the soldier-writer phenomenon to the fore certainly is to examine the nexus of politics and literature (which, unsurprisingly, involved the lopsided subjugation of the latter to the former); however, invoking "the soldier-writer" is not to pass judgment on these writers' political (in)correctness by virtue of their complicity with the oppressive regime, as such critiques would have little value when we now have the benefit of historical hindsight. In terms of political correctness, I would argue, it is precisely because they were politically correct in that era (at least in the eye of the Big Brother) that they could afford to pursue, to a certain extent, some artistic freedom "in the trenches" or "in the stone chambers"—as under rather challenging, limited, and confined circumstances—and move beyond their predetermined "proper places."

Of course, the Cold War was a peculiar species of war. One was always at war—or at least was continuously reminded of the omnipresence of war—without formal declarations of war (except for the Korean War and the Vietnam War) and the direct engagements, devastations, and sweeping economic impacts of the World Wars. More often than not, the Cold War flexed its muscles by means of shadowing the real wars, with the potential nuclear catastrophe that could erupt at any moment looming large on one's mind. Though wars, for most Taiwanese at the time, were not exactly imminent and seemed to take place in a far-off land, they were not imaginary either—the threats of war were palpable and could hit home, as evidenced by the continuing bombardments of Quemoy, an offshore island that is located much closer to the southeast coast of China than to Taiwan. Exposed to the constant risks of war and death, as well as the hazards of living with the airtight control of one's words and deeds by the authoritarian regime, many soldier-writers who had recently relocated from China and didn't feel at home in Taiwan would reveal literary instantiations of claustrophobia in their writings, as critics have pointed out. Consequently, they tended to look for a way out, both materially and spiritually. "Looking for an exit," in fact, could arguably be a Cold War symptom that characterized the collective mindset of the postwar Taiwanese, Koreans, and, to a lesser degree, Japanese. The ideal exit, for most of them, would be to immigrate to the United States. A number of the modernist writers from Taiwan, including some soldier-writers, followed the crowd and filed to that exit once they could manage to do so, with many cases appearing to be voluntary, self-imposed exile. Hence the beginning of a group of "expatriate-writers" that had the semblance of the European-American expatriates of high modernism.

One thing that seems to be missing from the preceding introduction yet underlies and connects various facets of the Cold War phenomena would be the "American connections," which came in several forms—on the basis of family, relatives, and friends that multiplied as waves of immigration to the United States continued; business and professional associations; and, in the public sector and at the collective level, numerous government ties (diplomatic, military, educational, economical, institutional) that combined to undergird what could be called "the US Cold War Military-Cultural Machine," of which Taiwan was one of the key parts in East Asia. With this greater contextual framework in mind, I will examine the role and ramifications of one of the key cogs of the United States Information Agency (USIA) for the networks of US Cold War initiatives in Asia—the United States Information Service in Taipei (also known as USIS Taipei), which, by virtue of covert collaborations with some local intellectuals, spearheaded the reorientation of the literary scene in Taiwan and indirectly fostered the paradigm shift and the institutionalization of the studies of American literature based on the US model, enhancing the cultural prowess (of the higher-brow stratus) of the postwar United States in the process as well. Connecting to this integral part, but not as covert as USIS, are other cultural and educational institutions that are more likely to enter into the history of postwar Taiwan literature or, more specifically, that of Cold War modernism—for instance, the International Writing Program at the University of Iowa (IWPI), where most major Taiwanese writers, as well as many from other Asian allies of America, have spent their share of time during the Cold War era, with the funds and resources that flowed from the institutional channels working in concert with the abovementioned Cold War Machine, and functioned as the material conditions upon which the "culture of US aids" depended.

THE SOLDIER-POET PHENOMENON AND THE FIRST INSTANCE OF THE MODERNIST MOVEMENT

The main content of the rest of the book can be divided into three parts and will be arranged roughly in the following order. The first part of my book takes as its point of departure the manifesto of modernist poetry published in 1956 by Ji Xian, leader of the literary modernist movement in Taiwan. While most of his statements in the manifesto are compatible with the tenets of Euro-American modernism (whether it be formal innovation or the purity of poetry), the last item on the agenda—underscoring the buzzwords "patriotism" and "anticommunism"—strikes one as a telltale sign of Taiwan's Cold War modernism, which epitomizes at once these modernists' unsuspecting allegiance to the dominant ideology and their pragmatic strategy of negotiating a limited autonomy of artistic freedom under an authoritative regime. The tension inherent in the bifurcation of this movement was rendered prominently in the presence of a disproportionally large number of soldier-writers who were part of the propaganda machine yet partook in the modernist endeavors as their true vocation, renouncing the edifying function of literature and championing a breakaway from tradition. This part of the book will delineate, examine, and expound on how the soldier-writer phenomenon emerged as an offshoot or unintended consequence of state-run literary agencies in the military that promoted patriotic, anticommunist literature, or "combat literature" (*zhandou wenyi*). I argue that the soldier-writer's surprisingly antiestablishment posture was first tolerated by the state partly due to his embeddedness in its apparatus. His strong role in driving the modernist movement was in turn magnified at once by such embeddedness and the exploitation of his self-image as "freedom fighter" (for the individual's artistic freedom and against communism—the archenemy of freedom). His pragmatic negotiations for a certain degree of artistic "autonomy," however, would not take him as far afield as to envision brand-new heights of literary adventure, not only because of the parameters laid out by the state but also thanks to his unwitting, genuine subscription to parts of the dominant ideology.

As I have briefly explained in the previous section, the designation "soldier-writer"—and, apropos of the modernist poetry movement, the "soldier-poet"—highlights the curious disjunction or even ostensible conflict between the modernist's two identities, between his mundane profession (which, nonetheless, says a lot about the Cold War) and his artistic vocation, between the worldly order he helped to maintain and the rarified sphere of literature re-created and accessed only through his devotion to his "other" (and true) craft. The said disjunction and/or conflict is aptly instantiated in the much-celebrated magnum opus of modernist poetry in Taiwan by the poet-warrior Luo Fu: "Death of a Stone Cell." Since it is widely considered an epitome of the Cold War sensitivity of being exposed to the constant threat of war and death, as well as the hazards of living with the airtight control of one's words and deeds by the authoritarian regime, I will offer an extensive "alternative" to the paradigmatic close reading—i.e., reading the context closely in conjunction with the text—of some excerpts of "Death of a Stone Cell" so as to give the reader a basic sense of Taiwanese Cold War modernist literature. Taking into account Luo Fu's claim that writing poetry is a kind of "revenge against reality" for him, I propose that Cold War partitions of the world and the concomitant reframing of what is perceivable/visible—especially in the context of postwar Taiwan—turned out to be conducive to such obliteration of immediate realities and the well-known modernist disdain of the mimetic or realist treatment or representation of reality.

TWO STATES OF THE SECOND MODERNIST INSTANCE AND THE CULTURE OF US AIDS

If the first appearance of Cold War modernism in Taiwan was sanctioned (though ultimately kept in check) by the Nationalist government, it also was partly legitimized by one aspect of the US aids that wasn't yet institutionalized (as little more than a nascent cultural milieu). When this modernist movement gained more visibility and drew more participants in the second instance of breaking into the literary and culture scene, the institutional clout of USIA (also known as USIS in Taiwan) was already in place, and the culture of US aids had gained decisive momentum. I shall explore the other pivotal moment of this Cold War modernist movement, the formation and culmination of the culture of US aids in Taiwan, and the state-sponsored institution(s) within the Cold War framework that facilitated all this. This part of my book delves into the founding of the influential literary magazine *Modern Literature* in 1960 by a group of undergraduates in the Department of Foreign Languages and Literatures, National Taiwan University (*Taida waiwenxi*), who nonetheless pioneered in creating and advocating modernist literature and have now become literary luminaries themselves. I will bring to the fore and critically reexamine the antiestablishment character at the beginning of this second instance, as the student-writers rebelled against both the tradition upheld by their elders and the curriculum handed down to them by the department (which rarely included the modernist texts newly recognized in American academia), and will look into the rather swift and significant institutionalization of modernist literature in the following years, thanks in part to what Chen Chien-chung has called "the US-aided literary establishment" (*meiyuan wenyi tizhi*).[7] Based on research findings of others and the archival and textual evidence gleaned from firsthand sources, it is plausible that the magazine *Modern Literature* wouldn't have lasted long enough to spearhead, from the vantage point of academic prestige, the paradigm shifts to modernism and New Criticism and reshaped, respectively, the literary scene and the discipline of *waiwenxi* in Taiwan academia, if not for USIS's timely financial reliefs (in the form of purchasing the bulk of printed copies of some issues) and its active promotion of American literature and culture.

I shall reflect on a nuanced kind of "American dream" for many of the aspiring modernist writers, which helped foster and strengthen the US-aided literary establishment in Taiwan and testified to the prevalence of the culture of US aids: University of Iowa's Writers' Workshop (IWW) and its International Writing Program (IWPI), where almost every key figure of the modernist movement has spent his or her share of time, through the connections directly or indirectly opened up by USIS. Chapter 4 makes clear that the formative years of the core members of this second peak of modernist movement coincided with the emergence and consolidation of the culture of US aids and the visible impacts USIS exerted, at the institutional level, over a number of key parts of this new literary establishment. As the culture of US aids necessarily points to the involvement of more than the state in the local context, Iowa's International Writing Project has to be examined in the larger Cold War framework as well. As recent studies on related subjects have shown (most notably in Bennett's *Workshops of Empire* and, to a certain degree, corroborated by Barnhisel's book), the IWP either covertly or unwittingly worked in conjunction with the aforementioned Cold War Machine for a considerable period of time.

In terms of the development of the US-aided literary establishment at the local level, this chapter probes the institutional history of *waiwenxi* as a discipline, and particularly the institutionalized studies of American literature (and, to a lesser extent, of British literature, as mediated via the American model) in Taiwan as it pertains to the introduction, dissemination, and canonization of modernist ideas and literary practices. Taking into consideration both the cultural capital of the IWP and the "reformist" urge of the new literary establishment, I will, on the one hand, examine the workings of the conjunctions of institutional forces, as elaborated earlier, and, on the other hand, reflect on the complex and nuanced ways in which local writers and scholars responded in tandem, and occasionally in conflict, with the hegemonic process initiated by the Cold War Cultural Machine. At issue here, I would argue, is whether a certain degree of localization and attempts to maintain some agency while playing the roles of both agent and reformer equipped with US-sponsored legitimacy could be discerned in that period. In addition, I shall review the erstwhile experience of inter-pollination or cross-fertilization (a quite natural process at the time) involving literary knowledge and literary practices between the literati and academia, which also contributed, among other factors, to the prestige of *Taida waiwenxi* yet could no longer be seen. This certainly was one of the drawbacks of the institutionalization of American literary studies enabled and, at the time, inhibited by the American connections under the Cold War framework.

THE EXPATRIATE AND THE TRANSITION TO PERPETUAL EXILE

To mark the closure, or the phasing out, of the defining phase of the modernist literature in Cold War Taiwan, which is inextricable from the "phasing out" character of US aids in Taiwan undergirding the culture of US aids there, the last chapter of this book will examine what became of the modernist writers in the wake of their "pivots" in response to the seismic changes since the 1970s to the preceding geopolitical contexts that forced them out of a certain Cold War "bubble" by reflecting on the ramifications of the trajectories of their spatial and spiritual displacements as well as their textual practices. Though the transitions of their literary outputs and career paths are not necessarily linear, they most likely emerge or shake out in terms of "exit-return-exile," which will be elaborated in more depth in the last chapter and will be illustrated by a reading of the short story "Winter Night" in Pai Hsien-yung's *Taipei People*. I argue that, even in a zigzag fashion, the pivots appeared to revolve around a certain China imaginary instantiating their persistent attempts at reconceiving Chineseness and its aestheticization. The formerly dormant or fledging traditionalist undercurrent in the movement phase of this modernism manifested itself much more prominently in the subsequent decades, matching their canonical status in the literary establishment they helped to shape, and with retrograde moderations so pronounced that the "modernist" appellation had little meaning in the latter stages without the Cold War framework. It moves, I venture to say, toward a literature of exile foregrounding an acute or contented sense of uprootedness in the face of emerging challenges to that which seems a priori in their conception of collective identity in a rapidly changing Taiwan.

The connection of this last part and the previous one is that the reformist thrust of this modernism (broached in the preceding part), which had reshaped the literary scene, ended up neutralizing itself after it underwent a US-sponsored institutionalization in academia and sought its agency of localization via an ethos of alienation and the aestheticization of perpetual exile. At stake here is the attempt at theoretical justification of such exile and the valorization of expatriate writing by the poet-scholar Chien Cheng-chen—what he terms "poetics of exile" (*fangzhu shixue*).[8] As with the discussion on the soldier-writer, I do not seek judgment calls on these writers' politics and notions about their "homeland" as the transition transpires into a new reality, another world. I would reexamine the aspects of their celebrations of (self-imposed) exile and the bulk of such expatriate writings where a certain romanticization (ironically, as antithetical to modernist penchants) relies on turning a blind eye to institutional forces from which they cannot extricate themselves.

NOTES

1. Greg Barnhisel, *Cold War Modernists: Art, Literature, and American Cultural Diplomacy* (New York: Columbia University Press, 2015), loc. 224, Kindle.

2. See, for example, Chen Chien-chung, "Meixinchu yu Taiwan wenxueshi zhongxie: Yi meiyuan wenyi tizhi xia de Taigang zazhi chuban wei kaocha zhongxin" ["USIS" and the Re-writing History of Taiwan Literature: A Study on the Publication of Taiwan and Hong Kong's Magazines on U.S. Aids under the Literary & Artistic Institutions], *Guowen xuebao* [Bulletin of Chinese] 52 (December 2012): 211–42; Jin-li Nikki Lin, "Lengzhan yishi xingtai yu xiandai zhuyi de wenhua xiangxiang: yi zhanhou Taiwan yu Zhongguo de xiandaishi lunshu wei guancha zhongxin" [Cold War Ideology and Modernism's Cultural Imaginations: Observations on the Discourse of Modern Chinese Poetry in Post-war Taiwan and China], *Chung Wai Literary Quarterly* 46, no. 2 (June 2017): 119–60; Tsai Ming-yen, "Yijiu wuling niandai Taiwan xiandaishi de jige mianxiang" [On Some Facets of Taiwan Modern Poetics in the 1950s], *Taiwan wenxue yanjiu xuebao* [Journal of Taiwan Literary Studies], no. 11 (October 2010): 89–112; Wang Chi-ming, "Lengzhan renwen zhuyi: Yan Yuan-shu ji qi piping shijian" [Cold War Humanism: Yan Yuan-shu and His Critical Practices], *Chung Wai Literary Quarterly* 43, no. 1 (March 2014): 121–68; Wang Mei-hsiang, "Meiyuan wenyi tizhi xia de Wenxue zazhi yu Xiandai wenxue" [Literary Review and Modern Literature under the U.S. Aid Literary Institution], *Taiwan wenxue xuebao* [Bulletin of Taiwanese Literature] 25 (December 2014): 69–100; Wang Mei-hsiang, "Wenxue quanli yu lengzhan shiqi Meiguo zai tai gang de wenxue xuanchuan (1950-1962)" [Literature, Power and American Propaganda in Hong Kong and Taiwan during the Cold War (1950-1962)], *Taiwanese Journal of Sociology*, no. 57 (September 2015): 1–51.

3. See Sung-sheng Yvonne Chang, *Modernism and the Nativist Resistance: Contemporary Chinese Fiction from Taiwan* (Durham, NC: Duke University Press, 1993), loc. 107–108, Kindle. The "factional" critical discourse reflected more the lack of intellectual rigor of many of the arguments, and the commentators' engagement in what one may call a Gramscian "war of positions" in the shifting and relatively open (compared with the previous decades) literary scene since the early 1970s. Such deficiency also had something to do with the meager institutional endorsement of and scholarly credit given to serious scholarship on contemporary works of literature in a generally conservative academia at the time. The institutionalization of the studies of Taiwan literature in the 1990s significantly remedied the aforementioned predicament. In the long run, the fierce debates and critiques on modernist literature in the 1970s did not undermine its canonical status in Taiwan; if anything, they might have further enhanced it.

4. Ibid, loc. 119.

5. Greg Barnhisel, *Cold War Modernists*, loc. 208.

6. See Michael Berry and Chien-hsin Tsai, eds., *Chongfan xiandai: Pai Hsien-yung, xiandai wenxue, yu xiandai zhuyi* [Return to the Modern: Pai Hsien-yung, Modern Literature, and Modernism] (Taipei: Rye Field, 2016), 74–75.

7. See Chen Chien-chung, "Meixinchu."

8. See Chien Cheng-chen, *Fangzhu shixue: Taiwan fangzhu wenxue chutan* [The Poetics of Exile: An Inquiry into the Literature of Exile in Taiwan] (Taipei: Unitas, 2003).

Chapter One

"Speech after Long Silence"

THE 1956 MANIFESTO AND THE OBSCURE(D) BEGINNINGS OF A COLD WAR MODERNISM

During the height of the Cold War in East Asia, not long after the Korean Armistice Agreement was signed (with no real end of the Korean War in sight), and in the wake of the military conflicts between Taiwan and China in 1954–1955 on the outpost island of Quemoy that foreshadowed the more intense and better-known 1958 Artillery War in frontline Quemoy,[1] a bombshell of a manifesto seemingly coming out of the blue rocked the literary scene in Taiwan in early 1956. The movement it inspired would go on to reconfigure the literary landscape of Taiwan, alter the trajectories of its cultural life, and usher in a new era of its literary history, even though the ripples the manifesto stirred were felt mainly among literati or limited circles of the reading public and its lasting impacts wouldn't become fully visible until a later historical juncture.

    The manifesto in question marked the occasion of the founding of the "modernist school" (*xiandaipai* in Chinese) in postwar Taiwan, rendering it even more outlandish in the context of a largely monolithic cultural scene subjected to official policies preoccupied with fighting communism and legitimizing the rule of Chiang Kai-shek's Nationalist government. Its exceptional character and the abruptness of its emergence as an *event* was thrown into sharper relief against the backdrops of an impoverished society lacking in all kinds of resources and still receiving US aids in more than military forms;[2] an authoritarian regime tightening its control by rounding up dissidents in increasingly heavy-handed ways; and, last but not least, the real-life scenarios of the outbreak of wars, as exemplified by the aforementioned battle in Quemoy, that threatened to obliterate all other endeavors in life. I argue that it is under such extraordinary circumstances, which cannot be extricated from the Cold War, that the "modernist" statements proclaimed in the manifesto of 1956 by an emerging, self-described "modernist school" not only became a momentous event in Taiwan's literary history, but could also shed light on recent scholarly efforts to examine the transmutations of literary modernism after the heyday of Euro-American "high modernism," and in a non-Western, transnational setting.[3] As will be illustrated in the following pages, the literary practices of the writers involved in this particular modernist movement in the ensuing decades can serve as an exemplary case for more critically nuanced examinations of the "afterlife of modernism,"[4] which certainly extends temporally into the postwar years and entangles geopolitically with the global Cold War order. Our readings of and reflections on these "modernist" texts and their attendant contexts seek to explore their possibilities and limits with an acute awareness that one cannot approach them merely through a recourse to the apparent source or model they themselves acknowledged[5]—namely, the Euro-American modernism that had been translated and transmitted to many parts of the non-Western world along with the expansion of capitalist modernity yet rarely led to more than one-way traffic of ideas and practices, despite its allegedly internationalist outlook. Nor can one simply fall back on the set of conditions facilitating the onset of "modernity" and the rise of modernism in Europe between the second half of the nineteenth and the early twentieth century, as the ultimate referent or the default comparator against which other manifestations are to be measured (or, for that matter, resort to a "postmodern" globality in which everyone outside the advanced capitalist societies is still cast as a latecomer or derivative, however the prior dyads of center/periphery and origin/copy are said to be undermined). In other words, the spatial realignments and the temporal complications (for instance, both the interruption and the reentry of modernism due to the Cold War) necessarily entailed in the discussions in this book will likely require us to rethink what we are accustomed to calling "modernism" and some of the critical common sense about the concomitant issues. To that end, it behooves us to begin with (or return to) what announced the advent of modernism in Taiwan, and presented itself as a brand-new start (and has been hailed as such): the 1956 modernist manifesto in Taiwan.

Modernism with a Cold War Stamp

The aforementioned manifesto was first printed prominently on the front cover of the thirteenth issue of *Modern Poetry Quarterly* (*Xiandaishi*),[6] which had been founded in 1953 by the leading poet Ji Xian (1913–2013), who single-handedly ran and edited all but a couple of issues of the journal and spearheaded this first wave of modernist movement in the early postwar years.[7] Although it is important to unpack the significances of this modernist manifesto with reference to its more detailed explications included in the opening pages of the same issue (titled "Explicating the Tenets of the Modernist School"),[8] here I shall take as my point of departure its "six principles," which were brought to the fore—literally—and befitted the declarative and summary nature of the manifesto:

1. We are a group of modernists who selectively promote the spirit of all new poetic schools since Baudelaire.
2. We believe that New Poetry is a horizontal transplant, not a vertical inheritance. This is a general assumption, a fundamental starting point, whether in theory or in practice.
3. Explore new continents of poetry, express new contents, create new forms, discover new tools, invent new techniques.
4. Emphasis on intellect.
5. Pursuit of pure poetry.
6. Patriotism. Anticommunism. Support of freedom and democracy.[9]

While most of the "principles" listed above are compatible with the tenets or traits widely attributed to those of Euro-American modernism (whether it be the championing of newness through the pursuit of formal innovation or the emphasis on artistic purity and intellect), the last item of the agenda—underscoring the buzzwords "patriotism" and "anticommunism"—strikes one as incongruous with, or even antithetical to, such modernist characteristics. Nonetheless, it betrays one of the articulations or manifestations of modernism that is symptomatic of the Cold War era; in other words, it may well be a prime example of "Cold War modernism."

The term "Cold War modernism," of course, has been treated at great length by Barnhisel, as mentioned in the introduction. My use of the same term to characterize and analyze postwar literary productions in Taiwan certainly is indebted to Barnhisel's work on this front, but with at least the following caveats: First of all, the specific "case" of Taiwan's Cold War modernism obviously falls outside the purview of Barnhisel's book-length study, as it does outside the radar of many Western scholars of modernism studies. Secondly, the designation "Cold War modernism," as deployed by Barnhisel, functions to name a phenomenon or a conjunction of historical, geopolitical, cultural, and social forces and institutions that repackaged modernism, or even redirected its trajectories, for Cold War strategic purposes, rather than a theoretical model which can be seamlessly applied to other particular cases under the aegis of the US camp of the Cold War order, despite Taiwan's structurally subservient position in it. Last but not least, there is a difference between a Cold War modernism that lies in what Barnhisel calls the "reinterpretation of the modernist movement,"[10] which had seen its heyday and was liable to evolve into something other than its former self, and the one in Taiwan that seized on the Cold War conditions favorable to its interpretation of modernism and presented itself as at once a clean slate to begin anew—even though modernist literature had emerged in stunted, eventually short-lived fashions in both prewar Taiwan and China—and a challenge to the status quo.

These nuances notwithstanding, it is clearly helpful to examine the seemingly odd juxtaposition of anticommunism, patriotism, freedom, and democracy with other modernist statements in the aforementioned manifesto by situating it, momentarily, in the framework of Barnhisel's "Cold War modernism." For the manifesto emerged in a broader Cold War constellations of discourses, ideas, institutions, and practices that linked the Cold War bywords (along with all their trappings) with modernism (as newly reinterpreted) and had earnestly valorized and consolidated such linkage since the end of World War II. Some of the shifts in political climate, cultural currents, and sentiments enabling the confluence of Cold War initiatives and modernism in the United States were, of course, palpable in Cold War Taiwan under US military tutelage (in the name of "ally"), even with the free flow of information limited by distance and government control. Geopolitically and culturally speaking, they were the greater conditions of possibility which paved the way for the emergence of this Cold War manifestation of modernism. Nonetheless, the impetus behind Taiwan's modernist movement, I argue, was born at the crucible of conjoining and intertwining forces, each of which, by itself, was not necessarily conducive to modernist literature: the American influences due to Taiwan's strategic position at the forefront of the US-backed Cold War machine; the ever-present prospect of war with communist China, brought home vividly by the outbreak of the military conflicts on the frontline island Quemoy; the Nationalist government's policies of promoting patriotic and anticommunist literature, as well as its unrelenting censorship, paranoid about communist infiltration; the depletion of the local literary scene in the wake of the February 28 Incident in 1947 that led to the death of many local intellectuals and the silencing of a generation of Taiwanese writers who, having adapted to writing in Japanese, had to relearn Chinese;[11] and, last but not least, the arrival in Taiwan of an amalgam of both experienced and novice writers among the mass migration of the Nationalist government's followers, who found themselves in a *leveled* local literary and cultural landscape ripe for a fresh start. With reference to the "six principles" quoted above, I shall examine how the signature characteristics of Taiwan's Cold War modernist movement were intertwined with these contextual forces.

Let me first begin with what appeared to mark this modernism with a specifically Cold War stamp: the inclusion of patriotism and anticommunism in the 1956 manifesto. While it would be tempting and reasonable to treat it as another telltale sign of the commonplace underlying ideological "baggage" of many proponents and practitioners of modernism in the United States in the earlier Cold War era, it was not common for these writers to elevate such terms—so ubiquitous in the Cold War that they sounded worn-out at times—to the height of a manifesto, or place them in the same context as their utterances of modernist aesthetics. For, as Barnhisel notes, the literary figures who actively participated in the Cold War projects of cultural diplomacy (for example, James Laughlin's editorship of *Perspectives USA*) were wary of being implicated in the propaganda campaign or sought to avoid such impressions even while they were, in a sense, actually engaged in one.[12] The invocation of anticommunism and patriotism in the manifesto, however, could arguably be out of necessity, at least *strategically speaking*. Given the fact that Taiwan had been declared under martial law by the Nationalist government since 1949, as well as the stabilization and consolidation of Chiang Kai-shek's rule in Taiwan thanks to the influx of US aids after the outbreak of the Korean War, the political climate under an essentially authoritarian regime (despite aligning itself with the camp of "freedom" and "democracy" in the Cold War) allowed for very little room of dissenting voices, with available cultural resources almost exclusively controlled by the government and government-funded organizations that had the semblance of private entities.[13] It is, therefore, easy to understand the pressure to go along with the anticommunist slogans in a homogeneous, stagnant cultural scene due largely to the Nationalist government's policy of aggressively promulgating "combat literature and art" (*Zhandou wenyi*),[14] and when the world—or at least half of it—was flush with anticommunist sentiment. Nonetheless, the rationale behind the talk of strategy deserves further nuanced critical attention.

It is important to note most literary historians' consensus that the bulk of 1950s literary outputs in Taiwan can be characterized as predominantly anticommunist, patriotic, and nostalgic (about pre-communist mainland China) literature, especially in terms of quantity, even though a significant portion of the literary works still worthy of scholarly discussions today do not necessarily fall neatly under any of those three categories.[15] As critics observe, the massive scale of mobilization led by the Nationalist government, which was intent on turning every facet of public life into an organ of the state apparatus and a part of an effective Cold War anticommunist machine, relied not only on censorship to prevent undesirable content but also multiple incentives to coax aspiring writers into toeing the party line: awards and prize money, workshops and correspondence courses, venues of publication, and leadership positions in literary and cultural establishments that had formal or covert ties to the Nationalist regime.[16] The extensive impacts of such cultural policies could be evidenced not only by the pervasiveness of anticommunist and combat literature in the entrants of literary prizes sponsored by government agencies and publications but also by the individual works of literature and public discourses about literature that were not directly involved in government initiatives in any official capacity. One good example of the latter can be found in the inaugural editorial of *New Poetry Weekly*, which Ji Xian briefly coedited with other poets as early as 1951. While they claimed to strike a balance between "art for art's sake" and "art for life's sake," the emphasis on the refinement of "technique" was intermixed with anticommunist rhetoric such as "aiming our literary weapons at the bosoms of the hideous Bolshevik."[17] Under these circumstances, public shows of support for the Nationalist state, ranging from anticommunist and patriotic statements to specific utterances in line with policies or government-mandated slogans, were so widespread that they could arguably be interpreted as either voluntary expressions of thoughts and feelings or, more likely, the familiar cultural practice called *biaotai* (in a literal sense, "openly displaying one's attitude") as part of the conformist ritual of publicly declaring one's loyalty to the power that be.

The practice of *biaotai* or *shucheng* (which literally means "delivering allegiance to a specific person or entity of power") certainly isn't unique to 1950s Taiwan. It could be a proactive, calculated move targeting one among competing options in some contexts, but when the political power is nearly monopolized, as in the case of Chiang Kai-shek's Nationalist regime in postwar Taiwan, the gesture of *biaotai* may well be a prerequisite for survival, or at best a routine passively carried out before one can do anything else deemed meaningful. As many critics contend, such was the rationale behind the raising of the anticommunist flag by the modernist poets on occasions where it appeared to be irrelevant to their true pursuit. The poet and scholar Liu Zheng-zhong, for example, clearly assumes that Ji Xian was simply "going through the motions"[18] when he prominently featured "the twin banners of anti–Soviet Union and anti–Communist China"[19] in the first paragraph of the inaugural editorial of *Modern Poetry Quarterly*. Aside from the military imagery and militant rhetoric in this editorial (e.g., "our short poems are rifles on the frontline") and in the abovementioned *New Poetry Weekly* editorial, the most telling sign of the perfunctory nature of such proclamations would probably be the glaring absence of further explication of the sixth principle of the 1956 Modernist Manifesto in the essay "Explicating the Tenets of the Modernist School," which is meant to accompany and explain the six modernist principles or tenets of the manifesto that are boldly printed on the cover of that February's issue of *Modern Poetry Quarterly*. For the other five tenets are explicated and elaborated in far greater detail, clarity, length and depth—or as far as declarative statements allow. The sixth, by comparison, is followed up with sentences of brusque self-evidentiality: "We promote patriotism and anti-Communism. We support freedom and democracy. These need no explanation."[20]

Michelle Yeh, who focuses on the 1950s poetic works themselves, points out the fact that Ji Xian, too, repeatedly took part, and won prizes, in poetry competitions or awards funded by the Nationalist regime, including a military-sponsored contest, composing overtly patriotic, anticommunist, or nostalgic poems that would be favored by the ruling elites but bore little resemblance to the kind of modernist poetry he himself championed elsewhere. Based on Ji Xian's first book of poetry after his relocation to Taiwan, which was originally published in 1951 and advertised as a "collection of political lyrics" (or, shall we say, politically correct lyrics?), and in light of his devotion to the privately-funded *Modern Poetry Quarterly* and the modernist movement, Yeh argues that Ji Xian, who epitomizes like-minded poets with similar backgrounds and maneuvers in this period, "participated in the official discourse mainly to obtain the cultural resources that would have been otherwise unavailable" to him, consciously using the symbolic capital and "the economic capital [he] thus obtained to sustain the private poetry journals" and the endeavors to which he committed himself instead.[21] Evidently, Ji Xian makes a deliberate distinction between his modernist writings and, more broadly, his literary oeuvres, and those he wrote for "political purposes," which, he would later admit, he used to write regularly but excluded them from all (but one) of his books of collected poems because he considered them propagandistic and of no artistic value.[22] Herein lies, I argue, the first sign of *bifurcation*, which signals not only the trajectories of this Cold War modernist movement and its practitioners but also their underlying mode of existence while accommodating to the profound contradictions constitutive of the Cold War order—to which I shall return and further elaborate in this and subsequent chapters.

Antiestablishment Discontent, Self-contained

Liu, Yeh, and other scholars defend and justify such strategic deployment of anticommunist or propagandist writings as a "cover" or "smoke screen"[23] by underscoring Ji Xian's and fellow modernists' antiestablishment character and, thereby, the groundbreaking significance of their literary practices. Ji Xian's tone-setting collection of politically correct poems as the point of departure of his postwar career in Taiwan, Liu conjectures, may have established his reputation (or cover) as an anticommunist poet, hence a "safety valve" for his modernist undertakings hereafter.[24] Yeh also observes that winning those state-sponsored literary contests might also give the modernist writers "some symbolic capital in the eyes of the establishment, which could protect and help them in their private endeavors."[25] Of course, what set them apart from the majority of the prize-winning, conformist writers of the same period was the supposedly antiestablishment character of their literary practices, even though they, too, were practically involved—to varying degrees—in the literary establishment itself. As Yeh says of their peculiar means of advancing their modernist agenda, "[p]olitical correctness was the strategy, radical experiment the goal."[26] The "radical experiment" in question, which was embodied in the manifesto by the typically modernist pursuit and celebration of the new ("create new forms, discover new tools, invent new techniques"), was meant to be conducted in a now safe, well-delimited, self-contained, or allegedly purified domain of literature (the foregrounding of "pure poetry" in the manifesto). In other words, the Cold War modernists in Taiwan *took care to include a conformist gesture in order to be nonconformist in a different register or realm*. With regard to the odd juxtaposition of Cold War bywords and modernist precepts in the 1956 manifesto, it is therefore plausible to argue that the precaution or safety net built into their statements could not be dispensed with, precisely because those who drafted the manifesto were aware of the overall polemical nature and the antiestablishment gesture of their manifesto.

How, then, did this modernism present itself as an antiestablishment movement, or could be perceived as such, if it preemptively spared, for instance, the sweeping anticommunist imperative that eclipsed the pursuit of the new, thereby defanging itself of any head-on attack on a status quo in which the body politic set up by the Nationalist regime almost exclusively predetermined every order in life, where the personal could very well be the political, and anything political could only be politically correct? The challenge the modernist movement posed to the status quo of the literary scene could be understood as threefold: First and foremost, it targeted Old Poetry, or classical poetry, which, composed of rhymed verses in the classical Chinese language with long-standing poetic conventions, was still the dominant form of poetry writing, as opposed to the marginal position occupied by New Poetry or Modern Poetry, which is written in modern or vernacular Chinese (*baihuawen*) and had been practiced since the 1910s, albeit with limited success until after modernist poetry gained mainstream recognition in the 1960s. In terms of social status, cultural and economic resources, publication venues, and inclusion in curriculums, New Poetry paled in comparison with Old Poetry. Due to the "long tradition of consecration of classical poetry," Yeh notes that while "the classical genre was associated with erudition and cultural refinement, modern poetry was considered unsophisticated" and commonly belittled by conservatives and highly educated intellectuals alike.[27] Which is why Ji Xian once lamented in an editorial for *Modern Poetry Quarterly*, "Old Poetry is in the court, New Poetry is in the wild. Those of us who write modern poetry have neither power nor connections. Further, we are hard-pressed financially; we use our own money to publish poetry journals and can barely afford it."[28] Ji Xian's challenge to the supremacy of Old Poetry had been launched well before the manifesto first appeared—even prior to the founding of *Modern Poetry Quarterly*—relentlessly casting Old Poetry as the primary obstacle to their advocacy of modernist poetry, mainly on the ground that it had become outdated and unfit for the expression of the spirit of modern times, yet it still embodied a certain ingrained notion of poetry and commanded most of the available resources.

Secondly, this modernist movement directed much of its discontent of the status quo at "new regulated verse" (*xin gelushi*), which is generally categorized under the umbrella term "New Poetry," as it is written in *baihuawen* or the living Chinese language but consists of rhymed lines of identical or mostly standardized lengths. Due to its formal regularity and the fame of Xu Zhimo (1896–1931), who, together with other Crescent Moon School writers (*Xinyueh pai* in Chinese), pioneered in such styles and was best known for his sentimentalist works in 1920s China, new regulated verse appeared to be more accessible to the common reader than both modernist poetry and the classical genre, which requires advanced learning in Chinese classics. Although its thematic concerns seemed drastically different from those of combat literature, new regulated verse was tolerated by the ruling elites because it resembled the political lyrics in terms of the "formulaic language and predictable content," thereby constituting no threat to the official ideology.[29] With its regular forms, *xin gelushi* also proved to be more popular with the newspaper editors who catered to the largely conservative taste of the general public and were keen in filling in the spare or loose blank spaces on their literary supplement pages with the rectangular or square shape formed by its lines of equal lengths, once mockingly dubbed by Ji Xian as "tofu cake style."[30] Ji Xian and other modernist poets renounced new regulated verse not only for its formal rigidity but also for a certain "sentimentality and shallow lyricism"[31] from which the modernist poetry in their conception sought to distinguish itself by virtue of its "emphasis on intellect"—the fourth principle listed in the manifesto.[32] In the early postwar years, New Poetry was still a generic term assigned to poetry that wasn't written in classical Chinese, as part of the *baihuawen* movement (a push for vernacularization) since the May Fourth era, and could be applied loosely and indiscriminately to Modern Poetry and new regulated verse alike. Given the aforementioned prestige of Old Poetry and the clout and symbolic capital of those who still practiced it at the time, new regulated verse could compete with Old Poetry in terms of its popularity or impact (reaching a wider swath of the readership and making New Poetry more acceptable to mainstream media), though it could not—and did not envision to—overtake Old Poetry's high place in the existing cultural hierarchy. By highlighting its critical distance from new regulated verse, the modernist school of poetry also resolutely refused the potential of New Poetry's mainstream recognition and greater popularity in Taiwan—thereby

Modern Poetry's acceptability and legitimacy—on those terms represented by new regulated verse. Such distancing, I argue, prefigures this modernism's elitist orientation that would intensify during the Cold War years as it evolved toward its eventual apotheosis in subsequent decades. Even though Ji Xian would later dissociate himself from the incremental "difficulty" of modernist poetry perceived and deplored by critics from within and outside the literary circles a few years after the 1956 manifesto,[33] the well-known image of a modernist artist peering down the philistine crowd and pursuing his artistic ideal in a defiant gesture, or at least one that is indifferent, toward the naysayers began to gather strength.

As far as the modernists were concerned, the serious and "professional" attitude with which they approached their literary practices distinguished them from what they deemed as a dilettantism prevalent on the poetry scene at the time, whether it be Old Poetry, New Poetry, or literary criticism in general.[34] To some extent, the professionalism upheld by these modernist poets paralleled or were modeled after the well-known Western modernist pride in their "impeccable professionalism in contrast to their predecessors."[35] "If classical poetry," as Yeh writes, "was a hobby in which the elites dabbled at leisure, then modern poetry was a vocation, a calling requiring the poet's wholehearted dedication."[36] New Poetry, on the other hand, was plagued not only by new regulated verse's sentimentalism, shallowness, and penchant to become crowd-pleasers (instead of following a higher calling) but also by the commonplace misconception that it was easy to write—since it is composed in *baihuawen*—and therefore unsophisticated and lacking in learning and craft. Central to this emphasis on professionalism is not merely an advocacy for setting new golden standards of creative writing or recognizing the dignity of writers, as the profession had long existed with attached symbolic capital. As a matter of fact, virtually all of the modernist poets (except some students) had other full-time jobs or livelihoods (mostly as teachers, soldiers, and government employees), so, technically speaking, they could not claim to be full-time professional writers, at least not in the earlier stages of their careers. Nonetheless, it was their aspiration toward an ideal of poetic creation and purportedly unswerving devotion to perfecting their craft in such creation that instantiated the "pursuit of pure poetry" stressed in the manifesto, even though the vague and seemingly arbitrary definition of what is pure and impure in poetry, as stated in the explication of this principle, could prompt further contention.[37]

The third, and arguably the most daring and controversial challenge posed by the modernist manifesto to the status quo—hence its most pronounced antiestablishment gesture—would be the second of the six principles, which asserts: "New Poetry is a horizontal transplant, not a vertical inheritance,"[38] effectively championing the Western modernist models at the expense of the "tradition" these poets supposedly inherited. Such a statement not only flew in the face of the conservatives, who decried the self-conscious break from a time-honored poetic tradition, but also generated uneasiness among other practitioners of New Poetry who also were exploring alternatives to establishment literature and who, despite frequent disputes with Ji Xian on these tenets, would typically be categorized as one of the factions of Taiwan's postwar modernist poetry movement.[39] Its radicality could extend beyond the self-contained and purified artistic realm it so painstakingly focuses on and overstep the politically safe boundaries it prudently delimits, since such a disavowal of the "vertical inheritance," in tandem with its valorization of models from abroad, could very well be construed as an iconoclastic renunciation of tradition by the Nationalist authorities, thereby potentially eliciting unwanted censors or even greater risks.

Moderation, Modernization, and Mobilization

So far this chapter has enumerated the purportedly cutting-edge or even radical statements and practices of this modernist movement as well as their underlying paradoxes and inconsistencies: the formal experimentation of modernist poetry vs. the triteness of anticommunist clichés; its fierce insistence on artistic autonomy vs. its self-imposed curtailments on the freedom such autonomy envisions; its self-image as a nonconformist in the cultural circles vs. its practices as a conformist under an oppressive regime. All these are manifestations of a transplanted (and translated) modernism inflected by the Cold War circumstances in Taiwan, while such paradoxes are somehow reflected in the latter-day debates about and evaluations of the modernists in post-war Taiwan.[40] This Cold War modernism, I argue, can be characterized in terms of *moderation, modernization, and mobilization*, which also undergird and fuel the next phases of postwar modernist literature in Taiwan, as indicated in the following chapters.

First, moderation as a tendency characteristic of Taiwan's modernist movement. As relentless as its pursuit of the new (third principle of the manifesto) seemed, and as rebellious as its severance of the "vertical inheritance" may sound, the practitioners of modernist poetry did not stage an all-out or straightforward effort to tear down the existing literary establishment or strike down establishment literature itself—assuming that they set their sight on "literature" *only*, without any consideration of its institutional entanglements or social ills at the time. For instance, the third front on which the modernist movement's antiestablishment character was unleashed had to be taken with a grain of salt, since the modernists' resistance and uncompromising stance vis-à-vis Old Poetry and new regulated verse did not exactly extend to government-sanctioned combat literature, against which, many scholars claim, modernist literature railed.[41] Although the pro-Nationalist slogans in the manifesto and the anticommunist statements in many of their writings could be interpreted as reluctant and/or strategic, as explained above, the modernists' varying degrees of complicity in the propaganda machine was unmistakable. It has to be noted, therefore, that the challenge mounted by the modernist movement in Cold War Taiwan almost always proceeded *within the bounds of self-imposed limitations* of its literary adventures, or what might be dubbed a certain "safety net" that indicates not only its adaptation to the repressive political order but also its *modus operandi*, which will be discussed in this and subsequent chapters. Such a mode of operation was clearly demonstrated in the aforementioned anticommunist "cover" as the practitioner's conformist gesture for nonconformist poetry in a separate, allegedly autonomous or sealed-off sphere. In addition to this "trade-off" character of its operation, "moderation" in my conception of Cold War modernism also refers to many of its proponents' moderations or revisions, over time, of their positions on the key terms of their modernist discourse, including the term "modernist" and the hotly contested second tenet of the manifesto.[42]

Second, modernization, in practice, served as the permeating, though not often foregrounded, theme and legitimizing ground. Underneath the advocacy for and contestation about modernist literature lay a certain idea of modernization, which was presupposed, taken for granted, and seldom clarified—hence a kind of ideology of modernization.[43] It is noteworthy that this declaration was couched in, and implicitly justified by, the discourse of modernization, which chimed in with the state's official exhortation or injunction of modernization that in turn could be incorporated into a nationalist discourse and was legitimized by the symbolic capital of US cultural influence as a force of progress toward "the modern." In "Explicating the Tenets of the Modernist School," Ji Xian wrote of the stated goal to "accomplish the modernization of poetry."[44] Elucidating, in the same piece, the controversial second tenet, he further resorted to the familiar, decades-old call for "catching up" that had driven modernization initiatives as well as a range of modernisms in various fields, and had worked in conjunction with a certain nationalist discourse of self-strengthening:

> When in the realm of science we are eager to catch up with the world, why are we content to remain closed-minded and complacent in the realm of literature and art? We should realize that, like science, literature and art know no national boundaries. If someday our New Poetry achieves international acclaim, I guess even stubborn traditionalists will praise us for bringing glory to our country.[45]

Apart from the obvious appeal of modernization, the rationale for modernist poetry that aspired to be a transplant of the more modernized poetry from abroad also borrowed the authority and high esteem of science in mainstream society, which looked up to science for progress toward a better future. Here the celebration of science is, moreover, linked to the stress on intellect in the fourth tenet, citing (European) modernism's characteristic opposition to romanticism, which, as Ji Xian interprets it, is tantamount to "an emphasis on reason and rejection of the direct expression of emotion."[46] By way of a commonsensical understanding of science, Ji Xian thus skillfully grafted the modernization discourse to a modernist one that could be more accessible to a greater number of readers and, at the same time, could function as a safety valve against potential censorship, since it to some extent tied in nicely with the kind of nationalist ideology powered by the imperative of modernization. Modernization discourse, which inevitably comprised nuanced conceptions or imaginations among different groups, hence emerged as a common denominator for people of various positions not just on politics but also on literature and art. Which is one of the reasons, as far as those who were immersed in this Cold War cultural milieu and ideology and thus tended to identify with the right side of modernization (read: the modernized and anticommunist West) were concerned, there appeared to be no contradiction between modernism and anticommunism,[47] despite the inconsistencies or paradoxes listed above. Importantly, the explicit connection between modernism and modernization highlighted by Ji Xian also heralded similar calls for modernization in literature and art at the next defining moments of Taiwan's modernist movement, when other major players sought to advance their own agendas with slightly different means and emphases,[48] as the following chapters will show.

Last but not least, this modernist movement emerged and thrived on a peculiar form of mobilization that is indicative of the Cold War era. Granted that all movement requires mobilization to gather enough momentum to become a movement in the first place, the Cold War, however, would be unthinkable and unrecognizable without mobilizations at multiple levels (inter-state or provincial) and in various forms (top-down or bottom-up, forced or voluntary)—which is true even for the individualists in the "free world" who warned against "sloganeering amidst slogans run amok" but tended to be united by an often vague idea of "freedom" as a necessary rallying cry to combat the evils of a likewise vaguely conceived communism that forbade in-depth discussion.[49] What is interesting about the modernist mobilization in 1950s Taiwan is the phenomenon that the movement, on the one hand, answered the interpellation of the state (reluctantly so, while betraying a certain extent of compatibility with the latter's ideological underpinnings) and, on the other, initiated a smaller-scale mobilization that appeared to be out of step with, if not at odds with, the official one. In addition, it leveraged an even larger scale of mobilization (at the international level) to its advantage by invoking a modernism geared toward modernization in its scrupulous navigations through a literary scene highly mobilized and tightly monitored by the Nationalist government. The Cold War, as recent research indicates, was waged more on ideas and beliefs than anything else (including conflicting national interests, which is what most tend to presume).[50] True to form of Cold War Taiwan, the modernist mobilization gravitated toward a single idea or a key term, reflecting the monolithic culture trending toward oneness rather than diversity, convergence instead of individuation, especially in this early phase of the movement, even though this tendency resulted in fierce competition for predominance over the field, hence momentary divergences in the process. As the critic Xie Kun-hua argues, in this specific case the contestations revolved around the idea of the modern, which, due to its inherently malleable definitions, evoked variegated imaginations and conceptions among the modernists in Taiwan's Cold War contexts.[51]

Returning to the point of departure of this chapter, I would like to point to the 1956 modernist manifesto as a bona fide testament to the significance, momentum, and impact of this modernist mobilization. It served as a watershed event that ushered in a series of crucial moments in Taiwan's postwar cultural history that proclaimed anew the arrivals of newness in the form of manifestos as well as literary practices and public debates; it galvanized a recently depleted and barren literary field to swiftly coalesce around an alluring banner like modernism amid the anticommunist banner and myriad obstacles and limitations imposed by the authorities. Furthermore, because of its ostensive incongruity—in both content and form—with the culture and political climate of 1950s Taiwan (rallying followers around an "-ism" not endorsed by the government could be politically risky), such a mobilization exemplified an alternative route and mode of literary production that was not only previously unimaginable but also viable and seemingly safe (at least not immediately dangerous), thus enabling an outlet for the pent-up creative energies in a stifling culture scene.

Mobilization, of course, presupposes a certain collectivism—regardless of the nature of its binding—and the dedication to its cause in order to become effective. On the fronts of collectivism and the adherence to its cause, the initial stage of this modernist movement to some extent resembles military mobilization, especially the volunteer, militia type, given its staunch defense of its "banner," which consisted of statements or ideas that sometimes had not yet been backed up by its own literary outputs, and its often vehement attacks on its detractors (with enough moderation to avoid directly provoking the authorities, though). If the modernist veneration of the individual and artistic autonomy is antithetical to this postwar manifestation and mobilization of modernist ideas, it at the same time sheds light on the constitutive contradictions lurking beneath many of the Cold War conditions and modes of existence in general. Such contradictions could hardly be more salient, and the underlying tensions scarcely more intense, than in the formation of the group of soldier-writers who turned to modernism for a new path forward in the second phase of the modernist movement, as will be discussed in the next chapter.

NOTES

1. The name of the island Quemoy, located less than ten miles from the city Xiamen on the Southeast coast of China, is today frequently spelled "Jinmen," in accordance with the pinyin system. To be consistent with the Cold War contexts with which this book engages, I will spell it "Quemoy" henceforth, unless otherwise indicated. For the strategic importance of Quemoy, the ramifications of the artillery wars mentioned here, and the overall significances of Quemoy in the Cold War history in Asia, see Michael Szonyi, *Cold War Island: Quemoy on the Front Line* (Cambridge, UK: Cambridge University Press, 2008). Szonyi's book, in my opinion, is the most comprehensive book-length study on the island's Cold War history to date.

2. Aids from the United States of America to Taiwan began in 1951 and officially ended in 1965. They became "loans" instead of relief funds in 1961.

3. Regarding book-length studies on literary modernisms in non-Western and/or transnational settings, I am particularly indebted to Margaret Hillenbrand, *Literature, Modernity, and the Practice of Resistance: Japanese and Taiwanese Fiction, 1960–1990* (Leiden, Netherlands: Brill, 2007), and Shu-mei Shih, *The Lure of the Modern: Writing Modernism in Semi-colonial China, 1917–1937* (Berkeley: University of California Press, 2001). Both touch on some of the issues raised in Fredric Jameson's landmark essay in 1986 as well as a follow-up essay in 1990 that spawned debates and critical attention on the relationship between modernism and colonialism. For studies on the intersections between postcolonial and modernist literatures that have become much more visible in recent scholarship, see, for example, A. James Arnold, *Modernism and Negritude: The Poetry and Poetics of Aimé Césaire* (Cambridge, MA: Harvard University Press, 1981), Richard Begam and Michael Valdez Moses, eds., *Modernism and Colonialism British and Irish Literature, 1899–1939* (Durham, NC: Duke University Press, 2007), and Rajeev S. Patke, *Modernist Literature and Postcolonial Studies* (Edinburgh, UK: Edinburgh University Press, 2013). For works directly related to the vicissitude of Western modernism in the Cold War era, long after its heyday earlier in the century, I draw on Greg Barnhisel, *Cold War Modernists: Art, Literature, and American Cultural Diplomacy* (New York: Columbia University Press, 2015), Kindle, and Roland Végső, *The Naked Communist: Cold War Modernism and the Politics of Popular Culture* (New York: Fordham University Press, 2013). It has to be pointed out that, despite the fact that Végső's book was published earlier and features "Cold War modernism" in the book title, the term isn't further developed or elaborated in the text itself. In the case of Barnhisel, the term is central to its main arguments and is given a clear definition.

4. Tim Armstrong, *Modernism: A Cultural History* (Cambridge, UK: Polity Press, 2005), 40.

5. It was also customary for earlier critical attempts to assess or study Taiwan's modernist literature in terms of its presumed Western model, even when some of them sought to critique the latter along with the former by adopting a Marxist position that favors a very different viewpoint on the representation of reality. Lu Cheng-hui's article is a prime example of this approach; see Lu Cheng-hui, "Xiandai zhuyi zai Taiwan: cong wenyi shehuixue de jiaodu lai kaocha" [Modernism in Taiwan: From the Perspective of Literary Sociology], *Taiwan shehui yenjiu jikan* [Taiwan: A Radical Quarterly in Social Studies] 1, no. 4 (Winter 1988): 181–210.

6. Following Michelle Yeh's translation of the Chinese title, I keep the word "Quarterly" in the English title, but it has to be noted that the official Chinese name of the periodical did not include such words to indicate the frequency of its publication, and it was briefly published bimonthly, with its English title *The Modernist Poetry Monthly* (*Xiandaishi yuekan*) printed on the front cover of those issues. See Michelle Yeh, "'On Our Destitute Dinner Table': *Modern Poetry Quarterly* in the 1950s," in *Writing Taiwan: A New Literary History*, eds. David Der-wei Wang and Carlos Rojas (Durham: Duke University Press, 2007), loc. 2331–803, Kindle. Michelle Yeh works as a scholar in American academia but goes by her Chinese name Hsi Mi when writing in Chinese. When citing her Chinese-language publications in this book, I will refer to her as Hsi Mi. This has to be clarified from the outset because this quoted essay, as one of her essays on Taiwan's modernist poetry in the 1950s and 1960s, first appeared in Chinese in 2000 and was later on collected in her 2009 book *Taiwan xiandai shilun* [Reflections on Taiwan's Modern Poetry] (Hong Kong: Cosmos Books, 2009). The English version is not exactly a literal translation of the original, although with largely the same content.

7. Issues 22 and 23 of *Modern Poetry Quarterly* were edited by Ji Xian's protégé, Huang He-sheng, whose interim editorship began in 1958 and lasted until Ji Xian came back from his hiatus to resume editorship from issue 24 onward. The journal remained a privately funded publication throughout its existence, supported financially by subscriptions, purchases, advertisements, and in large part the founder Ji Xian's own money. It had experienced periods of financial difficulties as well as glory days since its inception in February 1953 and, after producing forty-five issues, eventually folded in February 1964.

8. Ji Xian, "Explicating the Tenets of the Modernist School," trans. Paul Manfredi, in *The Columbia Sourcebook of Literary Taiwan*, eds. Sung-sheng Yvonne Chang, Michelle Yeh, and Ming-Ju Fang (New York: Columbia University Press, 2014), loc. 4158–96, Kindle. For the original Chinese text, see Ji Xian, "Xiandai pai xintiao shiyi" [Explicating the Tenets of the Modernist School], *Xiandaishi* [Modern Poetry Quarterly] 13 (February 1956): 4.

9. Yeh, "Destitute," loc. 2353.

10. Barnhisel, *Cold War Modernists*, loc. 201.

11. Lin Heng-tai, one of the core members of the modernist school, is the most well-known representative of such a difficult linguistic transition facing the native Taiwanese writers in the immediate postwar years, who he himself describes as "the

translingual generation" (*kuayue yuyan de yidai*). See Lin Heng-tai, *Li shikan* [Li Poetry] (June 1985): 127. For English-language references on this situation, see, for instance, Yeh, "Destitute," loc. 2546; Sung-sheng Yvonne Chang, *Literary Culture in Taiwan: Martial Law to Market Law* (New York: Columbia University Press, 2004), loc. 1643–1713, Kindle.

12. Barnhisel, *Cold War Modernists*, loc. 3991. The book also provides similar examples of the roles government agents played in initiating the literary magazine *Encounter* in Europe (chapter 4), and Faulkner's central place in the American Book Programs and USIA goodwill tours abroad (chapter 3).

13. As it is often referred to as the Kuomingtang government (*Guomindang zhengfu*), the Nationalist regime ruled Taiwan via the three arms of the party, the government, and the military (*dangzhengjun*). Two prime example of these nongovernment organizations that were, in effect, controlled or directed by representatives or proxies of the Nationalist regime were the Committee on Chinese Literature and Art Prizes (*Zhonghua wenyi jiangjin weiyuanhui*), and the Chinese Literature and Art Association (*Zhongguo wenyi xiehui*). For more detailed expositions on such organizations, their roles, and influences, see Yeh, "Destitute," loc. 2436–72; Hsi Mi, *Taiwan*, 48–55; and Ying Feng-huang, *Huashuo 1950 niandai Taiwan wenxue* [An Illustrated History of 1950s Taiwanese Literature] (Taipei: Vista, 2017), which is by far the most comprehensive account in this regard.

14. The term "combat literature and art" (*Zhandou wenyi*) had appeared much earlier than it was officially adopted and announced by Chiang Kai-shek in January 1955 as the Nationalist government's signature cultural policy of the time. For a concise timeline of this particular genre, see Lin Rui-ming, "*Taiwan wenxueshi nianbiao*" [Timeline of Taiwanese Literature], in *Taiwan wenxue shigang* [*History of Taiwanese Literature*], by Yeh Shih-tao (Kaohsiung: *Wenxue Jie* magazine, 1987), 181–352.

15. Published in 2000, Chiu Kuei-fen's article "Cong zhanhou chuqi nüzuojia de chuangzuo tan Taiwan wenxueshi de xushu" [History Writing and Women's Literature in the Early Post-War Period], *Chung Wai Literary Quarterly* 29, no. 2 (July 2000), addresses both the tendency to generalize, often in dismissive terms, this period's literature as "anticommunist literature" in the earlier attempts at writing the history of Taiwan literature, and the concomitant criticism of such a characterization. "Anticommunism" is featured prominently in Yeh Shih-tao, *Taiwan wenxue shigang* [History of Taiwanese Literature] (Kaohsiung: *Wenxue Jie* magazine, 1987), and Chen Fang-ming, *Taiwan xin wenxue shi* [A History of Modern Taiwanese Literature] (Taipei: Linking, 2011), which are two of the most definitive, textbook-like accounts of the relatively young discipline of Taiwan literature studies. Chang Su-zhen's pioneering essay on 1950s literature, for example, lists nostalgia (*huaixiang sijiu*) as one of the main characteristics of this period's literary production, along with policy-driven anticommunism and combat literature; see Chang Su-zhen, "Wuling niandai Taiwan xinwenxue yundong" [The New Literature Movement of Taiwan in the 1950s], *Chung Wai Literary Quarterly* 14, no.1 (June 1985): 130. These three terms are all conducive to the kind of nationalist sentiment and "patriotism" promoted and legitimized by the Nationalist government. While acknowledging the limits or pitfalls of such sweeping generalizations, I use these terms as illuminating contexts

through which to critically examine the collective movement and individual works of the period, which, as the reader shall see, cannot be exhausted by any of these characterizations.

16. With regard to the last incentive, Edwin A. Winckler offers an incisive analysis of what he calls the "establishment cronyism"; see Edwin A. Winckler, "Cultural Policy on Postwar Taiwan," in *Cultural Change in Postwar Taiwan*, eds. Stevan Harrell and Huang Chün-chieh (Boulder, CO: Westview Press, 1994), 41. For a concise, English-language review of the cultural policies that bore on the poetry scene in the 1950s, see Yeh, "Destitute," loc. 2442–66. Ying Feng-huang's illustrated history of literature in this period also shows in great details how the policies overwhelmingly shaped the literary scene at the time. Also see Sung-sheng Yvonne Chang, *Literary Culture*; Chang Su-zhen; Chen Fang-ming, *Taiwan*; and Cheng Ming-li, "Dang dai Taiwan wenyi zhengce de fazhan, yingxiang yu jiantao" [The Development, Influence and Critique of the Cultural Policies of Contemporary Taiwan], in *Dangdai Taiwan zhengzi wenxue lun* [Politics and Literature in Contemporary Taiwan] (Taipei: China Times, 1994), for other accounts of the fraught relationships between cultural policies and literature.

17. Quoted in Liu Zheng-zhong, "Jun lü shiren de shuli xintai: yi wuliulshi niandai de Luo Fu, Shang Qin, Ya Xian weizhu" [The Sense of Alienation in the Poets as Soldiers: Luo Fu, Shang Qin, Ya Xian and Others in the 1950s and the 1960s], *Taiwan wenxue xuebao* [Bulletin of Taiwanese Literature] 2 (February 2001): 115. The short-lived *New Poetry Weekly* (*Xinshi zhoukan*) was published in the literary supplement pages of the local newspaper *Independence Evening News* (*Zili wanbao*) on Mondays from November 1951 to September 1953.

18. Liu Zheng-zhong, "Jun lü shiren," 116.

19. Ji Xian, "Declaration," trans. Paul Manfredi, in *The Columbia Sourcebook of Literary Taiwan*, eds. Sung-sheng Yvonne Chang, Michelle Yeh, and Ming-Ju Fang (New York: Columbia University Press, 2014), loc. 4154, Kindle. For the original Chinese text, see *Xiandaishi* [Modern Poetry Quarterly] 1 (February 1953): 1.

20. Ji Xian, "Explicating," loc. 4196. For the original Chinese text, see Ji Xian, "Xiandai pai," 4.

21. Yeh, "Destitute," loc. 2528–32.

22. *Xiandaishi* [Modern Poetry Quarterly] 22 (December 1958): 2. The notable exception is, as mentioned in this paragraph, Ji Xian's very first book of poetry after moving to Taiwan, titled *Zai feiyang de shidai* [In the Soaring Age] (Taipei: Baodao Wenyi: 1951).

23. The Chinese equivalent to "cover" or "smoke screen," *huagnzi* is used by Chen I-chih, while other critics are not as explicit in characterizing this Cold War modernist strategy. See Chen I-chih, *Shengna: Taiwan xiandai zhuyi shixue liubian* [Sonar: The Evolution of Taiwanese Modernist Poetry] (Taipei: Chiu Ko, 2006), 52.

24. Liu Zheng-zhong, "Jun lü shiren," 116.

25. Yeh, "Destitute," loc. 2532.

26. Ibid, loc. 2583.

27. Ibid, loc. 2422. Also see Yeh, "Modern Poetry in Chinese: Challenges and Contingencies," in *A Companion to Modern Chinese Literature*, ed. Yingjin Zhang

(Chichester: Wiley Blackwell, 2016), for the historical significance of Old Poetry and the marginalization of poetry in modern times.

28. *Xiandaishi* [Modern Poetry Quarterly] 15 (October 1956): 80. The translation quoted here is Michelle Yeh's. See Yeh, "Destitute," loc. 2386.

29. Yeh, "Destitute," loc. 2510.

30. Ji Xian, "Editorial," *Xiandaishi* [Modern Poetry Quarterly] 11 (Autumn 1955): 89.

31. Yeh, "Destitute," loc. 2510.

32. It is clear that this stance is similar to and consistent with Western modernism's rejection of Romanticist celebration of passions and various forms of sentimentalism; however, when it comes to the definition, role, and representation of the intellect, consensus among the modernist poets in Taiwan wasn't as clear. See Liu Zheng-zhong, "*Zhuzhi, chao xianshi, xiandai pai yundong*: Taiwan, 1956–1969" [Intellectualism, Surrealism, and the Modernist Movement: Taiwan, 1956–1969], in *Ji Xian*, ed. Wen-wei Shiu, vol. 9 of *Taiwan xiandangdai zuojia yanjiu ziliao huibian* [Compilation of Research Materials of Modern and Contemporary Taiwanese Writers], ed. Te-ping Feng (Tainan: National Museum of Taiwan Literature, 2011), for an attempt to unpack this issue.

33. Such a tendency toward opacity is one of the main reasons that prompted Ji Xian to unilaterally announce the dismantling of the modernist school in 1962. There will be more discussion on this in the next chapter.

34. See Yeh, "Destitute," loc. 2595–635, for her comment on the kind of professionalism promoted by *Modern Poetry Quarterly*.

35. Armstrong, *Modernism*, 3.

36. Yeh, "Destitute," loc. 2604.

37. In "Explicating the Tenets of the Modernist School," there is little exposition on the question of purity beyond a deference to "international movements of Pure Poetry" and the analogy of "a small jar of beef concentrate." See Ji Xian, "Explicating," loc. 4187–196.

38. The quote here is Yeh's translation in "Destitute," loc. 2353.

39. The highest profile of public debates stirred by this manifesto were the multiple heated exchanges between Ji Xian and Qin Zhihao, who, like the former, was already an experienced poet emigrating from mainland China before leading the rival poetry society *Lanxing* [Blue Star], which was founded in 1954 and initially adopted a much more conservative approach to practicing New Poetry, or *baihuashi*. In terms of poetic genealogy, *Lanxing* poets appeared to model after the New Crescent School, on the one hand, and Symbolist and Romantic Poetry when it comes to Western influences. As Chen I-chih points out, Ji Xian and Qin Zhihao had had more overlapping and similarity than their open sparring suggested, including the Symbolist influence. This became even more noticeable after Qin revised his earlier positions regarding some of the tenets and Ji Xian later modified his stance on the controversial second tenet; see Chen I-chih, *Shengna*, 51–64. Also see similar comments in Chen Kang-fen, *Shi yuyan de meixue geming: Taiwan wuling liuling niandai xinshi lunzhan yu xiandai guiji* [The Aesthetic Revolution of Poetry: Debates and Trajectories of Modern Chinese Poetry in Taiwan from the 1950s to 1960s] (Taipei: Wanjuanlou, 2018), 38–62.

In addition, the founding members of *Chuangshiji* [Epoch Poetry Journal], another poetry society that started in 1954, originally highlighted their difference from the modernist school, especially on the issue of "horizontal transplant"; however, they, too, adjusted their positions over time, as it has become a critical common sense that they carried on and went even further on some aspects of the modernist experimentation initiated by *Modern Poetry Quarterly*. More related discussions on this will follow in the next chapter.

40. Most notably, the divergent and often polarized evaluations of the modernist literature have emerged since the debates surrounding nativist literature. See Sung-sheng Yvonne Chang, *Modernism and the Nativist Resistance: Contemporary Chinese Fiction from Taiwan* (Durham, NC: Duke University Press, 1993), Kindle, for a detailed and overall balanced account on related topics.

41. For instance, Tsai Ming-Yen, "Yijiu wuling niandai Taiwan xiandaishi de jige mianxiang" [On Some Facets of Taiwan Modern Poetics in the 1950s], *Taiwan wenxue yanjiu xuebao* [Journal of Taiwan Literary Studies] 11 (October 2010), contests this critical common sense, which for an extended period of time appeared to be the mainstream historical narrative.

42. Specifically, for Ji Xian's "moderations" of some of his positions and the nuances therein, see Chen I-chih, *Shengna*, 42–51, and Chen Kang-fen, *Shi yuyan*, 100–101.

43. This certainly is an allusion to Michael E. Latham's central thesis in his book *Modernization as Ideology*, which also focuses on the Cold War era. See Michael E. Latham, *Modernization as Ideology: American Social Science and "Nation Building" in the Kennedy Era* (Chapel Hill: The University of North Carolina Press, 2000).

44. Ji Xian, "Explicating," loc. 4164.

45. Ibid., loc. 4178.

46. Ibid., loc. 4187.

47. Lin Nikki Jin-Li, "Lengzhan yishi xingtai yu xiandai zhuyi de wenhua xiangxiang: yi zhanhou Taiwan yu Zhongguo de xiandaishi lunshu wei guancha zhongxin" [Cold War Ideology and Modernism's Cultural Imaginations: Observations on the Discourse of Modern Chinese Poetry in Post-war Taiwan and China], *Chung Wai Literary Quarterly* 46, no. 2 (June 2017): 136–37.

48. Ibid., 138.

49. See Eric Bennett, *Workshops of Empire: Stegner, Engle, and American Creative Writing during the Cold War* (Iowa City: University of Iowa Press, 2015), 2. The quotation here is taken slightly off the immediate context of Bennett's introductory chapter, which does not focus on the underlying paradoxes of the postwar era, but other parts of his book, particularly the chapter on Paul Engle as a Cold War era "warrior," will touch on this issue. Examples of statements and behaviors that belie or contradict the tenets of "freedom" and individualism in Cold War America abound in both Barnhisel, *Cold War Modernists*, and Végső, *Naked Communists*.

50. Arne Odd Westad, "Introduction," in *Reviewing the Cold War: Approaches, Interpretations, Theory*, ed. Arne Odd Westad (London: Frank Cass, 2000), 1.

51. Xie Kun-hua, *Zhuanyi xiandaixing: 1960–70 niandai Taiwan xiandaishi changyu zhong de xiandaixing xiangxiang yu zhonggu* [Translating Modernity: The Imagination and Revaluation of Modernity in 1960–1970s' Taiwan Modern Poetry] (Taipei: Taiwan Student Books, 2010), 47–85.

Chapter Two

A Double-edged Sword?

THE RISE OF THE SOLDIER-POETS AND THEIR MODERNIST TURN

From the long-range historical view, the alternative vision of poetry and the new possibility of literary production opened up by the modernist poetry movement not only survived under restrictive circumstances of Cold War Taiwan but also flourished into a new and dominant paradigm whose lasting impacts still remain palpable in Taiwan's culture scene today. The process, however, had scarcely been smooth. Since the aforementioned *xiandaipai* ("the modernist school") reached the apex of its momentum and reputation when more than a hundred poets joined the collective in April 1956, it elicited multiple rounds of heated debates from within the circle of fellow poets, drew uninformed criticism from lay detractors outside the poetry scene, and was once infamously and unilaterally declared "disbanded" by its proverbial leader, Ji Xian, in 1962.[1] The modernist poetry movement ended up being carried on under a slightly different banner. The critical consensus has long established a retroactive characterization of post-*xiandaipai* poetry as "modernist" and a certain degree of continuity between the first and second phases of the modernist movement,[2] but the twists and turns in the process warrant more critical attention if we are to better understand both the soldier-writer phenomenon and its predecessor. Before I further discuss the contexts, conditions, and other reasons for the rise and ensuing dominance of modernist literature in Cold War Taiwan in the next sections of this chapter and throughout this book, suffice it to say at this point that the first wave of the postwar modernist poetry movement succeeded in gaining ground on the leadership role within a literary establishment that was largely hierarchical and grew increasingly elitist, despite its initial antagonistic character and relative lack of popularity. This early successful challenge (to both Old Poetry and new regulated verse) paved way for the historical fact that since the 1960s, the designation "Modern Poetry" (*xiandaishi*) has replaced "New Poetry" (*xinshi* or *baihuashi*) to become a collective term that denotes the poetry of our times.[3] It also testifies to the groundbreaking significance of the modernist poetry movement and, as Hsi Mi rightly argues, of *Modern Poetry Quarterly*, since we witnessed an enormous and fundamental change in the poetry scene in the few years following the founding of the journal.[4] In hindsight, such a change appears to be irreversible, but the paradigm shift could not have consolidated its preeminent position in the post-*xiandaipai* years without the emergence of a revamped *Chuangshiji*—a poetry journal whose most well-known core members, Luo Fu, Shang Qin, Ya Xian, and Zhang Muo, were all young soldiers at the time. *Chuangshiji*, which was founded in 1954 and didn't adopt the official English title *The Epoch Poetry Quarterly* until several years after its inception,[5] had existed under the shadow of *MPQ* before filling in the void left by the gradual disintegration of the latter since late 1950s and emerging as the new pacesetter of the modernist poetry movement around the early to mid-1960s.[6]

From Conscripted Nationalists to Avant-garde Soldier-Poets

What made this second peak of the modernist poetry movement so extraordinary and worthy of further critical examinations here, I argue, is not only the culmination and canonization of modernist literature it helped to cement by late 1960s but also the trajectories and modes of operation and existence that parallel the first, reflecting or refracting their Cold War circumstances: *moderation*, or experimentation within self-imposed bounds, and the *bifurcation* of the poets' literary practices and life experiences in response to the movement's underlying tension and constitutive contradiction. First of all, the second wave of modernist poetry spearheaded by *Chuangshiji* was, too, characterized by its moves of moderations, initially as a mean of negotiating or compromising with the policies and initiatives of combat literature, then with revisions that appeared drastic but remained embedded in and secured by the safety zone whose groundwork had been laid by now. In its inaugural editorial, *Chuangshiji* vows to "accentuate the nationalist direction for New Poetry" (*xinshi de minzu luxian*) as part of the first of its "three precepts" that mostly echo or expand on the "party lines" propagated by the authorities without elaborating much on the journal's views on poetry itself and aesthetic issues,[7] on which the journal would concentrate almost exclusively after its modernist turn. Interestingly, the explications of these precepts in the same editorial champion the importance of politics to individual lives and the fate of the nation—while calling for the poet's interventions into "politics" and the occurrences of one's times—to the extent that they denounce the familiar "art for art's sake" claim and dismiss literature's autonomy apropos of politics.[8] Although such a perspective on the relationship between politics and literature revealed more the mobilization of statist politics, which is the opposite of the interventionist stance and grassroots approach of radical politics, than the poet's agency, it nevertheless represented, retrospectively, a far cry from the journal's latter-day isolationist attitude toward politics as they began to valorize, like the modernist school, the purity of poetry.

How did the representative poets of *Chuangshiji* get to that latter position and become surrealists—of all schools of thought—since their humble beginnings as soldier-poets still learning their craft while striving to rise above the unison of "combat poetry" (*Zhandou shi*) barely distinguishable from slogans? What appeared to be an abrupt and monumental alteration of the group's direction had in fact been preceded and shaped by multiple moderations of the abovementioned precepts. If Ji Xian and the modernist school came to terms with the Cold War imperatives of anticommunism and patriotism *under duress*, then the propagation of these messages and initiatives was simply part of the *job description* for the soldier-poets who, whether wittingly or not, were deemed—or expected to function—as an integral cog in the propaganda machine. To be sure, a poetry journal like *Chuangshiji* belonged to a slightly different category than such mouthpiece publications as *Youth Warrior Daily* (*Qingnian zhanshi bau*) or a more general, multi-genre literary magazine like *Literature and Art in the Military* (*Junzhong wenyi*)—all of which attested to the Nationalist government's aggressive drive to combat and contain communist influences since 1950 and to prevent a repeat of their crushing defeat in the propaganda war at the hands of the Chinese Communist Party during the Chinese Civil War, as mentioned in the previous chapter. Yet no publication founded by the military personnel could have come into existence without the approval of or endorsement by their higher-ups, despite the fact that these official policies had encouraged and mobilized the literary activities in the military to such an extent that almost each of its notable units had its own *wenyi* publication.[9] One can thus infer that *Chuangshiji* was *supposed* to perform the function of setting the standards on the front of New Poetry, even though the co-founders Luo Fu and Zhang Muo established the journal out of their own volition and apparently envisioned something else in addition to the stated goals in the editorials and ample examples of "combat poetry," especially in the first few issues.[10]

Nonetheless, the "something else" in question, though initially unclear to even the founding poet-soldiers themselves, eventually set them apart from the rank and file of soldier-writers after a series of trial and error. Unsurprisingly, most of the *Chuangshiji* poets have written samples of combat poetry, which seems a natural fit to their profession. Yet as early as the second issue, the editorial criticizes the crudeness and naivety of many "combat poems" that in effect trivialize the title "combat poet" (*Zhandou shiren*).[11] Two poems published in issue 3 and the "News on the Poetry Scene" column in issue 4 (which is a thematic issue on combat poetry) further call out a so-called "combat poet" who allegedly gives the fellow soldier-poets a bad name.[12] Expanding on the conventional associations of poetry with beauty, goodness, and freedom to highlight poetry's innate fighting spirit against their opposites—that which is ugly, cruel, dark, and oppressive (read: communism)—the editorial statement of issue 4 nevertheless does not lose sight of the indispensability of "artistic forms" in its somewhat stretched connection between poetic endeavors and warfare.[13] Such critical reconsiderations of the genre that was earnestly promoted by the authorities and that they, more than those in other walks of life, were expected to write or even specialize in already foreshadow the journal's first notable departure from the mission as well as baggage of combat poetry.

A Moderate Proposal: In Transition to the Surrealism Period

Five issues and less than two years into its existence, *Chuangshiji* published an editorial titled "A Proposal to Establish the New National Poetic Paradigm," which begins with its own survey of the poetry scene and categorizes the writings of New Poetry in "Free China" at the time into three "types" (*xing* in Chinese): sonnet type, alluding to the new regulated verse that mimics the centuries-old Western form; combat poetry type, referring to the sloganeering poems previously dismissed by the journal; and the modern type, with reference to poetic practices since Baudelaire. Save for the third type, the editorial argues, works in the first two categories do not even merit commentary, since they do not engage in the innovation of the genre—which the modern type does.[14] Significantly, it acknowledges the founding of the modernist school, which occurred less than two months before the publication of issue 5 of *Chuangshiji*, passing little overt judgment on the former beyond giving it credit for its effort to innovate, on the one hand, but, on the other, mentioning the "occasionally eccentric poems" produced by the modernist school and their own observation that there were differing views on poetry among those falling under the third category (which is why the term here is the broader "modern type" instead of "modernist type").[15] The editorial aims to propose an alternative to all these three types, however. What it calls "new national poetic paradigm" consists, first of all, in the foregrounding and valorization of imagery and ambience (*yijing*), insisting on, interestingly, the "purity" of poetic language, just as the modernists do. The second pointer underlined in the "Proposal" is a (rather vague) reference to "Chinese style,

Oriental taste" (*Zhongguofeng, dongfangwei*).[16] While stressing the "essence" of the new national poetic paradigm in order to undergird and complement the abovementioned emphasis on formal elements and techniques, the editorial's thesis on such essence, or the content of the new poetic paradigm it conceives for the nation, resorts to a quite commonplace discourse of cultural nationalism, albeit a more eclectic one that claims to synthetize different schools of thought in the Chinese cultural tradition, such as Confucianism and Taoism.[17]

This proposal for a "new national poetic paradigm," however, did less to establish a lasting model to follow or define this group of soldier-poets than to signal a transitional phase of *Chuangshiji*. Clearly moving further away from the official policy of contributing to the production of combat literature (whether they still regarded it as part of their soldierly mission or not), the visible departure from the inaugural "precepts" may have been motivated at once by the group's continued quest for that "something else" and by the radically changed dynamics of the poetry scene in postwar Taiwan—namely, the founding of the modernist school in early 1956. In fact, Luo Fu attended the launching ceremony of the modernist school, although in the capacity of "observer," unlike the other attendees, who signed up to become members of the modernist school. The event evidently had some impact on him, which may factor into the drafting of this proposal.[18] Again, moderation is key to understanding the fashions in which modern(ist) poetry developed in Cold War Taiwan. Although the proposal celebrates the sophistication of technique and the purity of poetic language as some sort of "difference-maker" in determining the quality of a politically correct poem, it counterbalances—as it were—the highlighting of formal elements and some measure of autonomy implied in such formulations with the weight and overall framework of a revised ("new") "national poetic paradigm." Similar to the modernist's maneuver of listing Cold War buzzwords such as "anticommunism" and "patriotism" in the last item of the 1956 manifesto, the soldier-poets' framing of their poetics in terms of national paradigm may well be a gesture of swearing allegiance to the powers that be, thereby deploying a safety valve, even if they sincerely believed in prioritizing the expression of national essence. Of course, if the modernist mention of those keywords were merely perfunctory, as they receded to the background of the modernist statements that rendered them irrelevant, then the soldier-poets still kept the flag-raising in the nationalist facade that appeared to be inextricable from the substance of their ideal paradigm of poetry. Overall, the proposal is nonetheless a modification of "the nationalist direction" in the inaugural editorial. The explicit reference to an overarching (and the only viable) politics at the very beginning of the journal is now replaced by "Chinese style" and taste, a relatively covert allusion to nationalist politics,[19] or what I would call a "soft-core nationalism."

Apart from staking out its moderated position in accordance with the constraints of political reality, the proposal also signaled the journal's moderation on the steps it had taken in the direction of the modernist movement. As indicated above, the proposal echoed the latter's pursuit of the purity of poetry, and apparently endorsed the modernist valorization of formal experimentation, with the trappings of implied artistic autonomy therein. Yet it also set a self-imposed limit on the extent to which it would go along the modernist movement by seeking to establish a "new national paradigm" for poetry—a revised or reformed "vertical inheritance" that the modernist school claimed to do without. To be sure, *Chuangshiji*'s response to this controversial tenet in the modernist manifesto was neither exceptional nor particularly pointed vis-à-vis the modernist school, since such a blanket jettisoning of tradition (as substituting "horizontal transplant" for "vertical inheritance" was usually perceived) not only didn't garner support from much of the cultural scene but also invited fierce and targeted attacks from the other New Poetry practitioners (especially the Blue Star poets) as well as conservative critics.[20] Indeed, it would be inconceivable for the soldier-poets, who by the nature of their profession were supposed to follow and carry out orders, to publicly endorse a stance on tradition many in the general public found iconoclastic, even though they, too, had developed a pattern of bifurcation of their textual practices—those of the soldier and those for the poet in the soldier—just like the modernists. It was as if the soldier-poets strove to navigate their path forward in the general direction of modernist veneration of newness, paused halfway to survey the landscape, and, in effect, wound up pitching their tent of "new national poetic paradigm" in the middle ground between the nationalist, blatantly tendential combat poetry and the modernist school's Western model.

Whether the middle ground in question was to be construed as a compromise or an eclecticism on their part,[21] it did not take the soldier-poets very far afield when it comes to breaking new grounds in Taiwan's postwar poetry writing. And it certainly did not foreshadow surrealist poetry, which seemed even more iconoclastic to the average reader than the presumption that literary modernity can only be transplanted from abroad, and which the group—Luo Fu, Shang Qin, and Ya Xian in particular—would inevitably be associated with a few years later. Before the appearance of issue 11 in April 1959, widely considered the starting point of the so-called "surrealism period" of *Chuangshiji*,[22] there certainly wasn't much inkling of surrealism in either the editorial remarks or individual poems published in the journal. Why, then, was there this sharp turn toward surrealist poetry, and how did it happen? I shall elaborate on the external factors in the context of the literary scene that contributed to the seemingly surprising "paradigm shift" in the next section; however, here it behooves us to first note a couple of key characteristics that may be considered "internal" to the core members' developments as young poets but are also related to the prevailing mindset befitting the Cold War cultural politics in Taiwan: (a) the increasingly central place of formal elements in both their textual practices and poetics; and (b) their highly selective appropriation and unwitting (or deliberate) misreading of some Western concepts/terms, including surrealism.

Firstly, the emphasis on artistic forms and the attendant aesthetic issues such as imagery and ambience even before the "Proposal" could retroactively be interpreted as bearing the potentials for radical experimentation in form approximating the surrealist precedents if this tendency and a desire for novelty unmatched by their peers were not reined in by something like a "national poetic paradigm." Though there were not enough formally innovative samples before the surrealism period of the journal to collectively substantiate such potentials, occasionally individual works did offer glimpses of what would, in the next phase, evolve into the shocking juxtaposition of life and death or of otherwise irrelevant scenes, with concrete and crisp imagery of conceit, evincing a sense of poignant irony, or the pervading ambience of helplessness and confoundedness. Take, for instance, Luo Fu's "An Abandoned Infant," published in issue 5 of *Chuangshiji*:

> A good-looking couple hurried by, covering their noses,
> Around the street corner, there lay a naked, abandoned infant.
> A group of swarming flies congregated, discussing in a hushed tone:
> Solemnly, they were arguing over an amazing issue.[23]

The poem goes on to compare the sight to "a work of art in another *les Fauves* exhibition that's in vogue," and ends by shadowing the good-looking couple with a pair of stray dogs copulating in a back alley.[24]

In another Luo Fu poem, titled "Rickety Buildings" and included in the same issue, the whole text—both the sentiment and the logic as well as meaning of the iteration—hinges on the intertwined images of the shaky buildings and the speaker's tentative movements as a mysterious "cold cobra" amidst the equally enigmatic "rickety buildings" that bear some uncanny visual likeness:

> I carried the world and walked into the world
> Like a limbless, cold cobra,
> Tentatively, yet with my head raised, slithering under the shadows
> Of these towering, rickety buildings.[25]

Readers who are familiar with Luo Fu's most famous poems in the "Death of a Stone Cell" sequence may be able to recognize in this early work a semblance of the recurring insinuations of the precariousness, predicament, or even conundrum of existence humans have no choice but to confront, as many critics have explicated in light of existentialism, complete with the opaque referents seemingly pointing toward some generic human conditions. Regardless of the extent of resemblance to surrealist poetry, the label that would be forever attached to *Chuangshiji*, examples like these attest to the gaps between combat poetry and the kind of poetry that is closer to their real pursuit outside of their soldier identity. It is in the context of the towering presence of anticommunist and patriotic literature in the 1950s that one can better grasp and appreciate the stark contrast between—and the tensions therein—the bifurcated textual practices of the soldier-poets. Against the backdrop of the brightness of future prospects supposedly illuminated by combat literature, such embryonic forms of surrealist poetry, or simply rudiments of something to come that is not yet nameable, may well be viewed as what the critic Hsi Mi characterizes as "poetry noir."[26]

Secondly, it is important to point out that the prioritization of formal innovation also underlay the reception and appropriation of the imported schools of thought and cultural trends writers in Cold War Taiwan were keen in modeling after, surrealism not the least. As Ya Xian recounts, he had some reservations about surrealism when he first read about André Breton and made revisions accordingly while adopting the so-called "surrealist technique" in his own writing. What he found to be worthy of studying and transplanting in surrealism was its technique rather than its spirit. Moreover, surrealist technique was but one of the techniques at his disposal, and it shouldn't be the only one. Otherwise, one would likely step into the dead end of extreme formal and linguistic experimentation. That is why he characterized his textual practices as "conditioned surrealism" (*zhiyue de chaoxianshi*) and further described Luo Fu's surrealist poetry in terms of the latter's "Sinicization of surrealist technique."[27] Although Ya Xian's remarks were written in retrospect, and around the time when the former surrealists and current canonical poets attempted to distance themselves from the label of surrealism,[28] anyone who suspects the utter incongruity between the left-leaning political propensities of the key figures of French surrealism and the solder identity of these poets working for a right-wing regime may be able to infer by now how the soldier-poets (mis)read surrealism, cherry-picked only the expedient components, and absolved themselves of the radical politics of the latter. The most significant difference between the surrealist poetry in Cold War in Taiwan and its French source of inspiration therefore resides in the absence of attempt or vision to bring about radical social and political changes via literary and artistic ones, as pointed out by Hsi Mi, who, despite the distinction mentioned above, acknowledges the potentially or comparatively radical ramifications of this surrealist turn under rather restrictive circumstances: establishing a greater degree of artistic autonomy when it had been historically weak or lacking up until then, and registering some measure of discontent against social norms.[29]

While their grounds for such a selective appropriation may not be tenable—technique and spirit, or form and content, cannot always be disentangled from one another—the soldier-poets' depoliticized transplantation of surrealism wasn't unique in Cold War contexts. We can recall how the originally antiestablishment character of European modernism in its earliest phase was diluted to little more than a "style" as it appeared more palatable to the bourgeoisie it historically rebelled against and became firmly ensconced in the canon in the postwar United States.[30] In Cold War Taiwan, even the unsettling, if not potentially subversive, call for a complete severing of "vertical inheritance" in the modernist manifesto would have to be counterbalanced by the Cold War byword "anticommunism" on the one hand and be supplemented on the other by Ji Xian's explication that clarifies what it means by being selective with regard to transplanting "all new schools of poetry from Baudelaire to the present": "What we reject are the sickly, fin de siècle tendencies; what we try to develop are those that are healthy, progressive, and uplifting."[31] It is important to note that the adjective "progressive" (*jinbude* in Chinese) in this available translation does not have the same connotations as associated with the progressive politics of historical surrealism or that of our times because, as elaborated in the last chapter, that which was, broadly speaking, "progressive" in the horizontal transplantation was couched by Ji Xian in the discourse of modernization—signifying *jinbude* and working mostly in tune with the official ideology. In addition, the modernist school's vision for being progressive and their call for reform were presented almost exclusively in terms of technique and formal innovation (e.g., against the backdrop of the orthodox Old Poetry and the popular new regulated verse).[32] One good and well-known example of such an allegedly clear-cut dissociation of technique and spirit (or essence), of form and content, can be found in Ji Xian's defense of the modernist manifesto, specifically concerning the mention of Charles Baudelaire. In spite of his fondness and appreciation of Baudelaire, Ji Xian has to make clear that he doesn't want Baudelaire's "behaviors and thoughts"—only his "means of expression" (*biaoxian shoufa*).[33]

Both Ji Xian's and the soldier-poets' selective appropriations of their respective sources may reflect, to a certain extent, the ineluctable alterations, approximations, and incompatibility involved in cultural translation. Nonetheless, I argue that their *bifurcation* of technique (or form) and essence (or content)—together with the valorization of the former—also significantly testify to their keen sensibility toward exploring and figuring out a literary practice that most befitted Taiwan's Cold War cultural politics, thereby resonating with the hearts and minds of the 1950s and 1960s literati and generating a great deal of momentum that propelled in two separate pivotal moments of the postwar modernist movement. In addition, when it comes to receiving and adapting to literary modernity, such a practice of bifurcating technique-method-tool on the one hand and essence-content-substance on the other is reminiscent of the long-standing discourse of national self-strengthening dating back to the late Qing dynasty, which advocated for applying Western knowledge as a tool or method only, while keeping one's firm footing in traditional Chinese learning (*zhongxue weiti, xixue weiyong*).[34] Bringing to the fore the underlying logic and modality of their peculiarly selective appropriations of imported terms/concepts, I argue, is key to a more in-depth understanding of their repeated moves of moderation (e.g., what they fall back on and why) and, more broadly, their radical potentialities as well as the politics of Cold War modernism in relation to resistance and power—topics I shall elaborate on in this and subsequent chapters. Suffice it to say at this point that the depoliticization of radical, or at least progressive, ideas from abroad was predicated on the founding exception of anticommunist and nationalist politics of the ruling Kuomintang that effaces its own politicization by defacing everything else admitted into its perimeters, or simply by keeping them out of people's reach with strict bans. What is interesting and requires further inquiry is how this mechanism is internalized (unknowingly misreading or censoring), responded to (knowingly and preemptively misappropriating), or a combination of both in individual cases of writing practices.

Unite and Fight: The Consolidation of the Modern Poetry Front

Apart from these intrinsic characteristics of the soldier-poets, I would also like to identity and examine the external contextual forces linked to the rise of the *Chuangshiji* poets and their momentous pivot to surrealism: first, the dynamics of the poetry scene circa late 1950s and, second, the gradual yet crucial shifts of cultural policies after mid-1950s. As indicated earlier, *Chuangshiji*'s "Proposal" was a moderated response to the 1956 modernist manifesto, which ushered in the first peak of the modernist poetry movement in the form of an unparalleled number of poets getting behind the banner of the modernist school in the next two months and validating the new paradigm it advocated.[35] There were, however, other responses to the manifesto that were not moderate at all. Among fellow practitioners of New Poetry, Qin Zhihao, who, like Ji Xian, had established his career as a poet in mainland China and was the leading figure of the poetry society *Lanxing* (Blue Star), initiated in August 1957 what subsequently became a very contentious series of debates on New Poetry (*xinshi lunzhan*) and resulted in a momentary rivalry between the modernist school and the Blue Star society. From outside the poetry scene, harsh criticisms or denunciations poured in shortly after the manifesto's publication and cropped up from time to time in the ensuing years, mostly coming from conservative critics clinging to the established criteria specifically targeted by the modernist school or lay readers irritated by the second tenet's seemingly outrageous implication of belittling tradition.[36] The first stage of these "controversies," from February 1956 to the time around *Chuangshiji*'s surrealist turn in 1959, inevitably put *MPQ* and Ji Xian (who wrote most of the "defenses" on behalf of the modernist school) in an embattled position and combative posture. Though enhancing the visibility and, in the long run, the influences of the modernist views, these debates appeared to have consumed the energies of Ji Xian and taken a toll on *MPQ*. Ji Xian announced in issue 23 (March 1959) that the journal would discontinue indefinitely, citing protracted financial difficulties.[37] Prior to that, he had gone into a period of hiatus from the editor position, passing it to his protégé Huang He-sheng for issues 22 and 23 before returning to editorship in 1960, when *MPQ* resumed publication.

Meanwhile, the attacks on New Poetry (not limited to the modernist paradigm) from outside the poetry circles intensified beginning in July 1959 and continued for about a year, as heated exchanges of rapid fire between poets and their detractors extended into the literary supplementary pages (*fukan*) of the major newspapers.[38] Voluntarily or reluctantly, with or without coordination, the poets formed a united front, as it were, against "outside enemies" as their varying perspectives on New Poetry converged. Interestingly, some positions of the modernist school can now be proven—though retroactively—to have been taken up or accepted to some degree by its former critics among the practitioners of New Poetry, based on their discourses about poetry circa these years of *xinshi lunzhan* and their textual practices thereafter.[39] We have mentioned the soldier-poets' acquiescence to some of the modernist school's approaches to poetry. It is also significant to note the gradual yet visible adaptations of the Blue Star poets to many of the views on New Poetry promoted by their modernist rivals. Qin Zhihao would use the modernist school's arguments on the questions of the purity of poetic language, the paramount place of literary modernity, the insistence on the modernization of traditional forms—just to name a few he himself had taken issue with—to refute an ultra-conservative critic of New Poetry; Yu Kwang-chung, who would turn out to be the most popular and celebrated poet of the Blue Star and had practiced the kind of regulated verse dismissed by Ji Xian, not only came to Qin Zhihao's defense but also embarked on a period of his own "moderate modernist experimentation" in the 1960s.[40]

Last but not least, the convergence of different groups of New Poetry practitioners happened at the heels of an impactful shift of cultural policy since the mid-1950s. Likely sensing the ineffectiveness of blatantly propagandist works, high-ranking cultural bureaucrats in the Nationalist government, as

Sung-sheng Yvonne Chang points out, "made a conscious, and rather abrupt decision to switch from hardcore anti-Communist literary mobilization" to official encouragement and endorsement of *chunwenxue* (literally, "pure literature").[41] Overtly tendential literature and art under the combat and patriotic umbrella evidently had run its course and become barren of appeal by the mid-1950s. This alteration of cultural policy, however, could also be part of the authoritarian regime's strategic adaptations to the changing political situations, specifically as a way of channeling the potentially underlying discontent into more innocuous subfields outside the realm of the political proper.[42] As the Nationalist government emerged from its relatively unstable control of Taiwan in the late 1940s and early 1950s to assert its ironclad grasp of power in the wake of the infusion of US military and financial aids, what could arguably be called a "soft authoritarian rule" was taking shape in the literary and cultural scenes.[43] While the term "*chunwenxue*" was never clearly stipulated and its conception could vary widely, writers conceivably saw the relaxation of official demands on politically correct and salient messaging as an opening for a new paradigm that suited their own literary orientation yet could still be tolerated by, or even safely entrenched in, the establishment. In other words, the time was ripe for the young soldier-poets to advance an alternative to the incrementally acquiesced modernist model as well as the hitherto politically adjusted experimentation they had proposed.

Rebel without a Cause? Surrealism sans the Name

The official sanctioning of *chunwenxue*, as Sung-sheng Chang writes, did not necessarily result from or reflect a widespread and taken-for-grated belief in art for art's sake.[44] Likewise, the label "surrealism" points less to the consistency between the *Chuangshiji* poets' transplantation and the French original—let alone their endorsement of the ideas and politics behind surrealism—than its viability under the circumstances, its appeal via their presentation (for example, touted as one that goes the farthest in formal experimentation), and the desire for differentiation born out of the dynamics of the competing visions of Modern Poetry in late 1950s. Surrealist poetry in Taiwan did not suddenly emerge from a vacuum.[45] As one of the imported schools of Western poetry, it was first introduced to the intelligentsia in postwar Taiwan *not* by the soldier-poets but notably by Ji Xian's associate Lin Heng-tai, among others, with some of the introductions and limited translations of its representative poets' works published in *MPQ*.[46] However, surrealism had not been high on the modernist school's agenda, and Ji Xian's position on surrealist poetry (which had been included as one of the new schools of poetry since Baudelaire in the manifesto) oscillated in the initial round of debates between 1956 and 1958.[47] According to Liu Zheng-zhong, the sticking point for Ji Xian lies in his insistence on the fourth tenet in the modernist manifesto, i.e., the emphasis on the intellect (*zhixing*), which commonplace reading tends to equate with rationality, while Lin Heng-tai, unlike Ji Xian, does not conflate the two, thereby reserving the possibility of accommodation for the irrational valorized by surrealism.[48] Of course the signature surrealist approach of "automatic writing," much maligned, too, in the ensuing debates in postwar Taiwan, seemed to Ji Xian indefensible and impractical to practice as a modernist technique he wished to focus on, irrespective of its "spirit" (the applicability of this technique or tool would later be addressed by the soldier-poets themselves). In any case, the *Chuangshiji* poets wholeheartedly subscribed to "the pursuit of pure poetry," as highlighted in the modernist manifesto, while they serendipitously worked in tune with the new initiative of "pure literature" (*chunwenxue*), but they ran counter to the modernists on the front of "the intellect"—based on their own (mis)conception of it as the opposite of the subconscious and the irrational. Although the differentiation the soldier-poets attempted to stake out appeared to be more of a nuance than a significant departure from the modernist model, it was the boldest move they had ventured thus far (before taking a couple of steps of moderation at a much later date), and it was enough to position *Chuangshiji* as the new enfant terrible, ready to replace the erstwhile and struggling radical—*Modern Poetry Quarterly*—in a cultural climate suddenly welcoming for a *specifically delimited range/type of newness*.

As noted above, *MPQ*'s temporary discontinuation was announced in March 1959 and had been preceded by the hiatus of Ji Xian's editorship the year before. In April 1959, as if by coincidence, *Chuangshiji* published its issue 11, which features revamped content and format and has generally been considered by scholars as the onset of the group's surrealism period, effectively filling the void left by *MPQ* at a perfect timing.[49] The soldier-poets, however, did not immediately overtake the leadership role (of the avant-garde variety, as far as poetry was concern) in the span of merely one issue, nor did they change the course of the modernist movement simply by raising the surrealist flag. As Xie Kun-hua points out, issue 11 heralds a new era of the journal mainly because it demonstrates a noticeable shift in editorial direction, including shedding completely any piece resembling combat poetry and giving a much more prominent space to the translations of poems and essays on poetics by Western authors,[50] as part of its bid for modernization (which had been exemplified by *MPQ*). Yet around this pivotal moment, the soldier-poets did not propose their own version of "surrealist manifesto," nor did the term "surrealism" surface in the editorials, calls for contributions, and other discursive pieces published in *Chuangshiji*.[51] According to Chen Yi-chih's fact-checking, the journal's first direct reference to surrealism appeared in the form of the translations of the French surrealist poet Philippe Soupault's poems in issue 19 (January 1964). By that time, multiple poetry journals had published translations and essays on French surrealism since *Chuangshiji* began anew in April 1959.[52] One cannot help but wonder whence came the ingrained impression that the soldier-poets carried the surrealist banner.

What was also new and noteworthy about *Chuangshiji*'s pivot to surrealism was how it veered off the predominant way of promoting new literary agenda up until that point by *not prescribing in advance* the principles, tenets, theories, or a label of what they meant to pursue,[53] other than its determination to change and experiment (within a pre-delimited "safe" parameter, of course). Rather, the soldier-poets immersed themselves in their textual practices—in the sense of experimentation as well as apprenticeship—bided their time, and eventually produced poems that speak volumes for what many perceived to be surrealist poetry in postwar Taiwan. The publication of Luo Fu's most significant defense and elucidation of his brand and vision of surrealist poetry, a long essay titled "The Poet's Mirror," coincided with that of his *Death of a Stone Cell* in 1965,[54] which is widely considered the grand milestone of surrealist poetry in Taiwan. However, the first of that sequence of poems collected in the volume originally appeared in issue 12 (July 1959) of *Chuangshiji*, which also includes Shang Qin's and Ya Xian's works that are usually categorized as "surrealist."[55] In other words, unlike their modernist school predecessors, and contrary to their own mode of operation prior to that point as well as the establishment's top-down mobilization, the soldier-poets undertook their surrealist textual practice sans the manifesto, amidst the cultural climate of flag-raising or "sloganeering" running amok in the Cold War. The surrealist pivot of the *Chuangshiji* poets thus marked a significant departure in terms of the mobilization of modernist literature in Cold War Taiwan, as they only announced that there would be changes to come without specifying or naming them.[56]

While it may be construed as an indication of the soldier-poets' aversion or disdain for doctrines, including those they were obliged to put forth and adhere to, hence signaling their antiestablishment nature or free spirit,[57] their textual practices and sporadic discourses on poetics during late 1950s and early 1960s neither explicitly turned against a certain paradigm nor espoused a specific model. Their radicality in this period, I argue, lies more in the fact that these poetic experiments proceeded without a fixed modality (their exclusive focus on form notwithstanding) and without a firm, preconceived definition of the banner they wished to carry (even though they clandestinely leaned toward a vaguely conceived surrealism). Indeed, one can even make the case that they didn't know what, exactly, they wanted to do and how they would go about doing it.[58] In the absence of a towering paternal figure like Ji Xian, or an overarching, leading "-ism," the young soldier-poets staged, for a short span of time, a certain *bottom-up mobilization* in which members of the coterie group fed off one another's energies and carried out experimentations that also visibly affected some readers in a momentarily decentralized poetry scene, even though they would go on to assume the leadership role they had once challenged and wielded institutional clout from within the establishment in a few years. Those fleeting years of wild formal experimentation, *retroactively portrayed as "surrealist,"* saw the most radical these poets would ever become and resulted in the best works they produced, which would never again be written by some of them.[59] In light of the curtailed and subdued circulation of liberalism among Westernized intellectuals, exemplified by short-lived magazines such as *Free China Review* (*Ziyou Zongguo*) and *Literary Star* (*Wenxing*) in the 1950s and 1960s, and contextualized in an often vague and idealized vision of "freedom" at the time, the soldier-poets' push for a measured liberalization and autonomy of their poetic practices can entail radical potentialities that they seemed unaware of, or that exceed what they envisioned to bring about.[60]

However, as with what appeared to be groundbreaking, original, and daring in Cold War modernism in postwar Taiwan, such raw radicality and creativity emerged as experimentation within self-consciously imposed bounds (e.g., depoliticizing surrealist poetry by severing its technique from its ideas and vision) and was characterized by moves of moderations delineated throughout this chapter. The soldier-poets' poetic adventures in this period, too, were already preemptively placed firmly in a safety net. Chronologically, they surfaced as the "second coming" of a movement by breaking new ground through the cracks in the literary establishment that had been pried open by the modernist school; ideologically, they gained legitimacy and circumvented censorship by grafting their discourses to the official narrative of modernization and capitalizing on the authorities' pivot to a presumably innocuous, depoliticized *chunwenxue*; institutionally, their literary practices were ensconced in the literary establishment of the military, which was part of the state apparatus and propaganda machine yet surprisingly tolerated, or did not strictly scrutinize, certain works by those from their own ranks, as long as the basic requirements of their day jobs were met and such writings did not blatantly turn against the establishment.[61] Clearly an unintended consequence of the state-run literary campaigns in the military that promoted anticommunist or combat literature, the rise of the soldier-poets and the paradigm shift they initiated nonetheless can be considered, more so than Ji Xian and his associates, the first instance of a state-sanctioned Cold War modernism—sanctioned in the sense that it had the acquiescence, if not the blessings, of the state—since the soldier-poets tapped into the resources of the state apparatus in which they were securely entrenched in addition to perfunctorily swearing allegiance to the official policies like most others at the time.

NOTES

1. Ji Xian's controversial move was announced in the Spring 1962 issue of *Modern Poetry Quarterly*. The journal continued under Ji Xian's editorship until 1964, despite his pronouncement of the death of the modernist school. For another public act of disowning and erasure by Ji Xian in 1964, much lesser known than the first, see Xie Kun-hua, *Zhuanyi xiandaixing: 1960–70 niandai Taiwan xiandaishi changyu zhong de xiandaixing xiangxiang yu zhonggu* [Translating Modernity: The Imagination and Revaluation of Modernity in 1960–1970s' Taiwan Modern Poetry] (Taipei: Taiwan Student Books, 2010), 49, note 2.

2. Lin Heng-tai was the first critic to propose the periodization of pre-and post-*xiandaipai* stages of the modernist poetry movement; see his "Xinshi de zai geming" [The Second Revolution of Modern Poetry], in *Lin Heng-tai quanji* [The Collected Works of Lin Heng-tai], ed. Heng-chhiong Li, vol. 5 (Changhua: Changhua County Cultural Affairs Bureau, 1998), 5–6. For the continuity, with nuances of course, between the modernist school and the surrealism period of *Chuangshiji*, see Hun Se Wook, *Xinshilun* [On New Poetry] (Taipei: Sanmin, 1998), 13–28; Chen Fang-ming, *Taiwan xin wenxue shi* [A History of Modern Taiwanese Literature] (Taipei: Linking, 2011); Chen I-chih, *Shengna: Taiwan xiandai zhuyi shixue liubian* [Sonar: The Evolution of Taiwanese Modernist Poetry] (Taipei: Chiu Ko, 2006), 102–103; Chen Kang-fen, *Shi yuyan de meixue geming: Taiwan wuling liuling niandai xinshi lunzhan yu xiandai guiji* [The Aesthetic Revolution of Poetry: Debates and Trajectories of Modern Chinese Poetry in Taiwan from the 1950s to 1960s] (Taipei: Wanjuanlou, 2018), 12, 84; Li Min-yong, *Zhanhou Taiwan xiandaishi fengjing: shuangchong gouzao de jingshen shi* [The Landscape of Taiwanese Postwar Modern Poetry: A Dual-Structural History of the Spirit] (Taipei: Chiu Ko, 2019), 58; Liu Zheng-zhong, "Zhuzhi, chao xianshi, xiandai pai yundong: Taiwan, 1956–1969" [Intellectualism, Surrealism, and the Modernist Movement: Taiwan, 1956–1969], in *Ji Xian*, ed. Wen-wei Shiu, vol. 9 of *Taiwan xiandangdai zuojia yanjiu ziliao huibian* [Compilation of Research Materials of Modern and Contemporary Taiwanese Writers], ed. Te-ping Feng (Tainan: National Museum of Taiwan Literature, 2011), 135–62.

3. Hsi Mi (Michelle Yeh), *Taiwan xiandai shilun* [Reflections on Taiwan's Modern Poetry] (Hong Kong: Cosmos Books, 2009), 48.

4. Ibid., 54.

5. Interestingly, the Chinese term *Chuangshiji* happens to be the standard Chinese translation of the *Book of Genesis* in the Bible. In addition to the "creation-out-of-nothing" connotation of this biblical allusion, whether it be coincidental or intentional on the founders' part, the literal sense of *Chuangshiji*, however, also points to a brand-new era being created and/or some kind of epoch-making importance. Owing to *Chuangshiji*'s indispensable role in the modernist movement as well as its longevity (it is still alive and well today), the journal's name not only befits but also reinforces the common impression of the lay reader that it created the now canonized modernist poetry from a slate wiped clean, if not out of nothing. Another layer of meaning of the term *Chuangshiji* could very well be associated with the sort of

rhetoric extravaganza prevalent in combat literature or propaganda tracts on the grounds of raising morale—which is part of the job description for almost all publications involving military personnel.

6. Xie Kun-hua, *Taiwan xiandai shi dianlü yu zhishi diceng de tuiyi: Yi Chuangshiji, Li shishe wei guancha hexin* [The Canonization of Taiwan Modern Poetry and the Alterations of Knowledge-scapes: The Cases of *Chuangshiji* and *Li* Poetry Society] (Taipei: Showwe Information, 2013) 31–34. Also see Chen, *Shi yuyen*, 12; Li, *Zhanhou*, 58.

7. See "Chuangshiji de luxiang—dai fakan ci" [The Path Forward for *Chuangshiji*—in Place of a Founding Statement], *Chuangshiji* [The Epoch Poetry Quarterly] 1 (October 1954): 2–3. The first precept unequivocally refers to the official nationalism promoted by the Kuomintang—the Nationalist government, even though the original term *minzu luxian* is not, nominally speaking, the same as the direction of the Nationalist government. As the explanatory parts of the editorial indicate, the third precept addresses the campaign for "cultural cleansing," which was encouraged and endorsed by government agencies but appeared to be voluntarily organized by the literary and cultural circles that sought to rid themselves of communist influences (the red elements) in culture and literature, as well as traces of pornography and decadency in literary and art forms. The second precept seems to be exempt from such reiterations of official policies and ideology, as it alludes to the rivalry and factions in the poetry scene (read: *MPQ* vs. the Blue Star) to urge a "steely unity" of poets and warn against mutual attacks and factions among them. Liu Zheng-zhong contends that this statement may well be considered a preemptive disclaimer, since soldiers at the time were particularly likely to raise suspicions when they formed their own group that set their own rules and demanded a certain level of allegiance. See Liu Zheng-zhong, "Junlü shiren de shuli xintai: Yi wuliulshi niandai de Luo Fu, Shang Qin, Ya Xian weizhu" [The Sense of Alienation in the Poets as Soldiers: Luo Fu, Shang Qin, Ya Xian and Others in the 1950s and the 1960s], *Taiwan wenxue xuebao* [Bulletin of Taiwanese Literature] 2 (February 2001): 118.

8. "Chuangshiji," 2–3.

9. Ying Feng-huang, *Huashuo 1950 niandai Taiwan wenxue* [An Illustrated History of 1950s Taiwanese Literature] (Taipei: Vista, 2017), 36–38. Chiang Ching-kuo, Chiang Kai-shek's son and heir apparent, served as the director of General Political Warfare Department, Ministry of National Defense (*Guofang bu zong zhengzhan bu zhuren*) from 1950 to 1954 and played a significant role in this aggressive and nation-wide campaign.

10. The fact that the first six issues were printed by the print shop at the navy headquarters suggests a certain level of control that comes with utilizing the resources from the navy; however, the editor(s) and the editorial board did have the latitude in determining the quality and publication of individual poems (which, of course, does not preclude the possibility of self-censorship).

11. "Editorial," *Chuangshiji* [The Epoch Poetry Quarterly] 2 (February 1955): 33.

12. "Editorial," *Chuangshiji* [The Epoch Poetry Quarterly] 4 (October 1955): 2. The two poems with the subtitles "to a certain 'combat poet'" are printed on page 8 and page 19 of issue 3, respectively.

13. "Editorial," *Chuangshiji* [The Epoch Poetry Quarterly] 4 (October 1955): 4.

14. "Jianli xin minzu shixing zhi chuyi" [A Proposal to Establish the New National Poetic Paradigm], *Chuangshiji* [The Epoch Poetry Quarterly] 5 (March 1956): 2.

15. Ibid.

16. Ibid., 3.

17. Ibid.

18. Luo Fu, "Shitan chunqiu shanshi nian" [Poetry Scene of the Last Thirty Years], *Chung Wai Literary Quarterly* 10, no. 12 (May 1982): 8–9.

19. Liu, "Junlü shiren," 119. Besides pointing out this modification, Liu also contends that in this proposal, what seems to be a continuation of the nationalist direction on the surface is already hinting at an attempt to distance itself from direct involvement in politics proper as well as the official version of nationalism.

20. For point-by-point reexaminations of the heated exchanges between Ji Xian and Qin Zhihao, see Chen, *Shengna*, 41–64. For *Chuangshiji* poets' nuanced attitude toward the modernist manifesto, as revealed in the "Proposal," see Liu, "Zhuzhi," 149–150.

21. Liu, "Junlü shiren," 117–120; Liu, "Zhuzhi," 151.

22. For the most schematic periodization of the journal's trajectories, see Xie, *Taiwan*, 31–48. Also see, for example, Liu, "Zhuzhi," 151; Chen, *Shi yuyen*, 12–13.

23. Luo Fu, "Qi ying" [An Abandoned Infant], *Chuangshiji* [The Epoch Poetry Quarterly] 5 (March 1956): 12. My own translation.

24. Ibid. My own translation.

25. Luo Fu, "Weilou" [Rickety Buildings], *Chuangshiji* [The Epoch Poetry Quarterly] 5 (March 1956): 13. My own translation.

26. Hsi, *Taiwan*, 98.

27. Ya Xian, *Zhongguo xinshi yanjiu* [Studies in Chinese Modern Poetry] (Taipei: Hong Fan, 1981), 14–15.

28. The strongest statement in this regard may be the one made by Zhang Muo, who wouldn't object to the characterization of "surrealist dimension" in the group's poetry but deemed it necessary to rid themselves of the label of surrealism. This remark is quoted in Chen, *Shengna*, 102.

29. Hsi, *Taiwan*, 85–87. Also see Chen Kang-fen, *Shi yuyen*, 120–121, for a similar argument and assessment.

30. See Greg Barnhisel, *Cold War Modernists: Art, Literature, and American Cultural Diplomacy* (New York: Columbia University Press, 2015), "Introduction" and chapter 1.

31. See Ji Xian, "Explicating the Tenets of the Modernist School," trans. Paul Manfredi, in *The Columbia Sourcebook of Literary Taiwan*, ed. Sung-sheng Yvonne Chang, Michelle Yeh, and Ming-Ju Fang (New York: Columbia University Press, 2014), loc. 4170, Kindle. Chen Fang-ming contends that Ji Xian's total rejection of the supposedly decadent and the "sickly" in modernism completely misses the point, ignoring and misunderstanding some quintessential characteristics of European modernism and its historically rebellious significance. See Chen Fang-ming, *Xiandai zhuyi ji qi buman* [Modernism and Its Discontents] (Taipei: Linking, 2013), 46–48.

32. For critiques of this sole focus on form and Ji Xian's lack of vision and attempt for reforms beyond the literary field, see Chen, *Xiandai*, 48–49, and Yang Tsung-han, *Taiwan xinshi pinglun: lishi yu zhuanxing* [Criticism on Taiwanese Modern Poetry: History and Transformation] (Taipei: Independent & Unique, 2012), 84–85.

33. Ji Xian, "Dui 'suowei xiandai pai' yiwen zhi dafu" [A Response to the Essay "The So-called Modernist School"], *Xiandaishi* [Modern Poetry Quarterly] 14 (April 1956): 72.

34. Xie, *Zhuanyi*, 68–69.

35. Chen, *Shengna*, 52–53.

36. See Chen Kang-fen's comprehensive timeline and documentations of these debates, *Shi yuyen*, 163–72. Particularly relevant to this part of the chapter is Yang Tsung-han's 2012 comments on such debates, *Taiwan*, 86–87, and Chen I-chih's 2006 account about the exchanges between Ji Xian and Qin Zhihao, *Shengna*, 51–56.

37. Ji Xian, "Bu shi ganyan" [Not a Sentimental Statement: On the Occasion of Our Journal's Sixth Anniversary], *Xiandaishi* [Modern Poetry Quarterly] 23 (March 1959): 1. Ji Xian's statement in question left many readers with the impression of announcing the cessation of the journal, since it came amidst the periods of discontinuation—which could be viewed as long delays—between issue 22 (June 1958) and issue 23 (March 1959), and again between issue 23 and issue 24 (June 1960). Liu Zheng-zhong's account ("Zhuzhi," 151) is an example. To clarify, Ji Xian disclosed in that short essay that the journal would have had no choice but to fold if not for an ad hoc arrangement: Ji Xian and the Taiwanese poet Lin Zong-yuan, who had been looking to found a poetry magazine, agreed that Lin would replace Ji Xian as the person in charge of *MPQ* financially as well as its daily running, while Huang He-sheng retained the editorship.

38. See Chen, *Shi yuyen*, 166–172 for the detailed documentation on some eighty entries related to this series of debates within the span of one year, which started with Su Xue-lin's critique of the Symbolist poetry and its Chinese advocates, including Qin Zhihao.

39. Hun, *Xinshilun*, 13–28. Yang Xiang, "Wuling niandai Taiwan xiandaishi fengchao shilun" [On the Trends of Taiwanese Modern Poetry in the Fifties], *Jingyi renwen xuebao* [Journal of Humanities] 11 (July 1999): 45–61. Similar remarks can be found in Chen, *Shengna*, 21–40, 83–108.

40. The terms Chen I-chih uses are "modernism in a broader sense" (*guangyi de xiandai zhuyi*) and "moderate modernism" (*wenhe de xiandai zhuyi*). See Chen I-chih's elaborations on these terms in *Shengna*, 83–90.

41. Sung-sheng Yvonne Chang, *Literary Culture in Taiwan: Martial Law to Market Law* (New York: Columbia University Press, 2004), loc. 1759–1784, Kindle. Chang points out how "a significant number of writers who supported the allegedly apolitical and genteel form of *chunwenxue* played dual roles as writers and literary bureaucrats" to facilitate this development. For prime examples of such cultural officials, see note 5. In addition, the term *chunwenxue*, as Chang observes, took on a "new significance" in Taiwan after 1949, despite its existence long before that.

42. It is worth noting that *Free China Review* (*Ziyou Zongguo*), a rare instance of dissent leveraging the American-style liberal democracy, had turned increasingly

critical of Chiang Kai-shek's monopoly of power since the mid-1950s, signaling its shift from an ally of the Kuomintang government's anticommunist politics to a more directly critical position under the liberalism banner. Its call for an opposition party is generally considered the last straw that contributed to the eventual banning and forced closure of the magazine in 1960.

43. See, for instance, Chang, *Literary Culture*, chapter 3 for the workings and impacts of the Nationalist government's soft-authoritarianism on the literary scene in Taiwan.

44. Ibid., loc. 1767–1776.

45. In colonial Taiwan circa 1930s, there had been Taiwanese poets who introduced and translated French surrealist poets and practiced their own brand of surrealist poetry, though their poetic experimentation never amounted to the scale of a movement. There have been plenty of research and scholarly outputs on this front since the 1990s. For a concise yet in-depth account of the most well-known surrealist poet in prewar Taiwan, Shui Yin-ping (Yang Chi-chang), see chapter 1 of Chen, *Shengna*. A quite similar situation also occurred in 1930s China, mostly limited to the group of poets based in Shanghai who promoted various schools of modernist poetry and art. See Shu-mei Shih's comprehensive book-length study on this in her *The Lure of the Modern: Writing Modernism in Semi-colonial China, 1917–1937* (Berkeley: University of California Press, 2001).

46. It has been widely known that Lin Heng-tai had briefly been exposed to modernist poetry, including surrealist works during the Japanese period of Taiwan. In his short piece "Guanyu xiandai pai" [About the Modernist School], Lin gives a simplified yet accurate periodization of a broadly conceived modernism in Europe, from cubism to Dadaism to surrealism; see Lin Heng-tai, "Guanyu xiandai pai" [About the Modernist School], *Xiandaishi* [Modern Poetry Quarterly] 17 (March 1957): 32–34. Besides, the earliest translations of poems by Guillaume Apollinaire and Jean Cocteau, who are associated with surrealism in terms of literary genealogy, albeit not directly, were published in *Xiandaishi* [Modern Poetry Quarterly] 13 (February 1956).

47. Liu, "Zhuzhi," 145–148.

48. Lin Heng-tai, "Zhongguo xiandaishi fengge yu lilun zhi yanbian" [The Evolutions of the Styles and Theories of Chinese Modern Poetry] in *Lin Heng-tai quanji* [The Collected Works of Lin Heng-tai], ed. Heng-chhiong Li, vol. 4 (Chuanghua: Changhua County Cultural Affairs Bureau, 1998), 177–179. Also see Liu's expositions in "Zhuzhi," 145–147.

49. Zhang Muo, "Bianjiren shouji" [Editor's Notes], *Chuangshiji* [The Epoch Poetry Quarterly] 11 (April 1959): 36. In his "Editor's Notes" in issue 11, Zhang Muo points out that the journal decided to make significant changes to not only its format but also its content back in February 1959, so the fact that this renovated version of *Chuangshiji* came to being right after *MPQ* suspended publication may have been just a coincidence—in a timely fashion for the former. Zhang Muo also acknowledges in this piece that *Chuangshiji* went through its own long delay in publication (for almost a year) and its struggles during that period. See Zhang, "Bianjiren," 36.

50. Xie, *Taiwan*, 33–34.

51. See Chen, *Shengna*, 103; Liu, "Zhuzhi," 152.

52. Chen, *Shengna*, 102–103.

53. Liu, "Zhuzhi," 152.

54. This essay was first published in issue 21 (December 1964) of *Chuangshiji* and appeared as the author's "Preface" to the very first edition of *Death of a Stone Cell*, published in early 1965. Although the term "surrealism" is mentioned in Luo Fu's 1961 article, "'Tianlangxing' lun" [A Commentary on Yu Kwang-chung's "Sirius"], *Xiandai Wenxue* [Modern Literature] 9 (July 1961): 77–92, this earlier and well-known piece is more a critique of the kind of poetics and textual practice represented by Yu than a plea for surrealist poetry. Nor does it elaborate on surrealism with the same length and depth as "The Poet's Mirror."

55. Issue 12 (July 1959) also includes Ya Xian's "Abyss" (*Shenyuan*)—probably his most well-known poem—as well as Shang Qin's "A Giraffe" (*Changjinglu*) and "A Fire Extinguisher" (*Miehuoqi*), widely considered among the representative works of surrealist poetry in postwar Taiwan. In addition, issue 11 (April 1959) had already published Luo Fu's "My Beast" (*Wo de shou*), which marked a significant stylistic change in his poetic trajectory.

56. See Zhang, "Bianjiren," 36.

57. Liu, "Zhuzhi," 153–54.

58. In retrospect, Ya Xian comes close to admitting that they understood "only about half" of what they read regarding surrealism, as indicated in his "Chuangshiji de piping xingge" [The Critical Nature of Genesis] in *Chuangshiji sishi nian pinglun xuan* [The Collected Reviews of Genesis in Forty Years], ed. Ya Xian and Chien Cheng-chen (Taipei: Chuangshiji Magazine, 1994), 357.

59. Ya Xian would produce virtually no more poetry after this period of intense and productive poetry writing and went on to immerse himself in the editorial work for one of the most prominent venues of literary publication, the literature and arts sections (*fukan*) of the newspaper *United Daily*.

60. Xie, *Zhuanyi*, 66. I shall return to discuss the soldier-poets' politics of depoliticization in relation to the actual existing political resistance in the next chapter.

61. To be sure, this does not mean that those in the military and the "deep state" could be exempt from censorship, nor was there any guarantee that they could not be incriminated or persecuted whenever they veered from the party line. They were only less likely to be suspected of anti-government sentiment or penchants when compared with the Taiwanese. That is to say, theoretically there were still risks in the soldier-poets' poetic experimentations, however "loyalist" their backgrounds and gestures appeared to be, and they certainly didn't have to go down that path.

Chapter Three

Breaking Ground in Splendid Isolation

DEATH OF A STONE CELL AND COLD WAR ETHOS

As indicated in the preceding chapter, the soldier-poets rekindled and intensified the modernist poetry movement by capitalizing on the resources accessible to them as part of the literary establishment in the military. Given that the rise of the soldier-poets was arguably an instance of state-sanctioned Cold War modernism, it stands to reason that one can cast their ensuing dominance of the poetry scene as the natural outcome of the inner workings of the state apparatus—to which, however, I deem it necessary to add two caveats: First, such a characterization loses sight of the fact that their emergence was an unexpected offshoot of the literary campaigns overseen by the military arm of the Nationalist regime rather than by design. Second, it does not fully account for why the authorities settled on modernism, out of other viable options (e.g., the more reader-friendly new regulated verse that, too, warrants politically innocuous content).[1] Likewise, attributing the ensuing valorization of the soldier-poets' brand of modernist poetry solely to the state's meddling in the literary scene—which was a rather commonplace perception among the detractors of modernist literature when the Nativist movement arose as a backlash against it in the 1970s—does not tell the whole story.[2] I argue that the epochal significance of the this Cold War modernism as well as its ramifications today lies not only in its entanglement with a typical Cold War regime like the postwar Kuomintang government but also in how it figures or refracts the ethos of these extraordinary times. To elucidate this argument, this chapter centers on Luo Fu's *Death of a Stone Cell*, widely considered "the representative work of Taiwan's modernist movement,"[3] together with some influential interpretations of it, and shall proceed by means of a two-pronged analysis.

On the one hand, I critically examine how the institutional forces, which could not be extricated from the state apparatus, legitimized and eventually canonized the newly emerging textual practices like *Death of a Stone Cell* while obscuring such extratextual maneuvers precisely via the establishment's single-minded focus on and preoccupation with its supposedly infinitely rich textual universe. On the other, I shall illustrate why the displacement of Cold War realities in the new paradigm resonated with an as-yet-unarticulated collective anxiety and longing, which would be preemptively compromised freedom promised and pursued in the allegedly self-contained confines of the textual bunker, thereby giving way to further grounds of justification for its canonization on account of its popularity among some circles, despite its daunting difficulty or opacity for the average reader.

Reality Fades—The Making of a Modernist Magnum Opus and the Cold War Realities

Death of a Stone Cell (*Shihshi zi shiwang* in Chinese; hereafter abbreviated as *Death*) is a collection of Luo Fu's poems that features sixty-four individual poems composing a sequence under this title. Most of these works had been serialized in the pages of *Chuangshiji* before they were collected (after revisions) and published in the first edition in January 1965 along with the newly added ones in the volume, with the individual poems being numbered 1 through 64 and each containing ten lines, which, however, are not of the same length (the English translation cited here does not always conform to the original number of lines).[4] Every one of the sixty-four poems can supposedly be read at once as an independent work and as part of the organic whole that is the long poem or poetic sequence named *Death of a Stone Cell*. Since the appearance of the first of the sequence in issue 12 of *Chuangshiji* in 1959, the sequenced poems had garnered much attention and prompted spirited, usually polarizing critical responses, which did not see any sign of abating after the publication of *Death* in 1965 and remained so until its landmark status in Taiwan's postwar modernist poetry was pretty much cemented after the mid-1970s, though dwindled reluctance to such recognition still persisted thereafter.[5] Regardless of the divergent receptions and assessments, one common ground between some of its defenders and detractors would be that *Death* is "difficult" or "abstruse" (*hui se* in Chinese), though the reasons they found this series of poems difficult or what they mean by the term "*hui se*" may be quite different.[6]

Here I would like to focus on one of the reasons this text has been consensually considered difficult: the indeterminate or unlikely events or scenarios unfolding or referenced through the images and descriptions in the poems, which, then, beg the questions about the unspecified or unspecifiable referents—except for the stone cell(s) as the main setting and probably an organizing metaphor. This often was (and still has occasionally been) explained away by the term "surrealism," whether it be used as euphemism by sympathetic readers or an epithet by critics. Take, for example, the opening lines from poem no. 1 of *Death*:

> Looking up, by chance, toward a neighbor's corridor, I was petrified—
> At dawn, that man turned against death with his naked body
> Allowing a black tributary to roar through his veins
> I was petrified—my eyes swept over the stone wall
> Two channels of blood were then gouged on its surface[7]

A careful reader would reasonably infer from this and other *Death* poems the thematic concern of death running through the larger text as well as the real or imaginary stone cell(s) repeatedly referred to in the sequence. Given the heated arguments over recondite passages like the last two lines of the quoted stanza above and the commonplace disorienting reading experiences of *Death*, the retrospectively identified reference, in the 1965 edition of *Death*, to the actual and prolonged bombardments of Quemoy that started in 1958—the circumstances under which Luo Fu, as a liaison officer there, composed his first few poems of the sequence[8] that also point to the larger historical-political contexts of Taiwan's Cold War realities at the time—would have better oriented the reader and helped lend a more concrete footing in imagining the constant existential threats in wars, as the text appears to consistently evoke the ambience of anxiety, alienation, and the liminal experience likely prompted by confronting the imminence of death. The allusion to the most brutal and fiercely contested site of military conflict in Cold War Taiwan, complete with the otherwise cryptic "stone cell" in the poem that corresponds to the burrowed stony tunnels designed to shield soldiers from the bombings, is therefore a credible and sensible one, rather than a far-fetched conceit. What is quite intriguing about the reception of *Death*, however, is that this allusion to an indispensable aspect of its times had virtually no bearing on the process of valorizing the text; instead, the bulk of critical literature on this text seems to be preoccupied with its formal elements—dense imagery, intricacy of poetic language, etc.—or the reconstruction of inner spirituality out of the ruins in the material world. In this view, the groundbreaking significance of *Death* lies in either its unprecedented formal experimentation (à la surrealism) or its representation of some universal angst of modern men (read: existentialist sentiment that was in vogue among intellectuals in 1960s Taiwan), but not in its implications in, and refraction (as distinct from a realist "reflection") of, the immediacy and peculiarities of Taiwan's Cold War realties.

While such effacement of real-life referents or disregard of referentiality—which is arguably one of the hallmarks of Euro-American modernism as well as certain critical approaches at the time—does not make *Death* a lone exception in postwar Taiwan, I argue that it happens to epitomize what the critic Tsai Ming-yen calls the "inward turn" toward the individual psyche—at the expense of turning one's back on external reality—in Taiwan literature that took place around late 1950s and early 1960s,[9] ushering in this epoch-changing trend both in terms of its textual example and at the level of its critical reception. Before further elaborating on *why* this was the case and *how* it unfolded, I would like to clarify the following: At issue here isn't a question about whether a realist approach and episteme should be prioritized over the one advocated and practiced by Luo Fu and other modernists in postwar Taiwan, since it would be a general direction in which they were bound to go once they modeled themselves after Western modernists, regardless of the modifications they had made out of various reasons, and irrespective of how, to be fair, their brand of modernism isn't merely mindless mimicry of the "original." Nor do I propose that the real-life referent at the front line would hold the key to unlocking the abstruseness or mysteries of the *Death* poems, hence its importance. In other words, what is at issue here is not whether the text should (have had) realistically or aesthetically represent(ed) the assumed referent, Quemoy at that historical juncture, but the implications of this Cold War condition that tends to be obscured in the text and the discussions it generates.

To begin with, Luo Fu himself appeared to be leading the way as to how his poetry is to be written and read. Shortly after the publication of the first of his *Death* series in issue 12 (July 1959) of *Chuangshiji*, the soldier-poet's essay in issue 13 contends that while art is a mirror onto which the temperament of its times is "reflected," such a reflection may well coincide with the expression of the poet's selfhood (*ziwo*) because the poet is the spokesperson of all minds or psyches (*xinling*), upon which all art is centered.[10] Although the claim that the poet alone can speak for all individuals is questionable and is still premised, to a great extent, on a certain notion of mimesis, the reflection to be valorized here is not reality or the sociohistorical conditions of its times, but the visions in the inner reaches of individual psyche, where the poet's personal "I" is conflated with or stands for the collective "I" in this view. In Luo Fu's long preface to *Death*, which is titled "The Poet's Mirror" and also serves as his defense of his poetics and textual practices, he further spells out and elaborates on the aforementioned 1959 argument by invoking (his understandings and "moderations" of) both surrealism and existentialism, seeking to justify the difficulty and opacity of the text with the former (e.g., as a necessary means of pursuing poetic "purity" and breaking free of the constrains of rationality in reality), and to fend off the accusations of being "nihilistic" by appealing to the search for modern men's "authentic being" in existentialist thought and by characterizing existentialist literature as "*littérature engagée*."[11] Interestingly, the "reflection" in question now becomes "the merciless destinies" of modern men rather than their or the poet's image: "What we see in the mirror is not the image of modern men, but their merciless destinies against which writing poetry is a form of revenge."[12] Placed, literally, at the very beginning of his long essay, this quoted statement evidently indicates the point of departure taken for granted, the rhetorical as well as ideational foundation on which Luo Fu's whole defense rests.

And yet one may well wonder, assuming that we are all on the same page about the cruelties of the modern world from which we moderns have no escape, whether such "merciless destinies" can be disassociated from the historical and geopolitical contexts of the ongoing war, the uncertain fate of the people implicated in it, the author's émigré experience of dislocations from his homeland as youth caused by a civil war coming at the heels of the Sino-Japanese war; we may ask whether the harsh realities and tragic fate in general can be instantiated more concretely by these said contexts. If the truth about the "merciless destinies" can only be sought along the inward-bound trails of individual psyches, it certainly cannot be found with recourse to the most generic references and the most esoteric insinuations *only*, and nothing in between. Furthermore, Luo Fu's own characterization of writing poetry as "revenge" against—rather than "representation" of—the cruel destinies in reality betrays his strong psychic cathexis on the specificities in reality that simply cannot be glossed over. Again, the query here does not mean to suggest that the text should have named the most pressing existential threat, among others, at the moment—one of the pivotal battles that cooled a series of actual military conflicts down to one protracted cold war across the Taiwan Strait. Nor does it intimate that it should *only* be about this battle. There are, however, alternative approaches to writing poetry about a specific war without resorting to a certain "realistic" treatment, as Luo Fu himself demonstrated in his "Saigon" series of poems, which were composed when he was assigned to a military consultant corps from Taiwan (as an US ally in the Vietnam War) or written retrospectively about his experience there, while referencing this historic war by ways more than the telling title of the series.[13]

To be clear, Luo Fu did not simply bury the allusion to the life-and-death situations in heavily shelled Quemoy amidst the most impenetrable crevices of the textual underworld. His few devoted readers could only indulge themselves in the guesswork without any authorial confirmation if Luo Fu himself did not go on record and reveal as much. The first edition of *Death* includes a review by Li Ying-hao in which Li mentions—by quoting Luo Fu, though in passing—the circumstances under which the soldier-poet wrote his initial works in the sequence. Besides the noteworthy content of the review (which I shall discuss in short order), what is equally noteworthy about this mention is that it is not only brought up as an afterthought but is also used to underscore the contention that the title of an artwork is not, or doesn't have to be, related to its meaning, since, according to the poet, titles of poems are like the decorative and redundant buttons on a coat, and the loose, or even stretched, connection in this case is his presence at the war zone when first trying his hand at these poems.[14] Similarly, Lin Heng-tai's commentary on *Death* endorses and further expands on this view of poetic titles by coining the term "Mahayana mode of writing" to elucidate what he perceives to be Luo Fu's formal experimentation on the creative process of *Death*, one in which the poet is not bound by a preconceived title or presuppositions while exploring the uncharted spiritual territories and portraying the landscape of the individual psyche.[15] Nevertheless, Lin does acknowledge the recurring images and ambience associated with war and death, despite spotting some others that do not fit neatly into the categories.[16] Which, in effect, disproves the claim that the loose connection between the frontline bunker setting in the Cold War context and the text resides *only* in the title.

The Cult of Interiority

Of course a title can neither dictate the meaning(s) nor exhaust the interpretations of a given poem, just as a real-life referent cannot, however well-established or realistic it is. To delve into the implications of their positions on the seemingly trivial issues of the title and the referent, we need to look at the main contents of these critical essays. As one of the most attentive readings and earliest defenses of *Death*, Li's piece emerged as an influential reference point in the critical literature of *Death* and, by extension, of Taiwan's modernist poetry movement not only because it concurs with Luo Fu's "explanation" about the title and the abovementioned allusion, but also because it sets the tone and precedent for critical approaches to this particular text as well as postwar modernist literature in general for the following reasons:[17] First, it heralds and exemplifies the bracketing, disregard, or even dismissal of the contextual knowledge, especially the Cold War contexts in which *Death* and most modernist works in Taiwan were produced, in interpreting literary texts, which was practiced in a long line of literary criticism that contributed to the valorization of *Death* and the eventual canonization of similar modernist texts that foreground (or can be construed to foreground) the inward turn toward the complex dynamics of individual psyche in Taiwan literature that Tsai speaks of. It corresponds to an inward turn, on the part of the critic and a sizable portion of the readership, to the "interiority of the text," if you will, at the expense of obscuring the immediate realities the writers ran away from and the constraints and possibilities conditioned on those contextual forces. In his essay on *Death*, for instance, Li argues that beneath the semblance of textual disorientation and unconventional diction and syntax of the text lurks the dynamics of an individual psyche, which undergirds the movements of the poetic language and imagery while featuring the tragic exposure and constant reshaping of selfhood.[18] Backing up such claims by citing textual evidences, Li goes on to commend Luo Fu for his unmatched ability, among his peers, to tease out the internal tensions in his images and rhetoric and maintain them at a self-contained status, without recourse to extratextual resources (e.g., the authority of philosophical concepts or contextual references).[19]

Second, in terms of the substance and discursive rigor of criticism, Li's essay appeared to distinguish itself from the overwhelming majority of commentaries on the *Death* poems at the time—indeed, from the bulk of "literary criticism" by the mid-1960s, for that matter—that often consisted of overtly subjective or arbitrary remarks and impressionistic (not impressionist) evaluations, guided by no consistent criteria except for ossified dogmas or the existing reputation (or the lack thereof) of the writer being commented on, hence by factors irrelevant to the work under consideration.[20] By contrast, Li demonstrates not only interpretations founded on his close readings of the text but also a measure of more consistent intellectual acumen borrowed from or inspired by relatively recent (by the standards of that era and the limited channels of access) scholarly works—which, however, did not resemble the showcasing of either quaint erudition in traditional learning or the grandeur of imported (Western) knowledge that oftentimes eclipses the text it is employed to throw light on. The scholarly works Li draws on, it may be clear by now, are those of the American New Critics, especially Allen Tate, Cleanth Brooks, Renè Wellek, Herbert Read, Joseph Frank, and John Crowe Ransom, whose ideas Li was among the first in the Chinese-speaking world to introduce, explicate, and put into one's own practice as a literary critic.[21] Likely due to the presumed autonomy and the inherent profoundness and complexity afforded to the text, as a self-contained universe, by this school of thought (e.g., Tate's "literature as knowledge"), together with Li's highlighting or expansion on the critic's respect for the text's own internal criteria, "New Criticism" quickly caught on among postwar writers in Taiwan, including the modernists, who had to first seek grounds of justification for the challenges their own writings posed. For example, Luo Fu's preface to *Death* enlists Cleanth Brooks and Robert Penn Warren, in addition to surrealism and Sartre's existentialist thought, to shore up his defense.[22] Li's emphasis on the dynamic and creative nature of criticism, rather than its prescriptive propensity, struck a chord, particularly with those who regularly played the dual role of poet/critic by commenting on fellow poets' works and editing anthologies and journals of poetry. Across generations, Li's writings on poetry and literary criticism—not limited to his essay on *Death*—have been routinely collected in those anthologies and included in accounts of the history of Taiwan's postwar literature, even though Li, as a Hongkonger, has never been based in Taiwan.[23]

Meanwhile, New Criticism would soon become the new and enduring paradigm of literary criticism and literary studies in Taiwan's postwar academia, advocated by its eminent spokesman in Taiwan, Yan Yuan-shu, an English professor at National Taiwan University. Through Yan's teachings and his interventions in the literary scene at the time, the presuppositions and basic principles of New Criticism (e.g., close reading as method), however adjusted in the local context, have had far-reaching and multiple-generation influences over readers and writers in postwar Taiwan (the parallel 1960s modernist literature movement, spearheaded by students in Yan's department but not connected with his time as faculty there, will be the main topic of the next chapter). The flagship status of Yan's institution and the cultural capital of academic discourse established the "dignity" of criticism as a "profession." Because of the shared single-minded focus on formalist interpretation and formal experimentation, New Criticism would, in turn, reinforce—not undermine—the air of professionalism exemplified by Li and modeled after by modernist poets/critics in Taiwan, who parlayed the signs of literary modernity (a literally "new" critical paradigm from the United States, a set of seemingly consistent criteria and methodical approaches, etc.) to distinguish themselves from the dilettantism of traditionalist men of letters—which, interestingly, mirrored the Western modernists' self-described "impeccable professionalism" vis-à-vis their predecessors.[24]

Although Yan did not show a definite predilection toward Taiwan's modernist poetry,[25] his 1972 essay "Close Readings of Two of Luo Fu's Poems," focusing on judicially discerning the difference between a "good poem" and a bad one in terms of the indispensable paradox of poetic language and organic unity, emerged as a classic textbook example of the kind of New Critical practices that contributed to further consolidations of *Death*'s place in the new canon[26] after the "movement phase" of modernist poetry had earned it legitimacy and recognition within the relatively "minor" circles of poets and readers. Following up Yan's essay were more academic endorsements at a noticeable institutional level, in the form of Chang Han-liang's often-cited 1973 treatise on Luo Fu's oeuvre (from *Death* up until his latest long poem)[27] that was published in *Chung Wai Literary Monthly*, a journal founded by Yan's department when he was the chair, and a book launch event, complete with a forum and recitations, that was organized by *Chung Wai* when the journal published Lo Fu's new book of poetry, *Magical Songs* (*Mo ge*), in 1974.[28]

Taken together, they marked the watershed of a long-running critical enterprise that preoccupied itself with the formal elements (imagery, language, etc.) and aesthetic renditions of certain timeless and universal conditions it perceives to be the primary concerns of *Death* and, indeed, of Luo Fu's and most serious poets' works. In the resurgence of critical interests in Luo Fu and well-established modernist writers in general since the mid-1980s, after the 1970s debates and backlashes against modernist literature posed by the Nativist movement (which gradually altered the landscape of the literary scene but not to the point of ending the entrenched dominant positions of modernism in the establishment),[29] an edited volume of *Death*, consisting of the entirety of the poetic sequence and the "important" critical essays about the text since 1965 and up until 1988, best testifies to the multigenerational impacts of the New Critical approaches in question. Nine of the ten representative essays selected by the editor focus on issues related to form, with Li's and Chang's pieces mentioning the frontline setting briefly only to sideline it without elaboration; the last essay, first appearing in this 1988 volume, unlike the other previously published essays, revolves around Luo Fu's mastery of imagery while denouncing, in a typically New Critical fashion, all kinds of "isms" as interpretive frameworks and admonishing the reductionism of thematic and contextual-historical readings.[30]

The Echoing Chamber of Cold War Ethos

The preceding discussions of the critical enterprise in question do not seek to nullify the merits of some of the approaches or the validity of its evaluations of the text; rather, they are meant to highlight the glaring absence of critical (re-)examinations of the Cold War contexts as *one* of the reasons for *Death*'s valorization and unique significance in postwar modernist literature. For there is no disputing the unprecedented nature of the text's formal experimentation, regardless of how one assesses the outcome. Nor do I propose that the text does not, or cannot, have extra layers of relevancy and appeals beyond the peculiar Cold War realities that implicated it and that appeared to be lacking in critical literature. It would be unthinkable for the soldier-poet to render the referent overt while representing the confrontation with the "merciless destinies" at the war zone in such a "noir" light, not long after combat literature, as promoted by the military, had been the order of the day—which means, literally, an order for the soldier in the poet. That would have posed a difficulty at a totally different register: Either such a text becomes incredibly risky, politically, for the author under the late 1950s and early 1960s circumstances, or it seems practically impossible to reconcile his soldierly mission and his "true vocation" as a modernist poet—his two identities that had been navigated through their modus operandi of bifurcation, like fellow soldier-poets and other modernists discussed in the previous chapters. Yet to foreground the frontline setting in the poem's exploration of the poet's "authentic being" would likely mean putting his two lines of work on a direct collision course. To understand the ramifications of the last point in more depth, one needs to take into account this piece of background information: As a liaison officer, Luo Fu, according to his own recollection, was tasked with regularly (as far as the frontline situations permitted) accompanying the foreign journalists to cover the Quemoy terrains, including visiting the burrowed tunnels and bunkers (the "stone cells").[31] In other words, part of his jobs there was to "handle" the press and to "represent" the Taiwan military to the "free world" headed by the United States, without whose military aides the subsequent success of that first line of defense in late 1950s would have been cast in doubt. The contradiction between the natures of these two representations could scarcely have been more pronounced, and the resulting tensions could hardly have been greater.

It therefore stands to reason that the soldier-poet, in keeping with the bifurcation as his customary mode of operation (thereby, probably holding in check the inner rage against the cruel fate in reality), wittingly or unwittingly circumvented the contextual, referential aspects of the "merciless destinies" from the outset, whether the aforementioned inherent contradiction and tensions dawned on him or not, or whether he really intended to represent or refract his experience at the front line (yes, to heed the "intentional fallacy" here). If, as far as Luo Fu is concerned, such a life-and-death, liminal experience, grounded in rather concrete and specific Cold War situations, had to be displaced or transported from an existential threat (and dread) to an existentialist aestheticization, from a response that cannot be extricated from the collective to the idiosyncratically individual, from that which concerns the local realities to what appears to be exclusively introspective, spiritual, and universal, then what do we make of the critical enterprise's shunning or disregarding the brutal and immediate realities by focusing on the intrinsic characteristics and formal elements of the text, or its introspective reflections on and inward gaze at the psychic, the innately spiritual, and the universal human conditions in the war-torn, fragmented modern world of discontinued pasts and dislocations? It is not merely a question of following the poet's or the text's lead, because the allusion had been made known since 1965 and the critical convention was a decades-long phenomenon in which the commentators and scholars certainly had incrementally more latitude to elaborate on it as Taiwan moved slowly but steadily toward liberalization.

I argue that *Death*, together with the literary criticism that contributed to the ensuing apotheosis of this text as a magnum opus of modernist *form*, epitomizes the prevalent Cold War ethos that outlasted the modernist movement. As indicated earlier in the chapter, *Death* isn't the only instance of such effacement or displacement of the immediate Cold War realities in Taiwan's postwar modernist literature, nor is it the sole example of the inward turn toward and preoccupation with the individual psyche. Nonetheless, the recurring image of stone cell arguably best instantiates the mixed senses of enclosure, isolation, and seclusion, probably with a tinge of secureness, coupled with those of entrapment, imprisonment, or even an ominous feel of entombment for *not only individual but also the collective psyche* of Cold War Taiwan in a stalemated yet potentially ever volatile state. This points to the first layer of what I would call "interiority complex"—which will be further elaborated in short order—in Cold War Taiwan that is figured by *Death*, a text preoccupied with the structure of interiority.

Without specifying the locales of the stone cells, *Death*'s ample mentions of war and war scenes in general, as illustrated by passages like the quoted lines below, would suffice to evoke death, violence, and the kind of dread, anxiety, confoundedness, and restlessness likely associated with such scenarios. After highlighting the paradoxical characteristics of those who are immersed in warfare—some sort of man-animal with the tameness found in the lizard's eyes but also with the toughness of its skin—the speaker goes on to reflect on war with even farther fetched comparisons:

> I thought of war—war is a black skirt that can't be folded
> When Death's steps kicked a rainbow off my roof
> I suddenly remembered your eyes devoured by cuttlefish[32]

As noted before, the much maligned abstruseness cannot always be resolved in light of real-life referents or allegorical readings, though the ambience of liminal, life-and-death experience and emotive reverberations could still conceivably be extrapolated and related to. The ineluctable difficulties in making sense of numerous passages in the text arguably reinforce the confoundedness palpably conveyed, thereby exemplifying the perplexities appearing to frequently besiege the speaker in the poem. The second layer of the "interiority complex" in question is related to the critical engagements with the *difficulties* of *Death* that features its effacement of referentiality and its gravitations towards the interiorities of the text and the individual psyche. In truth, the same abstruseness cannot always be convincingly explained by means of the painstakingly close "close readings" demonstrated by the New Critical approaches, either. However, as K. K. Leonard Chan says of Li Ying-hao's case, Li's over-expansive gloss on "tension" and the presumably inexhaustible plentitude and complexity of the text's meaning would serve to preemptively justify the obstacles in the reading process, goading or exhorting the reader to dive further into the depths of the text, projecting and co-opting various cognitive and affective activities not necessarily intrinsic to the text into its imagined interior.³³ In other words, readings premised on such presuppositions may well become self-fulfilling prophecy or proceed as an incessant quest for *das Ding* as an impossible object of desire with a quasi-religious piety and reverence for the text and the critic. In the event that a sensible interpretation cannot be attained (as Yan declares some of Luo Fu's oft-discussed lines to be),³⁴ or meanings to be uncovered through deference to further good-faith, diligent efforts (as in Lin Heng-tai's comparison of Luo Fu's metaphor in *Death* to a hard nutshell or kernel),³⁵ the reader has already been led to the bottom line: the bottom line here being an invitation, or even injunction, to participate in the authorial displacement, as well as the critical effacement and disregard, of Cold War realities by always looking deeper into the text and turning away from extratextual resources, except for a misconceived silo of individual psyche detached from the contexts that shape it. This brings to the fore the second layer of the interiority complex instantiated by what one may call the *Death* phenomenon.

While *Death* and the attendant critical enterprise may constitute a most extreme case in precluding a host of other approaches and possibilities of interpretation, the parallel, twofold "inward turn" in textual and critical practices, in fact, ran so deep and wide in the minds of writers and readers across generations that they combined to reflect, amplify, and legitimize a certain Cold War ethos linked negatively to (some aspects of) the Cold War realties they self-consciously or instinctively kept out of their pre-delimited and rarified sphere of poetic purity or modernist vision of "artistic pursuit" (e.g., *chunwenxue*). In Chen Fang-ming's revisionist account of Taiwan's literary history, which has made it into the mainstream since the 1990s, this postwar modernism is narrated in terms of a dual character: on the one hand, as an escapism from "reality," especially the repressive political reality and the people and lives in Taiwan, as opposed to those in pre-1949 China and elsewhere in the world; and on the other, as a form of "resistance" against the state's mandates of anticommunist literature and its tight control over people's thought and deed.³⁶ The Cold War ethos in question can therefore be characterized as the kind of "escapism" Chen describes, though escapism in itself is not unique to the Cold War era and, indeed, took nuanced forms or routes in Cold War Taiwan, even as we limit our scope to this particular time and space: The staging of flag-waving crowds and uniformed students marching to military music in ceremonies meant to be public displays of allegiance to Chiang Kai-shek could also be considered a form of escapism, as was the common practice of those with enough resources to seize on every opportunity to leave Taiwan for some other country, most likely by immigrating to the United States. From this perspective, if the widespread charge of "escapism," levied most visibly by the 1970s Nativist movement against the modernist predominance of the literary scene,³⁷ is to have a sharper critical edge in its critiques of modernism, the variances in the "escape routes" and the forms or natures of those "replacements" will have to be taken into account. Lest I be mistaken, such a reexamination does not to seek to absolve the modernists of such critiques; rather, it can help to shed light on the purported "resistance" of modernist textual practices—the other side of the duality Chen underlines—which is equally worthy of reconsideration.

To begin with, the modernist manifestation of the Cold War escapist ethos was not an easy way out, relative to other options available at the time, whether it be the more reader-friendly version of *chunwenxue* featuring genteel sensibility toward the personal and minute details in daily lives, or even the safest route of anticommunist literature, which, in the case of the soldier-poets, nevertheless would probably be credentials (despite being an inglorious genre for writers) good enough to land them posts as trusted agents in the literary establishment for the Nationalist regime in their post-military careers (more on this point shortly). That is to say, the act of displacement as well as that which replaced their default position were proactive instead of passive.

Meanwhile, it is plausible that their modernist textual practices to some extent shielded them from confronting the potential tensions or inherent conflicts between their soldier identity and their modernist pursuit, which could be brought to the fore by the *Death* poems, as illustrated above. Moreover, since Taiwan's postwar modernist writers consisted mostly of mainlanders who relocated to Taiwan with the Nationalist government, largely depended on it for their livelihoods, and wrote about their émigré experience that included senses of alienation from and uneasiness about the local setting in which they were inevitably aligned with the repressive rulers,[38] there were certain areas of the immediate realities and the Cold War context they unwittingly or self-consciously circumvented in spite of, or precisely because of, the gestures of nonconformity and the semblance of discontent evinced from their works (e.g., to disavow their own implications in the system against which their writings seem to register some veiled discontent). With the specifics of their "merciless destinies" being displaced to a very different register and sphere, it can be argued that the deeper and the more intricate the textual underground becomes, the further they can be removed from a potentially uncomfortable truth or reckoning. Although they do not appear to foreground some sort of "comfort zone" via their textual practices—anxiety being the predominant affect and alienation the prevailing experience emanating from their writings—the modernists gain a measure of solace or even redemption through their aestheticization. In this sense, the interiority complex, instantiated vividly in *Death* and figured, to varying degrees, in other modernist texts and New Critical textualism, can be understood as a defense mechanism.

The modernists, however, also took the offensive, as a proactive means of defense, by not only finding but also creating by themselves outlets and channels for their pent-up creative energies. Positioned differently to a regime of oppression than the majority of the population in Taiwan, the émigré soldier-poets likely perceived Taiwan's situations differently, thereby responding to them in their peculiar ways through their poetry. What they did have in common with most others was the perception of a general air of stultification and the anxiety that came with living the omnipresent and essential uncertainties of Cold War Taiwan that nevertheless remained unspeakable for most involved—hence the reverberations among the readers of *Death* outside this demographic group—even though they might have knowingly or subliminally located the sources of these sentiments elsewhere, without having to confront the prospect of their own implications in a system to which they could have fallen victim, in some sense.[39] Herein lies the dual character of the "interiority complex" that consumed many, though not all, in the literary and cultural scenes in Cold War Taiwan. Faced with the collective isolation and encroachment from outside the insular space, which threatens to breed claustrophobia, the modernist heralded and staged an indulgence in an intricate "secret garden" or self-made stone cell as an alternative mode of existence, a form of displacement that relieves oneself of some of the anxiety and uneasiness of confronting parts of the reality by, paradoxically, *reliving* the apprehension, confoundedness, pensiveness alternating with restlessness, and uncertainties in a secluded and *relatively safe* locale or setting (e.g., the text) with pursuits more complicated (e.g., difficult writing and reading) than the forced acts of taking sides and simplifying in real life.

The Institutionalization of Modernism and the Soldier-Writer Phenomenon without the Soldier

Given that Luo Fu makes clear in his preface to *Death* that writing poetry is a "form of revenge," as well as what Lin Heng-tai identifies as "critical consciousness" and a hint at protesting (whose target and content, however, remain unspecified) in some lines of *Death*,[40] one is tempted to argue that *Death* embodies the kind of "resistance" that is part of the said dual character of Taiwan's postwar modernism, per Chen Fang-ming. Nevertheless, the caveat to be heeded in this regard is that, first of all, the resistance against the official policy of anticommunist literature and the preceding literary conventions is not to be confused with the saliently political resistance in postwar Taiwan, which had been snuffed out before reawaking in the 1970s, and whose latter-day iterations were quite antithetical to what the solider-poets and other modernists became politically later on. Furthermore, even in terms of an expanded sense of "political," Luo Fu and his cohorts never aspired to effect changes in the most engrained social norms, as the French surrealists did (not to mention the latter's ties to communism, however fractured those were). As indicated in the previous chapters, Taiwan's postwar modernist movement was, up until this point, characterized by its boldest moves counterbalanced with its backsteps of moderations, or bounded within the preemptively compromised, self-delimited safety zone. Apropos of the modernist gestures of "resistance," including that of the soldier-poets, Xie Kun-hua offers a rather incisive portrayal: Under the constrained circumstances, the modernists "turned their backs on the powers that be without turning against them" (the catchy Chinese phrase being *beidui erbu fandui*).[41] In other words, they turned around, put their heads down, and pursued their artistic freedom in the trenches they had dug for themselves to ensure that they were politically safe in the first place. While the ramifications and relevancy of such a gesture of resistance can be cast in doubt, thanks both to modernism's preemptive concession and the authorities' unprompted relaxation on the foregoing campaign of anticommunist literature (mentioned in the previous chapter), the soldier-poets' "strategy of survival" and negotiatory outlook cannot be cited to take anything away from their literary endeavors—whether they be radical enough or not.[42] The main problem, I argue, lies rather in the textual and critical indulgence in modernist pursuits in the trenches that subsequently evolved into an elaborate, seemingly self-contained structure—an established institution. For the radical potential in the text itself—which I acknowledge and shall touch on shortly in this section—cannot be extricated from what one does with the text. That is to say, it is contingent on, or to some extent conditioned by, how the modernist text and its interpretation are institutionalized.

To reexamine the relevancy and validity of the modernist textual practices as a form of "resistance," I would like to return to the representative modernist text *Death*. In the process of the institutionalization of modernism, which was galvanized by the valorization of *Death* along with the consolidation of the New Critical paradigm, as elaborated above, two things about this critical enterprise at this historical juncture deserve more critical attention: First, the new paradigm initiated and then normalized the decoupling of surrealism and Luo Fu's poetry—a linkage the poet himself had sought to backtrack since 1969—in critical literature by underscoring the visible stylistic changes in his post-*Death* poems as well as the merits of the dreamlike scenarios (such as "bats eat the street lights / halo by halo") or shocking juxtapositions of images (e.g., "Standing far away, a baby faces the grave and smiles") in the text *apart from* and *in spite of* the tendency and possibility to attribute them to "surrealism," for better or worse reasons.[43] This went beyond correcting, on legitimate academic grounds, some misconceptions of surrealism in many readings and the misuses of the term on the part of the soldier-poets,[44] and led to what I consider the more consequential development: the sanitization of the radical potentiality of the text, reducing its epochal significance to formal experimentation *only* and ultimately highlighting the more moderated, less edgy poems that followed as the perfected works of a canonical author.

Instead of suggesting that whether *Death* can be *potentially* radical hinges on if one can establish its similarity to any French surrealist poem, I would like to take one example from the text to illustrate how its radicality can inhere in such passages but, at the same time, tends to be occluded in readings predicated on the New Critical approaches:

> Like a nude being sculpted by a passer-by
> I try to retrace how my body has taken shape in a giant palm
> How a certain kindness was arranged to beget a smile after being mocked
> Appearing in this mute stone cell for the first time
> How I distrust the serenity in the wake of the flames[45]

As with those passages with minimum referential specificities in *Death* (which means the overwhelming majority of the text), one may be tempted to interpret the quoted lines above in light of a certain religious quest in which the poet attempts to engage and query a presumed God (per Luo Fu's "Afterword" written years later),[46] or as an instantiation and dramatization of the Heideggerian term "thrownness." Nonetheless, by following only the text's prompts and its inner logic, in New Critical fashion, one cannot simply rule out the plausibility of projecting that pervading sense of confoundedness and powerlessness over the greater schemes of things *not only* onto the elevated or abstracted realm of a generic human existence in which they are by nature arbitrarily determined or willed by the Creator, *but also* onto the concrete Cold War conditions, where the individual's powerlessness and status comparable to a pawn in a chess match may well be indicative of the collective status of Taiwan as a vulnerable pawn in a high-octane Cold War geopolitical order with little say about its own fate. Moreover, the suspicion that one is being manipulated or handled like a puppet manifests itself so acutely that it arguably concretizes both the "merciless destinies" (Luo Fu) and "critical consciousness" (Lin Heng-tai) by adding the realization that one is even programmed to smile after being mocked. Granted that an allegorical reading like this doesn't make the text a well-wrought or even coherent critique due to its fragmentation in thought, the equivocation in speaking voice, and the impenetrable passages, it is more interesting to me that the critical enterprise in question, knowingly or unknowingly, did not explore readings along this line, even as they retrospectively acknowledged the text's situatedness in that particular time and space, seeking to pad on its resume as a masterpiece years later.[47] It appears that, as far as the critical enterprise is concerned, the scattered radical potentialities of *Death* would "move in a direction most people fear to mention," if we can take one of its lines out of context,[48] but it was more concerned with the depoliticization of the modernist canon it endorsed, just as its efforts in decoupling surrealism and Luo Fu sought more to depoliticize the aforementioned potentialities (especially in *Death*) than to call out his divesting the original of its political ramifications.

The second thing to note about this critical enterprise is that it cemented both the elitist image of modernism and its prestigious position in the literary establishment, which was freshly renovated thanks in part to the infusion of discursive power and cultural capital from its academic allies. As indicated in the aforementioned cases of Chang Han-liang's and Yan Yuan-shu's essays on Luo Fu's oeuvre, the scholarly interventions in that era made them participants in the literary scene as well as an integral part of the new literary establishment, the academic arm of which exerted its long-lasting influences largely on the basis of its institutionalization of modernist literature, enabled mostly by its New Critical approaches and exemplified by Yan's department (more on this topic in the next chapter). The entrenched institutionalization of modernism in academia and in a still relevant "high culture" back then was a pivotal development in that it helped modernist poetry withstand and outlast the Nativist movement's attacks on the modernist paradigm during the 1970s, before renewed critical interest during the 1980s, and yet a new generation of writers who had imbibed the modernist sophistication of technique in their formative years reaffirmed modernist preeminence in postwar Taiwan literature. Chang's and Yan's articles were published amidst a series of heated debates on modernist poetry (*xiandaishi lunzhan*), typically periodized as between 1972 and 1974, but with ripple effects percolating throughout the decade and culminating in the 1977 debates on Nativist literature (*xiangtu wenxue lunzhan*) that extended to implicate modernist fiction besides the poetry genre. In these high-profile back-and-forth exchanges, the modernist poets (including Luo Fu and Yu Kwang-chung) and scholars (e.g., Yan), who espoused the purity of aesthetic expressions and artistic autonomy and who usually shunned the more saliently political issues, took their turns to not only defend their positions on modernism but also to voice their stands on "proletariat literature" (*gong nong bing wenxue*), a politically toxic label commonly hurled at the other side that could get writers into serious trouble in 1970s Taiwan.[49] It was at this historical juncture and under such circumstances that any antiestablishment image or potentials of resistance in this modernism would have been neutralized if not nullified.

As timely and decisive a force the academic endorsement was for modernist poetry, whose movement stage had likely run its course by early 1970s,[50] it wasn't the only institutional support. Though it was a "shot in the arm" for the modernist poetry camp during the debate years and aligned the latter even more tightly with the establishment and the state's cultural policies when their politically conservative character was brought to the fore, it emerged much later than *Chuangshiji*, the poetry journal, bolstered by the soldier-poets' brand of surrealist poetry, had catapulted itself to the leadership role and the pace-setter of the poetry scene since the mid-1960s. Outside the academic institution, the soldier-poets themselves were already a formidable institutional force when it came to modernist poetry, and due to the disproportionally large number of "representatives" from the military in the literary scene at the time, they collectively amounted to what can be dubbed as a "soldier-writer phenomenon." The most well-known among them, especially the poets Luo Fu, Shang Qing, Ya Xian, and Zhang Muo and fiction writers Chu Hsi-ning, Duan Cai-hua, and Sima Zhong-yuan (the last two having no modernist orientations whatsoever), certainly were part of the literary establishment and could wield varying degrees of clout from within. Yet, as mentioned toward the beginning of this chapter, the rise of the soldier-writers cannot simply be explained away by viewing it as a testament to the state's *direct* interference in the literary field—not because the Cold War modernist movement could operate independently of the state apparatus (it's to some extent a state-sanctioned one, as broached earlier) but because this convenient explanation does not help to account for the inner workings of the literary establishment in more depth. To illustrate the *covert* nature of the institutional force that is the soldier-writer phenomenon, which is akin to the characteristics and workings of another, albeit related, instance of state-sanctioned modernism to be discussed in the next chapter, I would like to close this one by elucidating this arm of the literary establishment in terms of what I would call the "soldier-writer phenomenon without the soldier."

First of all, the 1950s combat literature campaign in the military had fizzled around the middle years of the decade, much like the nationwide promotion of anticommunist, patriotic literature, which meant one less incentive for the authorities to be as hands-on as before and issue another overt, top-down state initiative on literature, let alone give direct orders to the soldiers on the literary front. And while it was still on, "combat poetry" wasn't exclusively practiced by the soldier-poets—Ji Xian was a good example. If the preceding elaborations on bifurcation as the soldier-poets' mode of operation is any guide, the soldier-poets did not seek to link their writing practices to their identity as soldiers, nor did they establish any connection between the two identities that aims to break any stereotypes associated with the soldiers or outsiders' (mis-)perception of them as at once soldiers and poets.[51] Instead, they gained recognition as fellow writers in the wider literary field when they kept the two apart, thereby leaving a more positive impression—perhaps inadvertently—about their soldier identity. This is the first sense of the "soldier-writer phenomenon without the soldier."

The soldier-writer phenomenon without the solider also means that it is not directly related to the military, but this does not absolve the soldier-writers of their unwitting or knowing connivance in the "invisible hand," the inner workings of the state apparatus that now receded to the background but could opt to intervene when deemed necessary. Rather, the power and influence of the institutional dimension in the soldier-writer phenomenon was exercised through means that did not appear to be as "institutional," but more dissipated (à la Foucault) than people tend to expect from a Cold War regime still ruling by martial law. The diffusion and indirectness of power appeared to be particularly true when it came to the soldier-writers, since, crucially, the soldiers were discharged or retired from the military at a younger age than other professions, and in Taiwan, some of them moved into key posts in other walks of life through not only the networks built in the military but also channels facilitated by the Nationalist government, which took good care of them with pensions, benefits, and such placements: positions in both the public sector and the private sector (technically speaking only), including, more relevant to our topic here, editorships for literary magazines and literary pages of newspapers of varying importance and circulations, onetime or periodical anthologies or edited volumes functioning as standard-bearers for the literary scene,[52] and leading roles in various literary and cultural associations—all of which were owned or controlled by the government, the military, and the Nationalist party, or Kuomintang (defined as a "private" organization). Of the soldier-writers named above, Ya Xian has held the most important editor positions in postwar Taiwan's literary scene, having served in that capacity for both *United Daily* (*Lianhe bao*) and *Youth Literary* (*Youshi wenyi*) for decades; Duan Cai-hua also edited *Youth Literary* after Ya Xian. All of them were prominent actors in the literary establishment in their heydays (which were relatively long for some of them), often sitting on the judge panels of different literary prizes in the process as well. Structurally, they were the party-state's *trusted agents* in the quasi-autonomous literary establishment, with or without their soldier identity, which, in this sense, was still tacitly at work and outlasted their military careers.[53]

This is also why one can make a case for an even more expanded sense of "the soldier-writer phenomenon without the soldier," since a notable number of the non-soldier literary luminaries were *related* to the military: The soldier-writer Chu Hsi-ning, whose wife was a translator, raised a prominent "literary family," with his three daughters becoming famous writers in their own rights; the father of the modernist writer Pai Hsien-yung was a general allied with Chiang Kai-shek; Yan Yuan-shu's father graduated from a military academy founded by the Nationalist party back in China. And the list of military connections surely is much longer than the few named here who were linked to literary modernism in nuanced ways.[54] By no means does this suggest some sort of "guilt by association" and assume that they, too, were automatically trusted agents of the state apparatus. One would be able to point to some parts of their writings and argue otherwise, as one can with some of Luo Fu's works. The upshot of this (non-)soldier-writer phenomenon is that *military connections* were so pervasive that they became seemingly imperceptible, particularly for those involved (with no choice, as far as family ties are concerned) in its functioning, that one may easily normalize the embedded power structure, part of which was the literary establishment. Suffice it to say that the networking at stake in the said phenomenon went beyond *work*.

For the institutionalized modernism in postwar Taiwan did not merely exist in the soldier-poets' trenches like a secluded monastery for the devotees only. It made its presence felt on the literary pages of major newspapers and literary magazines (far beyond those publications in the military), in the entries and winners of literary prizes, in the periodical anthologies of poetry and fiction, and in discourses about poetry, literature, and art in general, scholarly or otherwise, that in turn served as the editorial directions and guidelines for many of the publication venues whose editorships went to the soldier-poets. I argue that the institutional power represented by the soldier-writers functioned as a *covert* exercising of power, but not in the sense that they worked as undercover agents to spy on other writers in a covert operation. Rather, it was precisely their limited measure of autonomy, together with their presumed loyalty and awareness or subliminal internalization of the "forbidden zone," that implicated them in the greater schemes of things from which they could not extricate themselves, and enabled conditions conducive to not only their own post-military careers but also the general direction(s) the ruling elites desired (which the latter may not have specified) or the minor deviations the authorities could tolerate, pending the dynamics between the agents and the state as well as the larger circumstances the authorities themselves must weigh in their control system (e.g., the nominal democracy and liberal ideas as part of the trappings of being a US ally in the "free world"). This is not to deny the soldier-poets their "individual talents," suggesting that they were not deserving of their statuses and positions as poets, editors, or other titles in the literary establishment.[55] By their own standards they were richly deserving, especially Luo Fu—the longevity and productivity of his poetic career appear remarkable by most criteria we know of. Part of the problem was that the criteria they stand for and perpetuate (with the help of others) were predicated on specific conditions of possibility that had to be disavowed by them. The bigger part of the problem in our Cold War context is that, paradoxically, their established individual talents made the institutional force of the soldier-poet phenomenon (without the solider) even more covert on account of the perceived autonomy of the soldier-poets, thus more powerful—for which they were not, however, solely responsible.

NOTES

1. Under the umbrella term "*chunwenxue*," there were definitely more accessible types of works available on the literary scene alongside modernist ones, especially in the genres of essay and fiction. However, the thematic focus on the personal and the everyday paired with the prevailing sentiments of contentment and serenity commonly seen in the reader-friendly type rarely characterizes modernist poetry in this era. For the authorities' pivot to a broadly conceived *chunwenxue*, see Sung-sheng Yvonne Chang, *Literary Culture in Taiwan: Martial Law to Market Law* (New York: Columbia University Press, 2004), loc. 1759–84, Kindle.

2. For a definitive English-language account of the Nativist movement's resistance to Modernist predominance of the literary scene, see chapter 5 of Sung-sheng Yvonne Chang, *Modernism and the Nativist Resistance: Contemporary Chinese Fiction from Taiwan* (Durham, NC: Duke University Press, 1993), Kindle.

3. John Balcom, Introduction to *Death of a Stone Cell*, by Lo Fu (Monterey, CA: Taoran Press, 1993), 1.

4. Luo Fu, "Houji: Shishi zi siwang zai tansuo" [Afterword: Revisiting Death of a Stone Cell], in *Shishi zi siwang* [Death of a Stone Cell] (Taipei: Unitas, 2016), 130–31. In his "Afterword," written decades later, in 1987, Luo Fu also clarifies the following: When appearing individually between 1959 and 1964, some of these poems did not always stick to the ten-line format, though they would eventually be changed to ten-line works because, according to Luo Fu, the ten-line sequence was his original plan. Luo Fu had occasionally used different titles for some of the poems previously published, but noted their connections to the "Death of a Stone Cell" project and documented the changes subsequently.

5. Luo Fu himself also acknowledges the said polarization as a "critical consensus" in his "Houji," 118–19.

6. Both Li Ying-hao and Lin Heng-tai elaborate on and adopt an overall sympathetic position on the "difficulty" of *Death*. See Li Ying-hao, "Lun Luo Fu shishi zi siwang" [On Luo Fu's Death of a Stone Cell], in *Luo Fu shishi zhi siwang ji xiangguan zhongyao pinglun* [Luo Fu's Death of a Stone Cell: The Text and Important Critical Essays], ed. Ji-liang Hou (Taipei: Han Guang Culture, 1988), 72–90; Lin Heng-tai, "Da sheng de xiefa" [Mahayana Mode of Writing], in *Luo Fu shishi zhi siwang ji xiangguan zhongyao pinglun* [Luo Fu's Death of a Stone Cell: The Text and Important Critical Essays], ed. Ji-liang Hou (Taipei: Han Guang Culture, 1988), 92–103.

7. Luo Fu, *Shishi zi siwang* [Death of a Stone Cell] (Taipei: Unitas, 2016), 52. The translation of these lines here is mine.

8. See Li, "Lun Luo Fu," 75. This mention of the frontline circumstances of the poet's writing was first brought up by Li Ying-hao, who quotes Luo Fu by relaying this reference in his essay, included in the 1965 edition of *Death*. Luo Fu himself would recount in more detail in his "Houji."

9. Tsai Ming-yen, "Yijiu wuling niandai Taiwan xiandaishi de jige mianxiang" [On Some Facets of Taiwan Modern Poetics in the 1950s], *Taiwan wenxue yanjiu xuebao* [Journal of Taiwan Literary Studies], no. 11 (October 2010): 96.

10. Quoted in Tsai, "Yijiu wuling," 97. The statement in this essay is, according to Tsai Ming-yen, the most prominent example that heralds and celebrates such an "inward turn" in Taiwan literature mentioned earlier.

11. Luo Fu, "Shiren zi jing" [The Poet's Mirror], in *Shishi zi siwang* [Death of a Stone Cell] (Taipei: Unitas, 2016), 11–13.

12. Luo Fu, "Shiren," 10. The English translation of these phrases, as quoted here, is John Balcom's. See Balcom, "Introduction," 1.

13. Luo Fu was stationed in Vietnam between November 1965 and November 1967. The entirety of the Saigon series poems were later collected in the volume *Magical Song* (*Muo ge*) after having been published elsewhere.

14. Li, "Lun Luo Fu," 75.

15. Lin, "Da sheng," 94–95. This piece was first published as a book chapter in 1968.

16. Ibid., 97–101.

17. For the role(s) of Li Ying-hao, as someone based in Hong Kong, in both the modernist literature movement in Taiwan and the parallel one in Hong Kong, see Kwok-kou Leonard Chan, "Xianggang wu liushi niandai xiandai zhuyi yundong yu Li Ying-hao de wenxue piping" [Hong Kong Modernist Movement in the 1950s and 1960s and Li Yinghao's Literary Criticism], *Chung Wai Literary Monthly* 34, no. 10 (March 2006): 20.

18. Li, "Lun Luo Fu," 74–75. Echoing such preoccupation with individual psyche, Lin Heng-tai begins his essay on *Death* by his presupposition: Poetry is, in essence, a sketch of the poet's psychic landscape. See Lin, "Da sheng," 94.

19. Li, "Lun Luo Fu," 81–82. For the linkage of Li's argument here and similar claims elsewhere to Allen Tate's elaborations on the term "tension," see Chan, "Xianggang," 24–27.

20. Lin Jin-li attributes this paradigm shift in the criticism of modern poetry mostly to Yan's intervention—which is basically true. But Li Ying-hao's review, which appeared earlier than Yan's influential essay on modernist poetry, as discussed in this chapter, impacted the core members of *Chuangshiji* much earlier and was therefore more directly related to the paradigm shift in the textual practices of modernist poetry, before Yan turned the tide among a larger readership and writers. See Nikki Jin-li Lin, "Xin piping yu xiandai shi: Yi Yen Yuang-su wei jujiao" [New Criticism and Taiwan Modernist Poetry: The Case of Yen Yuang-su], *Taiwan wenxue yanjiu jikan* [NTU Studies in Taiwan Literature], no. 15 (February 2014): 123–53.

21. Chan, "Xianggang," 21–22. Chan also suggests that while Li does not name nor directly quote the ideas of the New Critics in his essay on *Death*, synthesized versions of some of their well-known arguments are scattered throughout the piece, notably those about "tension" (Tate) and paradoxes as grounds of justification for the difficulty of the poems.

22. Luo Fu, "Shiren," 17–18.

23. Chan, "Xianggang," 20.

24. Tim Armstrong, *Modernism: A Cultural History* (Cambridge, UK: Polity, 2005), 3.

25. Because of Yan's gradual shift to a more sympathetic attitude toward realist and socially conscious literature since late 1970s, despite having blasted Nativist literature in those 1970s debates, some have come to align Yan with the anti-modernist poetry camp. For such a perspective, see, for example, Chih-ming Wang, "Lengzhan renwen zhuyi: Yan Yuan-shu ji qi piping shijian" [Cold War Humanism: Yan Yuanshu and His Critical Practices], *Chung Wai Literary Quarterly* 43, no. 1 (March 2014): 146–150.

26. Yan Yuan-shu, "Xi du Luo Fu de liang shou shi" [Close Readings of Two of Luo Fu's Poems], *Chung Wai Literary Monthly* 1, no. 1 (June 1972): 118–34. Despite his signature caustic tone and his identification of the negative instances or blemishes in Luo Fu's poetry, in this essay Yan unequivocally affirms Luo Fu's significant place in Taiwan's postwar poetry. Given Yan's change of positions later in his career, as mentioned in note 25, it is important to point out that since the mid-1960s, Yan had begun to introduce and explicate the critical works by T. S. Eliot, especially those most influenced by the American New Critics, who then famously established a special bond or compatibility between poetry and New Critical ideals. For a detailed account on this, see Chen Fang-ming, *Xiandai zhuyi ji qi buman* [Modernism and Its Discontents] (Taipei: Linking, 2013), 145–73. In an early attempt to conduct a historical review of the first twenty years of postwar poetry in Taiwan, the poet Ye Shan (today also known as Yang Mu) commented in 1972 that Yan played the role of a "Devil's advocate" in the development of modernist poetry. See Ye Shan, "Xiandaishi huigu zhuanhao" [Introduction to the Special Issue on the History of Modern Poetry], *Xiandai Wenxue* [Modern Literature], no. 46 (March 1972): 9.

27. Chang Han-liang, "Lun Luo Fu houqi fengge de yanbian" [Comments on the development of the later stage of Luo Fu's style], *Chung Wai Literary Monthly* 2, no. 5 (October 1973): 62–91.

28. *Chung Wai* became a quarterly in 2007 and renamed itself as *Chung Wai Literary Quarterly* after transitioning to a strictly academic and more conventional journal.

29. For a detailed account of the Nativist challenge to modernist hegemony, see chapter 5 of Chang, *Modernism*.

30. Chien Cheng-chen, "Luo Fu zuopin de yixiang shijie" [The World of Images in Luo Fu's Works], in *Luo Fu shishi zhi siwang ji xiangguan zhongyao pinglun* [Luo Fu's Death of a Stone Cell: The Text and Important Critical Essays], ed. Ji-liang Hou (Taipei: Han Guang Culture, 1988), 217–20.

31. Luo Fu, "Houji," 119–20.

32. This is from the second stanza of poem no. 24 of *Death*. See Luo Fu, *Death of a Stone Cell*, trans. John Balcom (Monterey, CA: Taoran Press, 1993), 28.

33. Chan, "Xianggang," 28.

34. Most of Yan's "negative" examples come from Luo Fu's "Saigon" series poems. Although there are a few lines in *Death* he considers incomprehensible, Yan, curiously, does not evaluate the latter as harshly as the former.

35. Lin, "Da sheng," 101.

36. Chen Fang-ming, *Dianfan de zhuiqiu* [The Search for a Paradigm] (Taipei: Unitas, 1994), 226.

37. "Escapism" can be said to permeate nearly all the Nativist criticisms of modernist literature, even when they do not use this exact term. For an example of the usage of this term in English-language critical literature, see Jing Wang, "Taiwan Hsinag-t'u Literature: Perspectives in the Evolution of a Literary Movement," in *Chinese Fiction from Taiwan: Critical Perspectives*, ed. Jeannette L. Faurot (Bloomington: Indiana University Press, 1980), 43–70.

38. To be sure, there were mainlanders who were persecuted and rounded up by Chiang Kai-shek and his inner circles for various reasons, including the prominent cases of political dissidence in Lei Zheng, founder of the liberalist journal *Free China Review* and the liberalist scholar Yin Hai-Kuang. In principle, however, loyalty to the Nationalist regime is presumed along the ethnic divide between the mainlanders and the Taiwanese.

39. After decades of silence or self-censorship on related topics, it has become common knowledge that a sizable portion of the young, lower-ranking soldiers who arrived in Taiwan with the Nationalist government had been "press-ganged" into Chiang's troops back in Mainland China rather than having voluntarily joined the military for some presumed patriotism or loyalty to the Nationalist party. Some of them "had enlisted so they would be fed," as Michele Yeh points out in the following essay: "'On Our Destitute Dinner Table': *Modern Poetry Quarterly* in the 1950s," in *Writing Taiwan: A New Literary History*, ed. David Der-wei Wang and Carlos Rojas (Durham, NC: Duke University Press, 2007), loc. 2605, Kindle.

40. Lin, "Da sheng," 101.

41. Xie Kun-hua, *Zhuanyi xiandaixing: 1960–70 niandai Taiwan xiandaishi changyu zhong de xiandaixing xiangxiang yu zhonggu* [Translating Modernity: The Imagination and Revaluation of Modernity in 1960–1970s' Taiwan Modern Poetry] (Taipei: Taiwan Student Books, 2010), 66–68.

42. Against the backdrop of the new trend of retroactive glamorization of the radical character of Taiwan's modernism since the 1990s (which can be exemplified by Chen Fang-ming's abovementioned account of Taiwan's literary history, though Chen does point out the modernist escapism as part of modernism's dual character), after it had been securely ensconced in the canon, it is important to contextualize the professed relevancy, efficacy, and radicality of any discursive practice as "resistance," which, theoretically, is relative to the characteristics, strength, and intensity of the power against which it resists, as well as the circumstances in which it emerges. Turning one's back on a panoptical overseer in a prisonlike setting can be a gesture of "turning against" this absolutist ruler. It is therefore important to assess the said radicality of Cold War modernists in the following examinations of such factors.

43. The first quoted example is from no. 5 of *Death*; the second quote is from no. 36. See Luo Fu, *Death*, 9 and 40, respectively. Chang Han-liang forcefully argues against the commonplace practice of attempting to decipher the recondite passages of Luo Fu in light of cursory understandings of surrealism, while Yan Yuan-shu tends to align what look like the "surrealist" parts of his poems with the weaknesses therein. In his preface to his 1969 collection of poetry, *A River without Banks* (*Wu an zhi he*), Luo Fu further distances himself from surrealism (which he previously endorsed, with minor reservations, in his 1965 preface to *Death*). The 1969 statement is quoted from

Chang Hang-liang's 1973 essay because the original poetry collection had been out of print, and no used copy could be procured by this author. See Chang, "Lun Luo Fu," 63. For a recent detailed account of this stylistic evolution, see Xie Kun-hua, *Taiwan xiandaishi dianlü yu zhishi diceng de tuiyi: Yi Chuangshiji, Li shishe wei guancha hexin* [The Canonization of Taiwan Modern Poetry and the Alterations of Knowledge-scapes: The Cases of *Chuangshiji* and *Li* Poetry Society] (Taipei: Showwe Information, 2013), 203.

44. As Liu Zheng-zhong points out, Luo Fu's conceptions of surrealist poetry would amount to an appropriation whereby the age-old notion of poetic inspiration via an otherworldly source (Muse) or a certain kind of poetic license can be categorized as surrealist. See Liu Zheng-zhong, "Zhuzhi, chao xianshi, xiandai pai yundong: Taiwan, 1956–1969" [Intellectualism, Surrealism, and the Modernist Movement: Taiwan, 1956–1969], in *Ji Xian*, ed. Wen-wei Shiu; vol. 9 of *Taiwan xiandangdai zuojia yanjiu ziliao huibian* [Compilation of Research Materials of Modern and Contemporary Taiwanese Writers], ed. Te-ping Feng (Tainan: National Museum of Taiwan Literature, 2011), 159–60. Also relevant here is the fact that the critical enterprise in question never entertained how cultural translation can divest the original of its political ramifications and appropriate it for a totally different politics—in this case, a politics of depoliticization.

45. Luo Fu, *Shishi*, 81. This poem is no. 30 of the sequence. The translation of these lines here is mine.

46. Luo Fu, "Houji," 122–26.

47. See, for instance, Luo Fu, "Houji," 119. The entire piece of Luo Fu's "Houji" can be said to offer the most authentic account (because it's by the author himself) of the contexts of writing *Death*, and a very detailed one at that. In addition, Zhang Muo's short piece, which was originally published in 1975, hence during the period when modernist poetry's dominance was seriously challenged, contends that the detractors couldn't understand *Death* because they didn't have personal experiences about real wars, unlike Luo Fu himself and other soldier-poets, who, he claims, immediately grasped some of the notoriously difficult lines of the text. See Zhang Muo, "Cong 'Ling he' dao 'Mo ge'" [From "Spiritual River" to "Magical Song"], in *Luo Fu shishi zhi siwang ji xiangguan zhongyao pinglun* [Luo Fu's Death of a Stone Cell: The Text and Important Critical Essays], ed. Ji-liang Hou (Taipei: Han Guang Culture, 1988), 164–66.

48. It is from the second stanza of poem no. 1 of *Death*, the first three lines of which read as follows: "My face spreads like a tree, a tree grown in fire / All is still, behind eyelids only the pupils move / Move in a direction many fear to mention." See Luo Fu, *Death*, 5.

49. For Yan's involvements in a series of debates during the 1970s, see Wang, "Lengzhan," 133–50. For other recently published detailed accounts of the series of 1970s debates on modernist poetry see, Xie, *Zhuanyi*, 85–109 and 133–74; Lin Jin-li, "'Ziwo' yu 'dazhong' de bianzheng: Yi xiandaishi lunzhan wei guancha zhongxin" [The Dialectics between "the Self" and "the People": The Discussion on the Modern Poetry Polemic], *Taiwan xuezhi* [Monumenta Taiwanica], no. 6 (October 2012): 27–52.

50. It is worth noting that the poetry journal *Chuangshiji* underwent a long hiatus between issue 29 (January 1969) and issue 30 (September 1972)—reportedly suffering from a fund shortage for more than three years. The soldier-poets of *Chungshiji*, however, were still active on the poetry scene during this period, and once the journal resumed publication, it (re-)started a remarkably long run for decades and is still alive and well today.

51. Liu Zheng-zhong ties the soldier-poets' soldier identity to their sense of alienation and self-image as heretics. See Liu Zheng-zhong, "Junlü shiren de shuli xintai: Yi wuliulshi niandai de Luo Fu, Shang Qin, Ya Xian weizhu" [The Sense of Alienation in the Poets as Soldiers: Luo Fu, Shang Qin, Ya Xian and Others in the 1950s and the 1960s], in *Taiwan wenxue xuebao* [Bulletin of Taiwanese Literature] 2 (February 2001): 113–56. While I concur with Liu's characterization, this doesn't necessarily mean the soldier-poets would try to establish connections between the two identities—in fact they rarely did in their writings—or make a point of their unusual combination of the two. Nonetheless, I think the heretics image would pose an interesting contrast to their latter-day image and textual practices as elitists, rendering them Janus-faced revolutionary/counterrevolutionary. I am also aware that Tsai Ming-yen even goes as far as interpreting the contradiction between, on the one hand, the class position of the mostly lower-ranking soldiers and, on the other, their status as elitist poets as their betrayal of their roots in the "masses," in addition to some kind of perverse takeover or annihilation of the role of the men of letters who were supposed to be socially superior to them. See Tsai, "Yijiu wuling," 97–98. Again, because of the aforementioned widespread "military connections" among the mainlanders who dominated the literary scene at the time, and due to the soldiers' disconnect with local Taiwanese communities, the kind of antagonism central to Tsai's argument would be questionable. Views such as Tsai's tell us more about how the soldier-poets irked others involved in the poetry scene in the 1960s and 1970s thanks to their domineering and collectivist behaviors that shaped the literary landscape—in other words, their maneuverings in the institutionalization of modernist poetry that were, ironically, acts of politicization based on a politics of depoliticization.

52. Li Min-yong, one of the most outspoken critics of the soldier-poets during their heyday, sneered at their practices of anthologizing "selected poems of the decade" every ten years at the beginnings of the decades—even before the decade began in one case. See Li Min-yong, *Zhanhou Taiwan xiandaishi fengjing: Shuangchong gouzao de jingshen shi* [The Landscape of Taiwanese Postwar Modern Poetry: A Dual-Structural History of the Spirit] (Taipei: Chiu Ko, 2019), 87–89. Xie Kun-hua also describes how the next generation of younger poets in early 1970s saw the editorial statements in these anthologizing practices as not only imposing the soldier-poets' own standards for the coming years but also as asserting the latter's paternalistic authority over the up-and-coming poets, thereby strengthening the hierarchy of the poetry scene. See Xie, *Zhuanyi*, 136.

53. Such a formation of the literary establishment based, partly at least, on military connections can be understood in terms of the "establishment cronyism" that Edwin A. Winckler characterizes as the mode of operation of the postwar Kuomintang regime. However, this system in the cultural field didn't appear to be as centralized

as usually assumed, particularly during the movement phase of modernist literature, when the core proponents' place in the establishment wasn't as secured and modernism arguably was an unintended consequence from the perspective of the ruling elites. See Edwin A. Winckler, "Cultural Policy on Postwar Taiwan," in *Cultural Change in Postwar Taiwan*, ed. Stevan Harrell and Huang Chün-chieh (Boulder, CO: Westview Press, 1994), 41.

54. For the modernist orientations in some works of Chu Hsi-ning, who usually is not considered part of the modernist camp, see Chen, *Xiandai*, 101–24.

55. Ya Xian, by many accounts, was the least contentious and most well-rounded critic among the soldier-poets, provoking the least debates and creating few enemies in his long career as as an editor. While the two main publications he edited—*Youth Literary* and the literary pages of *United Daily*—played key roles in promoting and enhancing the visibility of modernist poetry in mainstream media, overall they were not known as being focused on the editor's explicit agenda. Wu Sheng, a writer of very different persuasions, recently expressed in an interview his indebtedness to Ya Xian because of Ya Xian's appreciation of what and how he writes; see Wu Sheng, "Meng jian Ya Xian" [Dreaming of Ya Xian], last modified October 22, 2014, https://okapi.books.com.tw/article/3212. For a counterexample of how Ya Xian, early on in his editorship of *Youth Literary*, coordinated with Luo Fu's and Zhang Muo's editorial works in a not too subtle endeavor of self-promotion, see Xie, *Zhuanyi*, 89.

Chapter Four

Two States of One Peculiar Modernism

FROM THE US-AIDED LITERARY ESTABLISHMENT TO THE CULTURE OF US AIDS

Around the time when *Chuangshiji* (*The Epoch Poetry Quarterly*) and the soldier-poets were well on their way to dominate the poetry scene by mid-1960s after gaining strength in late 1950s, there was a parallel modernist literary movement that was so much more well received by the "mainstream position," hence more well known to the general public, that it often became synonymous with Taiwan's modernist literature in subsequent decades to the casual reader unaware of its immediate predecessors in almost the same historical period.[1] The second wave of this postwar modernism, which peaked in the 1960s, revolved around a group of fiction writers who, as students at an elite university, seemingly began on a clean slate of literary scene, as per the mainstream narrative, effectively emerging as the sole representative of Taiwan's modernist movement that eclipsed the first wave. The much greater visibility of this latter instance of Cold War modernism, I argue, cannot be extricated from the following factors: the presumed generic readability of storytelling (compared to poetry), despite the defamiliarizing formal experiments touted by its modernist practitioners; the changes and momentum brought about by its local precursors in the preceding postwar years; and the nuanced forms of institutional backing and cultural milieu on which this chapter focuses. Based on discussions of the earlier stage of the postwar modernist movement in the previous chapters, I shall examine the phased modernist movement in postwar Taiwan as two instances of *anti-establishment* literary movements in the name of modernism that not only wound up becoming central figures of establishment literature themselves (as Euro-American modernism did) but also was empowered—at least partly and respectively—by two different state-sponsored agencies undergirding the literary establishment at the time.

In the Beginning There Was Something . . .

Conventional wisdom has it that the "founding event" of modernist literature in Taiwan coincided, quite conveniently, with the founding of the influential literary magazine *Modern Literature* (*Xiandaiwenxue*) in 1960 by a group of undergraduates in the Department of Foreign Languages and Literatures, National Taiwan University, who nonetheless devoted themselves to creating and advocating for modernist literature, especially in the area of fiction writing, with core members Pai Hsien-yung and Wang Wen-hsing being two of its most prominent figures.[2] Armed with their youthful exuberance, the supposedly better position they, as students of Western literature, occupied in accessing, translating, and introducing most recent trends of Western knowledge (which for decades had been considered a catalyst for local progress and reform),[3] and an idealism seemingly untouched by—and unconcerned about—the calculated maneuvers of most of those involved in the literary establishment, these up-and-coming student-writers appeared to be poster boys (and girls) for a new generation of fresh literary voices that would break away from the historical baggage as well as practical considerations binding everyone else; lay claim to the title of the "modern"; and usher in much-needed newness in a literary landscape they declared to be "desolate." As they proclaimed in the inaugural editorial:

> We have no desire to live in the paralyzed mind-set of the good old days. We must acknowledge our backwardness; in the realm of new literature, even though it is hardly an empty space, it is at least a desolate scene. If the rich legacy of our ancestors cannot be put to good use, then it becomes an obstacle to progress. . . . We feel that the artistic forms and styles of the past are no longer sufficient to represent our artistic feelings as modern people. Therefore, we have decided to experiment, explore, and create new artistic forms and styles. . . . We respect tradition, but we do not need to imitate it or fiercely abolish it. However, by necessity we must carry out some "constructive destruction."[4]

Furthermore, the ivory tower's relative insulation from the utilitarian pursuits of society at large, coupled with the prestige of National Taiwan University as a top-ranking institution, tied into and enhanced the entrenched image of the elitist modernist artist (insofar as the Western model is concerned) peering down at the philistine crowd, ready to strike a defensive, if not defiant, pose in the interest of artistic purity, integrity, and autonomy. Given the fact that the European-American modernists these undergraduates modeled after were not yet included in the curriculum of the department, they also showcased their antiestablishment character by deviating from the "good student" type and exploring new frontiers of knowledge on their own, not to mention the iconoclastic protagonists and socially controversial subject matters treated in Pai's *Crystal Boys* and Wang's *Family Catastrophe* (homosexuality and a dysfunctional family, respectively).[5] The coterie they started, and the movement it spurred, thus appeared to fit the bill for "modernism"—rather than any other artistic school from abroad. Upon closer examination, however, this narrative about its founding is not as seamless as it seems.

Notwithstanding the inaugural editorial's unabashed statement of forging newness and literary modernity out of a figurative wasteland or an existing literary scene characterized as "desolate," these self-described modernists did not begin with a clean slate, or a ground zero brought to the forefront by their sweeping demolition of what had still been left standing. Nor did the vision and declaration at the outset of their movement constitute an absolutist gesture—at least not as total and resolute a break with tradition as Ji Xian's jettisoning of the "vertical inheritance" in favor of "a horizontal transplant" in the 1956 manifesto of modernist poetry.[6] Their emergence on the literary scene at the time did not happen in a vacuum. It wasn't exactly a sudden eruption (as European modernism tends to be presented), either. Instead, it could be considered the second wave of the postwar modernist movement whose earlier iterations (most notably the emphasis on formal and stylistic innovations) have been examined in previous chapters—a significant instantiation of similar endeavors whose groundwork had been laid by now, and a process of incremental evolvement or continuation of such modernist practices. It is noteworthy, too, that Wang Wen-hsing started his writing career with short stories; it took him several years before completing *Family Catastrophe* as his first novel in 1973 after much of his writing on this had been serialized since 1966. The initial serialized instalments of Pai's *Crystal Boys* didn't begin until 1977, followed by its first publication in book form in 1983. Their modernist movement has now often been celebrated, in retrospect, as an unexpected explosion or a radical break thanks largely to the gaps between the belatedly revealed radicality of these works and their secured places in the canon in later times, and through a time-compressed lens that projects the latecomer's desires, thereby glossing over the nuances between bygone eras. At the very least, they began anew what had been started by some other groups of people, both outside the ivory tower and within their own small quarter on campus, if one assumes that they either remained oblivious to recent predecessors (which is unlikely) or regarded such precedents as fading irrelevancies, even failed attempts.[7]

On National Taiwan University's campus, Professor T. A. Hsia, of the student-writers' department, had been sowing the seeds of modernism in the young impressionable minds of his students, especially the core founding members of this modernist movement, in the several years leading up its inception in 1960.[8] Hsia acclimated them to this particular school of Western literature not by teaching any course on modernist literature per se, which was still nonexistent there, but by sprinkling his lectures with certain views on literature that can be considered modernist, or at least conducive to some interpretations of, or approaches to, modernism. For instance, his characteristically modernist caveat against Romanticist overflow of emotions as well as a similar sentimentalism that emerged as a popular outgrowth of May Fourth literature developed in early twentieth-century China, and his valorization of form vis-à-vis content (e.g., "what to write" being outweighed by "how to write it") left lasting impressions on Ouyang Tzu and Pai Hsien-yung, two of his prized students, who became indispensable parts of the cohort that established *Modern Literature*.[9] Equally important, or even more so, was Professor Hsia's editorial work for *Literary Review* (*Wenxue zazhi*), which he founded in 1956 with a readership broader than the academia in mind.[10] Some of his precocious students, like many readers interested in literature and eager for an alternative to the officially sanctioned anticommunist literature and facile lyricism commonly seen in mainstream newspapers and magazines, had read and been clearly influenced by its contents.[11]

A Sobering Review: Literature at a Crossroads

It is important to point out, however, that *Literary Review* is not primarily a modernist journal, despite its founder's literary predilections (which are not entirely modernist either, as will be discussed later). And in spite of the fact that it ran, from time to time, translations of and introductions to works by Western writers who can be categorized under or related to modernism, such as Albert Camus and Henry James, it presumably centers on contemporary creative writings in Chinese, which include nothing that strikes one as recognizably "modernist" as seen in *Modern Literature*, since the translated materials constituted around one-sixth of its contents.[12] On the other hand, to the credit of the undergraduate modernists, they did not merely follow in the footsteps of their mentor when they started their own literary magazine, which noticeably was built on the foundation laid by *LR* and modeled after it in certain aspects. In this section I shall elaborate on *LR* as a figure of transition whose historical role and whose relationships to *ML* as well as other forces at play on the literary and cultural scene at the time can help us examine some of the characteristics of this second wave of modernist movement and unpack the institutional entanglements that tend to be obscured in mainstream literary historiography—what the scholar Chen Chien-chung has called a "US-aided literary establishment" (*meiyuan wenyitizhi*).[13]

Literary Review is to be viewed as a transitional publication in Cold War Taiwan in that its advent, alongside the modernist poetry manifesto in 1956, heralded the opening up of opportunities for alternative literary and cultural practices to those who fell in line with the Nationalist government's aggressive promotion and mobilization of anticommunist and combat literature, while also signaling the closure of some more radical potentialities that could be engendered by these opportunities around the time it folded in 1960.[14] It is a figure of transition also in terms of how it paved the way for a card-carrying modernist movement that Hsia's students initiated and that, over the next couple of decades, eventually grew into a full-fledged body of modernist literature in Taiwan. The journal eased the latter-day modernism into emergence with *its moderate, gradualist approach* to its goals and agenda, which seemingly leaves imprints of such moderations and ameliorativism in the said modernist movement, as will be elaborated later. Last but not least, *LR* is transitional in the sense that it instantiated the changing and nuanced workings of a literary establishment that was enabled by a vanishing mediator (in the form of covert US aids), while itself playing the role of a vanishing mediator to *ML*.

The "alternative" *LR* wishes to promote can be summed up in this sentence from its inaugural editorial, titled "To the Reader" and published in issue no. 1: "We are advancing a style of purity, rationality, and composure."[15] Compared with the flamboyant rhetoric of Ji Xian's modernist poetry manifesto, and the numerous "isms," labels, and terminologies brandished in the series of debates in the literary and cultural scenes in Cold War Taiwan, this statement of purpose, appealing to seemingly generic keywords, reads relatively down-to-earth and low-key, even though they evidently are conducive to the modernist precepts Hsia's protégés would uphold. True to the stylistic characteristics highlighted in the above-quoted sentence, the vision outlined in the editorial as a whole is as moderate as its tone is modest: "The journal was conceived by several friends who love literature. We don't plan to revolutionize the literary scene. We merely hope to keep our feet on the ground and do our best to produce a few good works."[16] What distinguishes the journal from the modernist penchant for sometimes overblown groundbreaking gestures and shocking effects goes beyond its rhetoric. The contents of the first issue include translated critical essays on nineteenth-century views of realism that do not square well with those commonly held by Western modernism,[17] and its "substance" in the ensuing years also features what can be deemed "realist" works (especially the creative writings in Chinese), with which *LR* vows to replace the "escapist" fiction popular in newspapers and magazines at the time.[18] The realist remnants, if not inclinations, can be corroborated by the claim in the inaugural editorial that "[w]e do not wish to escape from reality."[19]

While T. A. Hsia imparted to his students the modernist celebration of form, translated the American New Critic Robert Penn Warren's articles (published in *LR*), and even applied this kind of formal analysis to his own essays on Chinese texts,[20] the critical perspectives and textual examples provided by the journal do not always endorse or valorize the zealous experimentation with formal devices and acute self-consciousness of language characteristic of modernist writers. Rather, the aforementioned editorial sets the tone from the outset by making clear its dismissal of "idle wordplay" and by distancing itself from the presumed tendency to advocate for "art for art's sake," underlining instead that art "cannot be separate from life."[21] Its distance from Euro-American modernism, at least in certain regards, became more visible when compared with the burgeoning modernist poetry movement in Taiwan around the same time. When it comes to fiction, the genre of interest for the majority of both creative and critical writings in *LR*, the journal does not leave the impression that it favors the well-known modernist disdain of the mimetic or realist treatment of reality, and its poetry section shows rather conventional selections, or even conservative taste in poetry. Citing his own lack of specialty in New Poetry (or *baihuashi*), Hsia deferred the editorial responsibilities for this section to the poet Yu Kwang-chung, who belonged to the Blue Star Society, the rival group to Ji Xian's Modernist School prior to his own period of "modernist turn" in the 1960s.[22] This editorial move, around the years when debates about the modernist poetry manifesto were still intense, appeared to fit nicely into the moderate image and approaches of *LR*, even if it did not try to take its stand on New Poetry. As integral parts of the postwar literary scene trending toward varying degrees of liberalization subsumed under a quite broad and malleable conception of "modernism," modernist poetry and modernist fiction diverged on their separate starting points in the same year, 1956. Such divergence gives way to their respectively radical and moderate gestures (relatively speaking), but their divergent paths ultimately resulted from their differently conceived relations to "tradition," as the critic Tsai Ming-yen points out.[23] In contrast to Ji Xian's brazen call for wholesale Westernization in the manifesto,[24] *LR* states in the very first issue that "we hope to be heirs to the great, millennia-old heritage of Chinese literature and, by virtue of that, to extend its glory"—one of the few high-flown sentences in an otherwise composed and humble editorial.[25] Variations of this early sign of "traditionalist undercurrent" would resurface later in Taiwan's postwar modernist literature, most prominently when it moved past the movement stage and its representative figures themselves—both fiction writers and poets—became ensconced in the reconfigured literary pantheon.

Of course, the journal wasn't out to champion some traditionalist or ultraconservative causes—those would be part of the Nationalist government's campaigns to which *LR* sought to offer an alternative. In hindsight, the specific contents the journal featured (e.g., its brand of *chunwenxue*, or "pure literature") was less important than what it replaced or at least sidelined—propaganda promoted by the official cultural policies as well as the "markedly superficial pulp romances" surprisingly commonplace in a still underdeveloped market and highly regulated publishing industry.[26] Its lasting impacts lay, rather, in the manners in which it went about its business of establishing and running a literary magazine molded in its visions of aesthetic or literary *autonomy*, in the form of freeing itself of the directives from the Nationalist regime, and of a pursuit of its own agenda by means of a certain professionalism—in this case as professional writers and literary critics with criteria set from within their field of expertise instead of being imposed from without. By taking advantage of their dual roles as more traditional intellectuals with academic prestige and as representative scholars of Western knowledge that tended to carry with it an air of progress and legitimizing effects, Hsia and his scholar-writer friends, who were indispensable in founding the journal and keeping it afloat for more than four years, also managed to parlay such combined symbolic and cultural capital into the leadership position in a fast-evolving literary scene (*wentan* in Chinese) in which the literary establishment was undergoing minor transmutations as the Kuomintang government (or KMT) conceded some limited measures of its overreaching power into the cultural spheres after the mid-1950s. It was *LR* that initiated and instantiated the unique makeup of the literary establishment and its peculiar mode of operation made possible by Taiwan's Cold War circumstances in this transitional period. To illustrate how its modus operandi tied in with the putatively "modernist" traits—high seriousness, elitism, intellectuality, professionalism, and aesthetic autonomy—and how this watershed moment of Cold War modernism in Taiwan rehearsed decisively "moderationist" orientations that characterize the ensuing movement, one would need to examine the political contexts of a short-lived liberalism that contributed to the *apolitical* iterations in literature embodied by *LR* and inherited by *ML*.

From Cold War Liberalism to a Moderated Modernism

As mentioned in the previous chapters, the loosening up of the KMT's tight control on cultural productions and demonstrable ideological orientations in Taiwan took place around the mid-1950s, which resulted in relative liberalization of specific types and parameters of discourses and works (e.g., *chunwenxue*), cannot be attributed primarily to significant challenges to or resistance against the status quo, especially in the sphere of the political proper. This change in cultural policy may have stemmed, at least in part, from the authorities' realization that the effectiveness of the combat literature model, with its overtly tendential materials reeking of propaganda, had waned by then, as suggested by the account of a writer whose day job was a cultural bureaucrat working inside the propaganda machine.[27] Meanwhile, the cultural milieu befitting this relaxation of old policies and initiatives also had to do, to some extent, with the American-style liberalism that the authoritarian regime had to pay "perfunctory respect," as Sung-sheng Yvonne Chang puts it,[28] since Taiwan was supposed to be allied with the US-led camp of freedom and democracy in the Cold War world order, and because Chiang Kai-shek's government was receiving timely and enormous amounts of US military and economic aids during the 1950s after Chiang had suffered the consequences of American hesitancy in backing his grip on power since the immediate postwar years, particularly in the chaotic post-1949 period before the outbreak of the Korean War.[29]

It is in this context of a fledging cultural formation pried open partly by a US-aided liberalism that I would like to examine *Literary Review* alongside *Free China Review* (*Ziyouzhongguo* in Chinese), two journals that, according to recent scholarship on related topics, formed a certain loose or latent alliance based on a shared liberalism that was burgeoning in late 1950s Taiwan.[30] Founded in November 1949 by a small group of liberal-minded émigré intellectuals, most of whom had personal as well as conceptual reasons and ideological leanings to flee Communist rule in mainland China, *Free China Review* was a biweekly magazine featuring articles on politics, literature, and cultural commentary and advocating for liberal ideas of freedom and democracy.[31] Before the journal was forced to shutter following the arrest of its founder, Lei Zheng, in 1960, it was the only genuine and notable voice of dissent vis-à-vis the Nationalist government, as Chiang's regime grew increasingly authoritarian during the decade in which the US military and financial aids to Taiwan became securely committed and his grasp on power within the relocated state firmly consolidated. As indicated by numerous scholars, the "latent connections" or loose alliance between the two journals went beyond a coalition in liberal spirit and ideas, but struck one as strategic, practical, and at times coordinated, especially when it came to challenging the KMT government's top-down cultural policies and indoctrination campaigns: *LR* putting into practice *FCR*'s call for artistic activities free from the authorities' interferences, overlapping contributors to the literary section of *FCR* and *LR*, simultaneous pushes for nominating Hu Shih, the liberalist scholar and pioneer of New Literature who had been critical of Chiang, for the Nobel Prize in literature, etc.[32] Without contesting the critical consensus that *LR* was one of the rare bearers of the liberalist torch in Cold War Taiwan, at least the literary manifestation of it, I argue that it is important to reexamine *LR*'s place and role in this fleeting liberalist political movement in the last few years of the 1950s in order to better understand and assess the political ramifications and "radicality" of the literary modernism it inspired, especially when that critical approach tends to conceive it as the literary branch of a liberalism that loomed large in Taiwan's decades-long struggle for democratization.[33] My critical reconsiderations will proceed through the following three fronts on which the journal dealt with its Cold War circumstances: (1) literary autonomy and depoliticization; (2) the repercussions of the Nationalist crackdown on *FCR*; and (3) *LR* as an initiator and mediator of Taiwan's US-aided literary establishment.

First, the groundbreaking paradigm *LR* established, one that would have more lasting impact attributed to *LR* than the supposedly modernist one it ushered in, is the paradigm of literary autonomy—which is also arguably its greatest historical achievement. The autonomy in question was only vis-à-vis the Nationalist state, and not in the absolute sense (since there is no such thing as absolute autonomy, theoretically speaking). As underscored by an essay published in *FCR* right after the aforementioned inaugural editorial of *LR* came out, the literary autonomy envisioned and practiced by *LR* could be construed as a gesture of nonconformity, even of defiance, due to its significance as an alternative to the state-mandated "combat literature."[34] In other words, it was "radicalized" by the coercive nature of the cultural policies of a regime that did not (yet) extend its repressive rule to all facets of Taiwan society. Against the backdrop of the excessive and ubiquitous politicization—and only in the "right" and correct direction—demanded by the government, *LR*'s deliberate *depoliticization* of literature (i.e., those works it deemed as "pure" and worthy of the name "literature") as a way of practicing its idea of literary autonomy had, interestingly, an unmistakable *political* valence at that historical junction.

Meanwhile, it is also noteworthy that *LR*'s "defiant" practice of rehearsing a literary autonomy independent of the KMT regime's control was still rather moderate compared with *FCR*'s increasingly blunt and often pointed criticisms—which were "political" in the proper sense—of the government's various policies since the middle years of the 1950s. In addition to sticking to its self-delimited field of literature and literary criticism (which is a rather small circle, given its pretty high bar for the average reader) and refraining from opining on other issues, the journal did not directly dispute or complain about the stifling directives, initiatives, policies, and practices spearheaded by the KMT, even though it apparently sought to rectify the consequences they wrought upon the literary scene.[35] *LR*'s efforts in depoliticization could initially be seen as a form of passive resistance or noncooperation against the powers that be. However, this noncooperation move (rather than "movement," due to the subdued fashion and limited mobilization) was subsequently co-opted and neutralized during the transitional period in which the material basis of US military and economic aids had accrued enough symbolic purchase to seep into and reshape the still formative superstructure of 1950s Taiwan, so much so that both the Nationalist authorities and *FCR*, epitomizing the discontented elements in Taiwan, were exploring on the fly sensible ways to adapt to the emergent US-aided cultural formations as well as to respond to one another's maneuvers.[36] While *FCR* rightly attempted to leverage the cultural capital and legitimizing potentials of the key terms of liberal democracy to open up the political reforms they primarily fought for, it appeared that the KMT, quickly recognizing the relatively innocuous nature of depoliticized literature and the prospect of keeping up the vain appearance of open-mindedness without conceding something more substantial, pragmatically acquiesced and then eventually approved of *chunwenxue*, but balked at giving in to antiestablishment challenges on some other fronts, particularly the serious political demands mounted by *FCR*.[37]

Both *FCR* and *LR* pioneered in advancing one's agenda by tapping into the conceptual and cultural resources made possible by the prominent American presence in Cold War Taiwan. Juxtaposing the two journals, one can clearly see the different manners in which they furthered their main objectives, and how far (and in what direction) each could "push the envelope" with its approach: The crackdown and arrests related to *FCR* in 1960 signaled the "red line" Chiang's regime could never allow anyone to cross, regardless of—or precisely because of—the glaring contradictions of a so-called "democracy" that *FCR* had laid bare (questioning the constitutionality of Chiang's indefinitely extended presidency, its open call for and active participation in organizing an opposition party, etc.) in its last few issues, and in spite of the weight of the lofty ideals of democracy and freedom theoretically espoused by the United States and its allies.[38] On the other hand, the space the Nationalist government would concede, and even to some extent endorse, would be depoliticized literature (whether it be modernist or not) with self-imposed moderations and boundaries. Once the parameter of staying apolitical is established, even the more heretical modernist poetry and its wild formal experimentation could be tolerated, as shown in the previous chapters, let alone the "milder" version of modernism introduced and translated in the pages of *LR*.

If the litmus test conducted by *FCR* yielded a boldly marked forbidden zone that unequivocally indicated to all what *not* to do and spelled the hibernation of a liberalist movement before its reawakening decades later, *LR* came to signify a safety zone, which, despite the semblance of another certainty, found its bearings in a delicate balance in the following senses. First, the self-delimited perimeters of disinterested and pure literary pursuits outlined by *LR* can be interpreted *either* as signs of literary autonomy that sets its own rules *or* as those of self-censoring politically sensitive topics.

Judging, again, from what became of the two journals, the paradigm of autonomy *LR* bequeathed to *ML* strikes one as something in between. Second, true of its moderate character, *LR* presented itself as a "mediator" of sorts between tradition and Western literature (albeit heavily Anglo-American) by counterbalancing its role as a local representative of imported knowledge with its recourse to Chinese cultural heritage. In terms of "literature proper," it likewise chose to distance itself from the more "extreme" iterations, such as "art for art's sake" and radical formal experimentation the modernist poets were carrying out, as would the modernist fiction writers, most of whom, however, would still practice some measure of self-conscious moderations exemplified by their mentor, T. A. Hsia. Last, and most important, *LR* did not simply leverage the legitimacy and symbolic power of Anglo-American literature it brokered to its own advantage and for the good of its causes, as *FCR* and other entities and people at the time did. It literally received US aids in the material and practical forms, as recent research accentuates, giving rise to a US-aided literary establishment that enabled, to a significant extent, the swift ascent of the modernist movement led by *ML*, even after the US financial support was pulled.[39] In this sense *LR* can be said to mediate between the two states, between the institutional forces wielded, through official and unofficial channels, by the Nationalist state in Taiwan (Republic of China) and the United States of America.

Disentangling the US-aided Literary Establishment: *Literary Review* and USIS Taipei

First things first: Both *LR*'s and *ML*'s "American connections" had been known in some circles of Taiwan's literary and cultural scene and documented in critical studies prior to the latest findings by Wang Mei-hsiang, who scoured the decades-old archives and revealed to us what many could only speculate about: that the USIS (United States Information Service) did provide officially approved and regular financial support to *LR*.[40] That is to say, before the "hard evidence" uncovered by Wang, those American connections, based mostly on personal friendships and networks, involved such influential institutions as USIS Taipei, Hsia's department at National Taiwan University, and the Iowa Writers' Workshop (and its International Writing Program after 1967) and had so significant an impact on Taiwan's postwar literary landscape that they arguably warrant the characterization "US-aided literary establishment," even if they offered strictly symbolic and cultural resources that aided the causes of the journals. To point out the fact that *LR* was financially sponsored by the USIS post in Taipei is not the end of the story of Taiwan's Cold War modernism. It doesn't necessarily mean that the journal served as a mouthpiece or local agent of the American Cold

War propaganda machine, of which the USIS branches around the world were indispensable organs. For *LR* never existed formally or organizationally in that capacity, nor did Hsia and his friends found it with a view to filling such a role, even though hypothetically any publication could perform, or be used to perform, such functions simply by being implicated in monetary terms by American Cold War institutions or initiatives.[41] Nonetheless, the uncovered financial aids and the positivistic approach in archival research can help illuminate the nuanced and covert workings of this US-aided literary establishment and the ramifications of its mode of operation, in addition to the well-known American connections that will also be further unpacked in short order.

Most apparently, *LR*'s financial ties to USIS undercut the journal's claim to autonomy. Interestingly enough, however, we can now infer that the journal could, for four years, showcase a highbrow, elitist literature and retain a certain degree of autonomy from the market in such pursuits with little regard to a limited readership, largely thanks to the regular bulk purchases of half its printed copies by USIS Taipei, based on key internal documents cited by Wang, since *LR* folded in August 1960, shortly after USIS decided to withdraw its support in July 1960.[42] In addition to being semiautonomous from the market, *LR*'s relative autonomy from the KMT regime's pervasive interferences via the state apparatus or the existing literary establishment dominated by its trusted agents in the literary field was also bolstered by its well-known American connections. Not only did the journal evince some legitimacy and symbolic capital because of the Anglo-American literature and culture its contents featured or referenced, but T. A. Hsia and Wu Lu-qin (Lucian), a co-founding essayist and advisory board member, also had extensive working relationships with USIS—with Hsia being one of USIS's handpicked editors and translators for a series of anthologies of American literature (in Chinese) published by USIS and Wu working as a senior employee at USIS Taipei.[43] Fending off pressures from the market and the Nationalist state therefore came with a price, which was the journal's reliance on American resources of various kinds. This price or trade-off, unbeknownst to most outsiders, also betrays the *constitutive contradiction* of its "autonomy." Yet why did USIS stop supporting *LR* financially in 1960? And why did USIS want to sponsor a literary journal like this in the first place?

In an annual report, dated March 1961, by USIS Taipei to its headquarter USIA (United States Information Agency), the director of the Taipei post, Richard McCarthy, had this rather telling description about *LR* and its relations to his post: "USIS support to this Chinese literary magazine, begun in 1956 by a local publisher at our suggestion, always was confined to the purchases of 2,000 copies per issue at a special discount for distribution to nine other posts."[44] What clearly can be extrapolated from this quotation and corroborated by similar internal documents are as follows.

First, the USIS patronage was verified, but *LR* was neither directly published nor fully funded by the Taipei post, since the former was established by a local publisher (whose owner was also friends with Hsia and Wu) and the latter limited itself to regular bulk buying of 2,000 copies, out of the 4,500 copies, per issue "at a special discount" (without, for example, paying for its expenses or simply sending funds the journal could use at its disposal). This already distinguishes *LR* from other publications that had long been known to be affiliated with and published by USIS Taipei, such as *Student Review* (*Xuesheng yingwen zazhi*), which targets local students keen on learning the English language.[45]

Second, although it appears that USIS Taipei selected, for whatever reasons, an existing journal to sponsor without getting involved in its founding, much less its missions and editorial policies, the document quoted above reveals that the idea of starting a literary magazine like *LR* was actually suggested by USIS Taipei—"at our suggestion," as the post put it. Which strikes many, including those who were wary of the "American connections" of the journal's founders, as the most surprising part of the archival findings, since it contests the long-held presumption that *LR* was initiated by a small group of writers-scholars whose idealism and vision about the literary profession motivated them to found this journal, thereby undermining its image of autonomy and disinterestedness in the mainstream narrative.[46] To be fair, assuming that the cited archive states the truth (and there is little reason for the agency not to do so in this kind of internal papers), it is still plausible that Hsia and his associates had envisioned a journal like *LR*—or even fancied to challenge the status quo of the literary scene under KMT control with such a publication—but had no means to do so until USIS learned of their aspirations—likely through his friend Wu, the USIS employee—and stepped in to provide the timely push and indispensable financial support. Such a scenario, however, still begs these questions: Why did USIS Taipei want to see this journal come into being, and what did the post want from it? How much autonomy did Hsia, as the editor, have, given that USIS got involved from the very beginning? Before addressing these questions, I would like to bring up again *the indirect and covert nature* of USIS Taipei's sponsorship, because this did factor into the arrangements in question. USIS Taipei needed a local publisher to initiate—and partly fund—the publication, with which it didn't want to be formally and organizationally associated, limiting itself to the role of a significant yet secret patron of the journal via the practice of regular bulk purchases. This peculiar mode of operation, with the USIS sponsorship remaining steady yet unofficial, was also noted in an earlier report, submitted by USIS Taipei to USIA in February 1960, in which *LR* was referred to as an "unattributed" publication: "In September 1959, we initiated a survey of *Literary Review*, a USIS Taipei unattributed Chinese monthly publication, as part of this post's over-all program planning and evaluation."[47]

Not only does this quote from the report shed light on how the *LR* reliance on USIS support was supposed to look in the public eye—while betraying the inextricable ties between the two at the same time—but it also confirms that the "unattributed" (i.e., unattributable by outsiders) relation was by design, as part of the agency's broader plan, in which *LR* was but one of the publications expected to contribute to a grander program, according to whose goals the journal was to be periodically evaluated like other USIS publications. This leads us to the third important finding that can be gleaned from the *LR*-related USIS archives: No matter what *LR* purported to advocate, and regardless of whether Hsia and his coterie were aware of it, USIS Taipei, on behalf of USIA, had its own agenda apropos of *LR* that may or may not coincide with the journal's. The master plan for USIS branches around the world was, of course, to win the hearts and minds of millions over to the American side of the Cold War divide by combating Communist influences spread by the USSR and its allies as well as by propagating American values and culture. The "cultural Cold War," mostly understood in terms of defending and refurbishing American cultural standing in a battle raging across Europe against Soviet clout since the immediate postwar years through the 1960s, took on a nuanced form and approach in East and Southeast Asia.[48] Apart from exerting US prowess and rendering American culture and values in a positive light in this part of the world, the Cold War initiatives carried out by USIS posts in the region further took it upon themselves to "win the hearts and minds of overseas Chinese" over to the side of the Nationalist government in Taiwan (ROC), with which the Americans hoped the Chinese diaspora in Southeast Asian countries could identify culturally and politically, by means of publishing (or helping to publish) and distributing Chinese-language publications that could aid their cause. At the very least, the sizable minority populations of ethnically Chinese communities in those countries (approximately 9.6 million in total, circa 1950), with their disproportional economic wherewithal, would not be swayed into supporting the newly founded PRC in their ancestral land, thereby preventing, or at least containing, the potential Communist threat in the region.[49]

Keeping up with the ultimately anticommunist mission in the master plan, USIS Taipei expected *LR* to fulfill a rather specific function, as spelled out in the aforementioned 1961 report: "The magazine was designed originally to recruit Chinese writers from all over the world to contribute to it to show that Free China is the center of the Chinese-language literary scene."[50] While no literary magazine would oppose the perception that the transnational Chinese-speaking literary scene centers on itself, *LR* was, however, caught up in a larger anticommunist campaign at the international level that also encompassed the literary front, despite subtly declining to toe the party line in the KMT campaign of anticommunist literature. It has to be noted that Hsia and his associates, including the liberal-reformist allies at *FCR*, did not object to anticommunism per se. Ideologically aligned with the liberalist perception of Communism as inimical to individual freedom and electoral democracy, they were more concerned about what could be done in the name of anticommunism and the means to achieve anticommunist ends (e.g., mandating overtly anticommunist literature), though *LR* apparently bought into the idea that literary autonomy, as exemplified by the journal, puts to rout the textual practices behind the Iron Curtain that were reduced to servile tools of the state's ideological indoctrination.[51] Nevertheless, *LR*, in practice as well as theory, disapproves not only propaganda passed as literature, but also blatantly tendential works of literature. Yet the grander scheme of things into which *LR* was implicated was no other than propagandistic campaigns by the US Cold War machine, which knew better than to *directly* indoctrinate anticommunism through its broadcast or disseminated materials, as it tended to turn something seemingly irrelevant to anticommunism—a certain artistic form such as abstract expressionism or a mode of production like artistic autonomy or freedom of choice provided by the market—into an indirect and sophisticated instrument of the overarching anticommunist messages. Which is likely why an operation involving *LR* could only proceed in covert fashion and via unofficial channels, since it highlighted its form of literary autonomy, irrespective of the published contents. Such a *semblance of autonomy* is not only key to the functioning of *LR*, as far as USIS Taipei was concerned, but also was critical to the workings of the US-aided literary establishment in Taiwan, which was initiated by *LR* and was then inherited and further institutionalized by *ML*. Since we now know that it was the US government's common practice during the Cold War that it tended to work with—and through—collaborating actors in the private sector and went to great lengths to gloss over the appearance of propaganda in its messaging, it's not surprising that the USIS's clandestine funding, in the form of regular bulk purchases of *LR*, could remain secret for decades.

How much "real autonomy" did *LR* and *ML* enjoy, apropos USIS Taipei, under the aegis of US-aided autonomy? Given the lack of formal affiliation and the intent to obfuscate US interferences, it is unlikely that details about the responsibilities and powers of the local collaborators would be specified on record, even if the local USIS posts attempted to micromanage the "unattributed" publications. Nonetheless, if we examine *LR*'s relationship with USIS Taipei in conjunction with the other USIS publications (attributed or otherwise) under the rubric of USIS's official and unofficial networks, we may be able to gain some clearer perspective on it. For the anthologies of

American literature published directly by USIS Hong Kong, the group of "advisory editors," composed mostly of well-known and esteemed intellectuals from both Hong Kong and Taiwan, including T. A. Hsia, had a certain degree of latitude while working on the USIS projects—such as finding translators deemed fit and helping with the selections of anthologized works. There were back-and-forth discussions or negotiations between the local editors and USIS officials on both the contents and some editorial policies (e.g., keeping the original of the anthologized materials), with some suggestions from local collaborators adopted by USIS. In the end, the final product—the anthology of American essays, for example—differed significantly (in terms of the range and number of sources) from the two "model" English-language anthologies recommended by USIS. In addition, during the editorial process, Hsia, in the name of collecting and considering more potential materials, asked USIS Taipei to provide additional texts and references because it was extremely difficult to access those kinds of materials in 1950s Taiwan.[52]

All these point to some measure of partial autonomy on the part of the local advisory editors, who appeared to be active participants making the most of this opportunity to further their literary pursuits and acquire new knowledge, rather than passive subordinates taking and executing orders from their superiors. However, this precious window to new horizons of literature and foreign knowledge—which otherwise would be subject to the discretion of KMT censors in Cold War Taiwan—also came with a caveat: It was ultimately dictated by the Americans who granted this window, with limitations or premises undiscernible to the local collaborators,[53] however eye-opening and refreshing the view may look against the backdrop of a stifling cultural and political climate, in a time when transnational flows of information were slow, uneven, and often hindered by Cold War divides. Such a window and the USIS's firm control on selection of the advisory editors were among the few broad-brush means by which the United States ensured that its local collaborators, wittingly or unwittingly, met its agenda of anticommunism or cultural diplomacy, or at least rendered services that were conducive to US national interests. Thanks to such partial autonomy, the two sides may well have approached the collaborative projects with rather different purposes but wound up getting what each wanted in the process.[54]

If this is how USIS posts handled the "attributed" publications, then it would be quite unlikely that they dealt with the unattributed ones with more "hands-on" approaches.[55] Since *LR* also features creative writings produced by contemporary (and usually well-established) Chinese writers based in Taiwan and elsewhere in the "free world," USIS Taipei would have to rely more heavily on Hsia's expertise, judgment, and professional/personal network to maintain the quality and appeal of the journal. Even in the absence of detail-oriented interferences of editorial decisions, USIS Taipei obviously still held tremendous clout over the journal's financial lifeline, which it eventually terminated in 1960. Prior to that, USIS Taipei utilized another broad-brush approach, in the form of the intra-network survey mentioned in the post's reports cited above, to measure *LR* by the goals it expected the journal to meet, which was to "reach a small but influential group of the overseas Chinese elites," as indicated in the 1960 report.[56] The survey in question was to solicit the evaluations of *LR* by the nine other USIS branches in the region to which USIS Taipei distributed the purchased copies of the journal. Although *LR* received overall favorable reviews in the survey and in the Taipei post's reports, the number of copies requested or needed in those other posts steadily declined over those years. Such discrepancy between the qualitative evaluation and quantitative measurement, and between many of the positive readers' feedbacks reported and the final decision to withdraw USIS Taipei's support, brings to the fore, as Wang Mei-hsiang argues, the US network of propaganda campaigns in which *LR* must be placed as well as the *calculative reason* guiding these Cold War initiatives (making sure the Taipei post got a "special discount" in its bulk purchases of *LR* is one example).[57] In other words, the journal had to be assessed, like other attributed and unattributed USIS publications, ultimately in terms of its "effectiveness" in aiding US campaign goals. Such effectiveness involved not only the desired result—*LR* was well received by pockets of overseas Chinese teachers and students and was used as part of the teaching materials in some cases—but also the cost at which the result was attained: The small number of "elites" reading the journal (which had been anticipated) weren't worth the efforts after all.[58] For USIS Taipei did not give up on—but continued to push for—its stated mission of showcasing or helping to highlight Taiwan, or "Free China," as the center of the transnational literary scene for Chinese-speaking communities around the world, even after its withdrawal of financial support to *LR* that effectively ended the journal's run. In hindsight, we can infer that it transitioned to a slightly different and even more unattributable mode of collaboration with local intellectuals whose initiatives and practices, it hoped or expected, could assist in the agency's initiatives and American agenda overall, while proceeding at a lower cost and via means or channels that could further obscure its role and purposes in a larger Cold War propaganda campaign.

Towards a Culture of US Aids: A Short Story of Taiwan's Cold War Modernism

Specifically, USIS Taipei shifted gears and became more of a "promoter" than a sponsor for *Modern Literature*, heir apparent of *LR*, along with a few other Taiwan-based Chinese magazines of its choice, to be distributed to the aforementioned USIS posts in the region. This time, the Taipei post no longer committed to long-term and continual bulk purchases of these publications, which, after a "trial period," would cease to be free giveaways to readers connected with those posts, banking on the hope that the recipients of the free copies would subscribe on their own. Significantly, in an inter-post correspondence from Taipei to Singapore, dated 1961, this new practice by USIS Taipei was mentioned, with a caveat attached: "Publishers were advised not to mention USIS in any transactions."[59] That is to say, not only was the American (partial) financial sponsorship to be *phased out*, but its current promoter role was also to be effaced, laying the groundwork for the potential overseas markets for *ML* by utilizing the USIS networks in various locations, while allowing market forces to take over (part of) the fate of this publication, which was expected to gradually wean from the US financial aids. USIS Taipei's almost invisible—yet substantial and indispensable in the beginning—support for *ML* only further strengthened its valued image of being autonomous and apolitical—a position bequeathed by *LR* and subsequently rendered canonical along with the modernist predominance in 1960s Taiwan. Besides, it would also make more sense that the supposedly real "inheritors" of the Chinese tradition, instead of the Americans, take center stage in promoting a certain "Chineseness," whether in a traditional sense, as endorsed by the Nationalist government, or in more "modernized" manifestations, as exemplified by *LR* and *ML*.

Consistent with the general direction of American policies about foreign aids in the postwar years, US military and economic aids to Taiwan started nuanced schedules for phasing out around early 1960s, coinciding with the (relative) easing of cross-strait tensions and the modest economic improvement over the impoverished 1950s that enabled some in the emerging publishing industry to take advantage of and take over the market shares first opened up by US ventures and shored up by the public's growing interest in and ensuing gravitation toward most things American. These American goods signify not only imported material affluence but also new horizons otherwise inaccessible in Taiwan, including the niche market for the elitist, American-inflected literature represented first by *LR*, then by *ML*. In this context of phasing out and impending change, the folding of *LR* appeared to be a matter of when, not if, once it became clear that it couldn't pass the test of the market, which was part of the equation to measure its effectiveness for US propaganda objectives. Though the departure of editor T. A. Hsia for a new position in the United States in the summer of 1959 has been cited as the main reason for the withdrawal of USIS support, it may have been just the last straw that prompted the Taipei post to recalibrate, rather than the game changer that would reverse the trend and freeze the transition had he stayed on as editor.[60] Whether *LR* was too "heavy" for even the elites of diasporic Chinese due to its modernist undercurrents would be beside the point, as USIS Taipei would promote, at a lower cost and behind the scenes, the patently modernist *ML* soon afterward.

On the other hand, US support for an Americanized, reinterpreted modernism to claim an equal footing with the supposedly superior European culture, thereby debunking Communist critiques of the hollowness of American culture, wasn't as high on its agenda in Asia as it was in 1950s Europe, since the United States didn't feel the burden of proof for its "cultural superiority" in this part of the world and was generally received in Asia as the agent for change and progress in the wake of war devastations and, in Taiwan particularly, as the midwife to the drive for modernization, called for by people across various fields, from the ruling elites, to the US-educated economists and technocrats, to the modernist writers and artists.[61] USIS Taipei would be happy to showcase a Nationalist version of traditionalism if it proved to be what it takes to prevent millions of diasporic Chinese from leaning left. However, it could only burnish the image of the United States abroad if local young writers' enthusiastic embracement of modernist literature could be connected in any way to the perception of America as a spokesperson of cultural advancement and a benign benefactor. In other words, what mattered, as far as USIS Taipei was concerned, wasn't whether it meant to promote modernism. It was to retain *palpable yet unattributed* American presence and sway in many facets of Taiwanese society, especially in the elite circles of different fields, after the material US resources phased out. Such American presence, or the immaterial form of that which stays following the phasing out of US aids, is what undergirds "the culture of US aids" in Taiwan.

Since modernism in Taiwan appeared to be a success story for many involved in the USIS connections in the new phase, much like Taiwan was one of "the only sites of US Cold War intervention that achieved [its] desire outcome,"[62] in the remainder of this chapter I shall unpack the nuanced US entanglements that propelled *ML* and the modernist movement to its new heights, and examine how the workings of various institutional forces at play in this process came to epitomize the formation and consolidation of the culture of US aids.

First, USIS Taipei's transition to a more covert and sophisticated relationship with its local collaborators also sheds light on how the US-aided literary establishment, pioneered by *LR* and its brand of new literary paradigm, made a surprisingly seamless (given the fresh cessation of *LR*) transition to one that centered on *Modern Literature* and its cohort of new arrivals on the literary scene. The seamlessness and swiftness had partly to do with the similarities between *LR* and *ML* in orientation and approach: *ML* primarily expanded on, instead of setting itself apart from, the foundation laid out by *LR*, with the most notable difference being the section on creative writings by young and emerging writers (mostly from their coterie) that were meant to be experimental and modernist, while foregrounding the modernist inclinations of the critical essays, many of which were translations of scholarly essays compatible with the New Critical paradigm and sourced from the USIS window, as with *LR* under Hsia's tenure. Yet in addition to the individual talents of the student-writers (which are not to be trivialized here), it is also critically important to take into account the institutional forces enabled by *LR*'s and USIS Taipei's professional and personal networks when examining the phenomenon that the new journal could quickly overtake the leadership position vacated by *LR* and inquiring into how and why these novice writers could be catapulted to literary fame domestically and recognized and published internationally in a span of a few years. That is to say, the modernist movement cannot be extricated from the US-aided literary establishment and its Cold War context. The institutional clout and entanglements could not warrant a foregone success of the individual practitioners of modernism, but, in hindsight, they did set them off on a fast track and a vantage position to thrive.

The mode of operation of USIS posts in Asia, consistent with how US power tends to work, relied as much on the personal networks of their local collaborators, or those in the American private sector, as on the official and professional networks of government agencies—usually in various combinations of both, sometimes to the point of being indistinguishable.[63] The "People-to People program," begun in the Eisenhower years, was a prime example indictive of this mode and the thinking behind it.[64] Of course American officials did not simply make friends with the ordinary foreign "people" they came across, as the targeted or the "chosen" ones tended to be the elites among the locals, particularly during the Cold War. T. A. Hsia appeared to be a perfect match when it came to local collaborators for more than one reason—most significantly his status as an English professor at a prestigious university in Taiwan and his potential to influence more of the top students there to emulate his US-friendly propensity, and his friendship with Wu (who, being a USIS employee, might have been the originary and most indispensable link) that probably allowed for some form of unofficial channel of the collaboration. By the time Hsia left for America, the American connections and local network(s) established through his work with *LR* and USIS had been multiplied by his associates and other local collaborators, who in turn extended the USIS network.[65] Such multiplied connections were best exemplified by Hsia's protégés, who had been inspired by Hsia and whose literary orientations were molded by *LR*, since they would most likely become as invaluable to USIS Taipei as Hsia, while benefiting career-wise from this expanding network in the process (e.g., being recommended by the director of USIS Taipei to study at Iowa Writers' Workshop, where the most famous of them received their MFAs). All this forms the new material basis—sans the old monetary form—of what can be called the culture of US aids in the wake of the termination of previous material resources. Such a cultural formation was expected to aid US interests abroad, which now would preferably be spearheaded voluntarily and materialized by the "chosen" ones among the locals who could parlay the American connections, with their indirect or covert resources, into a new model of success, further enhancing the cultural capital of the US in Taiwan besides the power of the dollar.

Despite his journal's lack of market appeal overseas and the "alternative" literary paradigm he advocated, Hsia's moderate stance on modernism (which was rendered as a slightly different kind of *chunwenxue*, or "pure literature," by mainstream media) as well as his gradualist approach to his agenda ensured that he had a reasonable rapport with the KMT-sponsored local literary establishment of the time, enabling him and *LR* to gain a "mainstream" position in Taiwan's literary scene, as Sung-sheng Chang contends.[66] The US-aided literary establishment did not clash with the official one, with the latter gradually adapting to, or appropriating, some of the propositions of the former, such as allowing for literary autonomy (at least the semblance of it) and the championing of *chunwenxue*, which would then include the modernist variety. This turned out to be crucial groundwork—and network—for *ML* and the young modernists to flourish in Taiwan's literary circles, as most of them managed to publish works in other mainstream outlets besides their own journal (most notably, Wang Wen-hsing's iconoclastic *Family Catastrophe* being serialized for an extended period of time in a major newspaper amid controversies and outcries from some quarters). Now that the US aids receded further into the obscured background, the US-aided literary establishment, first grafted to but never imposed upon the local literary scene, could eventually and smoothly merge with the one sanctioned by the Nationalist state, which seemed to have learned a thing or two from the Americans about conceding some innocuous autonomy.[67]

On the other front, the American connections *ML* inherited from Hsia served the budding modernists of *ML* well not only in terms of facilitating the potential readership and recognition overseas through the USIS network in Southeast Asia, as mentioned before, but also by means of a series of "promotion campaigns" that entailed USIS's grander design. First and foremost, the "Book Translation Program," masterminded by USIS Taipei director Richard McCarthy (in that position from 1958 to 1962), aimed to publish—in that more unattributable mode elaborated above—English translations, in book form, of works by local writers, as a countermeasure against the outpouring of English translations of Chinese books from Beijing, and produced a number of edited volumes that collected some of the young modernists' short stories, billed as representative of the vibrant literary scene in "Free China," along with books on Chinese classical texts.[68] The second is the active networking, particularly in the early 1960s, with local artists and writers who, seeking alternatives to the KMT cultural policies, were keen in moving toward more "modern ways," hence likely to be receptive to the US postwar cultural diplomacy campaigns promoting American arts and literature. A prime example would be the dinner party hosted by McCarthy, where he invited the student-writers to dine with Eileen Chang, who was visiting Taipei in the fall of 1961 and had worked with McCarthy during his tenure as the director of USIS Hong Kong.[69] At the 1960 book launch party of one of the first publications from the translation program, *New Chinese Poetry* (edited and translated by Yu Kwang-chung), the US ambassador at the time met with the anthologized poets, including Luo Fu, along with such local luminaries as Hu Shih.[70] In the 1960s the exhibitions organized by USIS Taipei were always considered "can't-miss" events by the local art scene.

Last but not least, after establishing themselves as up-and-coming student-writers, the core members of *ML*—Pai Hsien-yung, Ouyang Tzu, and Wang Wen-hsing—went on to the famed Iowa Writers' Workshop (IWW), upon McCarthy's recommendations, shortly following their graduations from the university (a few others from the founding group who didn't continue on the creative writing path also went to various graduate programs of literary studies in the United States).[71] Together with the career path of Nie Hua-ling, who had edited the literature section of *FCR* before studying at IWW, settling down there and co-founding the International Writing Program at Iowa (IWPI) with Paul Engle, the trajectories of these young writers further reinforced the American connections and ushered in a new pattern or pathway for a long list of recognized writers in Taiwan, modernist or otherwise, to follow in the coming decade: One by one, they went through IWW or IWPI, constituting not only a formidable institutional presence of Iowa alumni in Taiwan but also a manifestation of an emerging *literary culture of US aids*. This, in fact, was still part of a bigger plan. Consistent with the US Cold War initiatives of promoting American studies abroad as well as stateside, US officials in Taiwan, as those stationed elsewhere, were keen in pushing for American studies across disciplines, including the studies and institutionalization of American literature, which would later take place in the Department of Foreign Languages and Literatures at National Taiwan University, where the young modernists had spent their formative years. According to the memoir of Chu Limin, who as department chair initiated and steered a series of curriculum reform in the second half of the 1960s that made American Literature part of the required courses, Chu had been approached by USIS Taipei in 1955, just the second year into his teaching career there, when the Americans inquired about his willingness to pursue a PhD in literature in the United States on a full-ride scholarship, since they had heard of his interest in American literature and realized that there was a dearth of specialists in this field in Taiwan. Chu would go on to eventually obtain his doctoral degree from Duke University and write, in Chinese, a book on American literature that was sponsored by USIS Taipei and published by a local publisher (again, in that post-*LR* mode of operation).[72] It was also during Chu's tenure that a set of grants, channels, and exchange programs were established and normalized to allow faculty members to go to various American institutions for research or higher degrees (it was still quite common then that junior faculty begin teaching at universities without a PhD or even a master's degree).[73] According to a Taiwanese historian's research, of all the disciplinary formations modeled after, to varying extents, the American institutions under the tutelage of similar postwar US educational and cultural exchange programs in Taiwan before the 1970s, the studies and institutionalization of American literature would be the most notable and full-blown example, illustrating the most profound imprints of US promotion of American studies in Taiwan.[74]

This contextualization of the rise of the parallel modernist literary movement under the aegis of a US-aided literary establishment and more entrenched American connections is not meant to belittle, let alone nullify, the significance of these modernists in Taiwan's literary history and the new literary grounds they broke in Chinese-language fiction writings—something that could not be demonstrated by any American model and could only be conjured up by the US-aided writers themselves. It is, rather, to underscore this modernism as part and parcel of its Cold War context and as *an epitome of the culture of US aids in Taiwan, which was never equivalent to the culture of the United States*, but emerged as a new pattern of success via American connections, the enhanced cultural capital with such connections, and a collective affinity and imaginary of the United States of America as a land of opportunities that suddenly could be materialized here. As an integral part of the evolving cultural formation in postwar Taiwan, which was dominated by the Nationalist government somewhat facilitating its American ingredients, the culture of US aids, however, was not exactly an instantiation of the triumph of Americanism in postwar Taiwan. For it is essentially, I argue, a *compromise formation* for all parties involved, proffering some measure of (partial) fulfillment of wishes or the seizing of opportunities, made available only by way of the American presence or connections, without overstepping the boundaries visibly delimited or unwittingly sensed under the authoritarian KMT regime. It is a relatively safe zone of adventure in certain spheres at smaller scales, although certainly with some caveats or trade-offs attached. For the young modernists and, likewise, reformers of varied stripes in Cold War Taiwan in the wake of the authorities' resolute clampdown on *FCR*, a certain form of depoliticized literature or an apolitical semblance of their endeavors appeared to be either a defense mechanism, deployed spontaneously, or a calculated move that ceded some grounds in advance in order to roam free in their respective terrains of relative autonomy, leveraged by their American connections but precluded from reforms that would entail deeper and wider structural changes of the Nationalist order.

Aside from the Nationalist state's pragmatic adjustments to or negotiations with the American presence it could not afford to do without, the US government also had to settle for Chiang's regime for multiple reasons, not the least of which was the stability and manageability of this Cold War front. Despite its presumed willingness to aid in local bids for reform—insofar as they could be steered into an American-style of modernization and enhance its image of modernizer and global benefactor—the United State would not throw its support behind elements that displayed too much of an antiestablishment disposition, not to mention those that called for a radical shake-up of the status quo in Cold War Taiwan, as in the case of *FCR*, even if their causes were advanced by means of championing the liberal and democratic principles supposedly represented by the United States.

In this context, the purportedly antiestablishment character that tended to be ascribed to this Cold War modernism in Taiwan due to both its European precedents and its reformist gesture of modernizing Chinese writing thus needs to be qualified, although its antiestablishment potentials cannot be denied. For it was firmly placed in the parameters of one establishment or the other, from the US-aided one that presented to them a latter-day, reinterpreted modernism devoid of politically radical tendencies and stamped with clear establishment character emanating from the updated postwar American canon, to the Nationalist one that eventually endorsed it as part of the concession the regime would come to terms with in this compromise formation, taking advantage of and gradually taking over the resources, channels, and connections first enabled by the Americans, including the ones that extended its literary establishment to the overseas Chinese diasporic circuits and bolstered, for a time, its legitimacy and appeal abroad. However cutting-edge the vision and claims of this modernism appeared to be, they were often couched in, or at least chimed with, the Nationalist-sanctioned modernization drives and characterized by its *moderationist approaches*. An early instantiation of such voluntary (or preemptive) moderation as a counterbalance move to its bold declarations of modernist experimentation would be the invocation of "traditional Chinese intellectuals" driven and tormented by a certain "ardent love" for "our country" and an idealized Chineseness in the concluding note of the inaugural editorial of *ML*,[75] tying in seamlessly with the age-old tradition of remonstrance long associated with intellectuals with the highest form of integrity. Such remonstrance, however, can just as easily be appropriated by the court or the modern state as cases of exemplary loyalty or patriotism as it can serve as the lens through which the underlying or overt social critiques of the well-known modernist works of fiction are understood, as Margaret

Hillenbrand argues.[76] Nuanced manifestations of remonstrance (e.g., as a ground of legitimization for modern-day reforms), modernization (e.g., as an updated version of remonstrance), and a palatable and "effective" presentation of "Free China" in Southeast Asia, the United States, and even different parts of the world then intersected to form an expedient common ground where the primary concerns of the modernists, the Nationalists, and the Americans converged and settled for what could be selectively extrapolated.

NOTES

1. For the "mainstream position" in the context of Cold War Taiwan, see Sung-sheng Yvonne Chang, *Literary Culture in Taiwan: Martial Law to Market Law* (New York: Columbia University Press, 2004), chap. 3 and 7, Kindle. To some extent, Chang's first book on Taiwan's postwar modernism, published in 1993, reflects the disregard of the modernist poetry movement in such mainstream narratives about Taiwan's modernist movement. See Sung-sheng Yvonne Chang, *Modernism and the Nativist Resistance: Contemporary Chinese Fiction from Taiwan* (Durham, NC: Duke University Press, 1993), Kindle.

2. The founding members include Pai Hsien-yung, Wang Wen-hsing, Chen Ruo-xi, Ouyang Tzu, Dai Tien, Leo Ou-fan Lee, Joseph S. M. Lau, and Wai-lim Yip.

3. For the reformist tradition in this context, see Li-Chun Hsiao, "Piping de changshi / changshi de piping: lilun, changshi yu gaige" [Theoretical Thinking on the Fault Lines of Theory, Commonsense, and Reform], *Chung Wai Literary Quarterly* 43, no. 1 (March 2014): 15–58; also see Chih-ming Wang, "Lengzhan renwen zhuyi: Yan Yuan-shu ji qi piping shijian" [Cold War Humanism: Yan Yuan-shu and His Critical Practices]. *Chung Wai Literary Quarterly* 43, no. 1 (March 2014): 121–68.

4. The English translation comes from Robert E. Hegel, trans. "Introduction to Modern Literature," in *The Columbia Sourcebook of Literary Taiwan*, eds. Sung-sheng Yvonne Chang, Michelle Yeh, and Ming-Ju Fang, loc. 4708–4718, Kindle. For the publication information of the Chinese original, see "Fakan ci" [Introduction to Modern Literature], *Xiandai wenxue* [Modern Literature] 1 (March 1960): 2.

5. For the English titles of these novels, I follow the translations of these versions: Hsien-yung Pai, *Taipei People*, trans. Hsien-yung Pai and Patia Yasin, ed. George Kao (Hong Kong: The Chinese University of Hong Kong Press, 2000); Wen-hsing Wang, *Family Catastrophe: A Modernist Novel*, trans. Susan Wan Dolling (Honolulu: University of Hawaii Press, 1995).

6. Ji Xian, "Xiandai pai xintiao shiyi" [Explicating the Tenets of the Modernist School], in *Xiandaishi* [Modern Poetry Quarterly] 13 (February 1956): 4. The English translation quoted here comes from Michelle Yeh, "'On Our Destitute Dinner Table': Modern Poetry Quarterly in the 1950s," in *Writing Taiwan: A New Literary History*, eds. David Der-wei Wang and Carlos Rojas (Durham, NC: Duke University Press, 2007), loc. 2353, Kindle.

7. Yip Wai-lim, who was a classmate of Pai Hsien-yung and whose creative writings consisted mostly of poetry, joined both the soldier-poets' *Chuangshiji* group and the cohort of *Modern Literature*. It is therefore unlikely that the young fiction writers of the latter, even as newcomers to the literary scene, were unaware of the modernist poetry movement the former was spearheading. Meanwhile, it is also interesting to note that the editorial work on the selections of poems to be published in *Literary Review* was mostly assigned to Yu Kwang-chung, who was from a rival camp within the small poetry circle. As *Modern Literature* modeled *Literary Review* in numerous aspects and inherited or utilized many of T. A. Hsia's resources and connections, its overlapping with the key figures of the parallel movement in modernist poetry was not significant when it came to poetry, which was never featured prominently in *Modern Literature* anyway.

8. Here I do not use the pinyin romanization Xia Ji-an, partly because his brother C. T. Hsia's works, published in English, are also referenced in this book.

9. These are based on Ouyang Tzu's and Pai Hsien-yung's recollections on the influence of T. A. Hsia and quoted in Chang, *Modernism*, loc. 746–50.

10. While it's edited by an academic and runs critical and scholarly essays on literature too, the publication is named a "magazine" (*zazhi*), and revolves around creative writers' works. There has been a long line of this kind of "academic" literary magazines, dating back to the pre-1949 era in China, as Mei Chia-ling points out. See Mei Chia-ling, "Zhongwai wenxue yu zhongguo/taiwan wenxue yanjiu: yi xueyuan pai wenxue zazhi wei shijiao de kaocha" [Chung Wai Literary Monthly and the Studies of Chinese/Taiwan Literature: An Investigation from the Perspective of "Academic Literary Journals"], *Chung Wai Literary Monthly* 41, no. 4 (December 2012): 145.

11. Pai Hsien-yung's very first published work of creative writing, a short story titled "Madame Jin" (*Jin danainai*), actually appeared in *Literary Review* under T. A. Hsia's editorship in 1958.

12. Ying Feng-huang, *Huashuo 1950 niandai Taiwan wenxue* [An Illustrated History of 1950s Taiwanese Literature] (Taipei: Vista Publishing, 2017), 66.

13. Chen Chien-chung was the first to coin the term. See Chen Chien-chung, "Meixinchu yu Taiwan wenxueshi zhongxie: Yi meiyuan wenyi tizhi xia de Taigang zazhi chuban wei kaocha zhongxin" ["USIS" and Re-writing the History of Taiwan Literature: A Study on the Publication of Taiwan and Hong Kong's Magazines on US Aids under the Literary & Artistic Institutions], *Guowen xuebao* [Bulletin of Chinese] 52 (December 2012).

14. For the significance of the year 1956 and *LR*'s founding, see Chang, *Literary*, loc. 1953, Kindle. For T. A. Hsia's role as a "critical bridge" to Taiwan's modernism, see Christopher Lupke, "Xia Ji'an's (T. A. Hsia) Critical Bridge to Modernism in Taiwan," *Journal of Modern Literature in Chinese* 4.1 (July 2000): 35–63.

15. This English translation comes from Xia Ji-an (T. A. Hsia), "To the Reader," trans. Christopher Lupke, in *The Columbia Sourcebook of Literary Taiwan*, eds. Sung-sheng Yvonne Chang, Michelle Yeh, and Ming-Ju Fang, loc. 4209, Kindle.

16. Ibid., loc. 4201.

17. See Hsu Chun-ya, "Huishou hua dangnian (xia): lun Xia Ji-an yu wenxue zazhi" [Talking about the Past in Retrospect (Part Two): On Xia Ji-an and Literary

Review], in *Huawen wenxue* [Chinese Literature] 54 (January 2003): 55. In addition, the special issue on Henry James can arguably be considered indicative of *Literary Review*'s transitional status between realism and modernism, since James is widely acknowledged as a transitional figure between the two.

18. Chang, *Literary Culture*, loc. 2041.
19. Xia, loc. 4209.
20. See Mei, "Zhongwai," 164, note 17.
21. Xia, loc. 4209.
22. See Yang Tsung-han, "Wenxue zazhi yu Taiwan xiandaishi shi" [Literary Review and History of Modern Taiwan Poetry], *Taiwan wenxue xuebao* [Bulletin of Taiwanese Literature] 2 (February 2001): 163–66.
23. Tsai Ming-yen Tsai, "Yijiu wuling niandai Taiwan xiandaishi de jige mianxiang" [On Some Facets of Taiwan Modern Poetics in the 1950s], *Taiwan wenxue yanjiu xuebao* [Journal of Taiwan Literary Studies], no. 11 (October 2010): 95.
24. To be clear, and as indicated in the previous chapters, Ji Xian backtracked on this position a few years later, and the seemingly heretical stance vis-à-vis tradition was modified quite a bit in the latter stage of the modernist poetry movement by the soldier-poets who once went with the most radical label in surrealism.
25. Xia, loc. 4201.
26. Chang, *Literary Culture*, loc. 2039.
27. The writer and cultural bureaucrat referenced here is Wang Ding-jun. See Chang, *Literary Culture*, loc. 1759–1784.
28. Ibid., loc. 2010.
29. See Hsiao-ting Lin, *Accidental State: Chiang Kai-Shek, the United States, and the Making of Taiwan* (Cambridge, MA: Harvard University Press, 2016).
30. See Chen Fang-ming, *Houzhimin Taiwan: Wenxue shilun ji qi zhoubian* [Postcolonial Taiwan: Essays on Taiwanese Literary History and Beyond] (Taipei: Rye Field, 2007), 173–96. Also see Hou Tzuoh-jen, *Ziyou zhuyi chuantong yu Taiwan xiandai zhuyi wenxue de jueqi* [The Search of the Relations Between the Tradition of Liberalism and the Rising of the Taiwanese Modernistic Literature] (PhD diss., Chinese Culture University, 2003); and Yang, "Wenxue."
31. According to Ying, *FCR* had a brief "honeymoon period" with the Nationalist government in the early 1950s, when it was also characterized by its anticommunist orientation, as evidenced by the journal's voluntary publications of works of anticommunist literature.
32. See Chen, *Houzhimin*, 179–80; and Yang, "Wenxue," 163, note 5.
33. Chen, *Houzhimin*, 173–96. Also see Chen Fang-ming, *Taiwan xin wenxue shi* [A History of Modern Taiwanese Literature] (Taipei: Linking, 2011), 339–64.
34. Quoted in Yang, "Wenxue," 160–61.
35. Where the inaugural editorial of *Literary Review* denounces propaganda as antithetical to literature, it refers to works of Communist propaganda without naming their counterparts in the Nationalist government's combat literature campaigns.
36. See the mention of the "permissible scope" in Sung-sheng Yvonne Chang, "Taiwan lengzhan niandai de 'fei changtai' wenxue shengchan" [The "Abnormal" Literary Production during the Cold War in Taiwan], in *Kuaguo de zhimin jiyi yu*

lengzhan jingyan: Taiwan wenxue de bijiao wenxue yanjiu [Transnational Colonial Memory and Cold War Experience: A Comparative Literature Study of Taiwanese Literature], ed. Chen Chien-chung (Hsinchu: National Tsing Hua University, 2011), 29. Chang mentions the cultural producer's strategies of sizing up the authorities and testing the delicate and supposedly flexible permissible scopes, while elaborating on the leverage enabled by the US presence.

37. Interestingly, the prototypical American product, Coca-Cola, was met with initial resistance by the KMT before it relented after the 1960s. See Tseng Ping-tsang, "Meiguo de ziwei: Lengzhan qianqi Taiwan de kekoukele jinling yu xiaofei (1950–1967)" [Taste of USA: Prohibition and Consumption of Coca-Cola in Taiwan (1950–1967)], *Taiwan shi yanjiu* [Taiwan Historical Research] 26, no. 2 (June 2019): 113–50.

38. To be sure, the United States has historically supported, openly or in covert fashion, autocratic regimes as long as they aligned with its national interests after weighing the pros and cons—Iran under the last Shah being the prime example. Having an embattled Chiang Kai-shek with the attendant political instability in Taiwan may not be seen by the US authorities back then as in its best interests.

39. See Wang Mei-hsiang, "Meiyuan wenyi tizhi xia de Wenxue zazhi yu Xiandai wenxue" [Literary Review and Modern Literature under the U.S. Aid Literary Institution], *Taiwan wenxue xuebao* [Bulletin of Taiwanese Literature] 25 (December 2014): 69–100.

40. Ibid.

41. It is worth noting that USIA (at the federal level, under the State Department) was founded with the view that it propagates US Cold War initiatives and campaigns overseas without the appearance and tone of propaganda. See Greg Barnhisel, *Cold War Modernists: Art, Literature, and American Cultural Diplomacy* (New York: Columbia University Press, 2015), 75.

42. Wang, "Meiyuan," 89.

43. Wang Mei-hsiang, "Wenxue quanli yu lengzhan shiqi Meiguo zai tai gang de wenxue xuanchuan (1950–1962)" [Literature, Power and American Propaganda in Hong Kong and Taiwan during the Cold War (1950–1962)], *Taiwanese Journal of Sociology*, no. 57 (September 2015): 13.

44. Quoted in Wang, "Meiyuan," 80.

45. Wang, "Meiyuan," 77–81. The publications directly published by USIS Taipei include *Student Review*, *Free World Pictorial*, and *Harvest Pictorial*.

46. This account of the journal's founding is mostly based on the personal recollections by Wu. See Lucian (Lu-chin) Wu, *Didiao qiantan——xiasan huasi ji* [Low-key Recital: Miscellaneous Works] (Taipei: Chiu Ko, 2006).

47. Quoted in Wang, "Meiyuan," p. 79.

48. For the scope and ramifications of the term "cultural Cold War," see Frances Stonor Saunders, *The Cultural Cold War: The CIA and the World of Arts and Letters* (London: The New Press, 1999). Also relevant here is Barnhisel's focus on the battle in Europe in the first two decades of the postwar years and the campaign for reinterpreting modernism in order to elevate the American cultural standing in Europe, its supposedly cultural superior. See Barnhisel.

49. Meredith Oyen, "Communism, Containment and the Chinese Overseas," in *The Cold War in Asia: The Battle for Hearts and Minds*, eds. Yangwen Zheng, Hong Liu, and Michael Szonyi (Leiden, Netherlands: Brill, 2010), 59–60.

50. Wang, "Meiyuan," 81.

51. Due to its anticommunist position, on the basis of which *FCR* briefly allied with the KMT for the first couple of years of its existence, and its persistently liberalist inclinations, *FCR* mirrored (and likely drew its inspiration from) the "Cold War liberalism" prevalent on American intellectual scene in the first two postwar decades, which came together from previously divergent ideological positions for the first three years and even published some characteristically anticommunist works of literature. Also aligned institutionally with the "Vital Center," its literary manifestations include those from the ones who were ideologically compatible with Hsia. For the unpacking of the relation between Cold War liberalism and anticommunist politics, as well as with postwar literature, see Roland Végső, *The Naked Communist: Cold War Modernism and the Politics of Popular Culture* (New York: Fordham University Press, 2013), 38–42; 99.

52. Wang, "Wenxue," 17–18.

53. Ibid., 18.

54. Ibid., 19.

55. As documented by Wang Mei-hsiang, USIS Hong Kong did include more meddling methods, such as specifying in advance a certain plot structure and content in some works of overtly anticommunist fiction it published around the mid-1950s, besides selecting finished texts for publication. See Wang Mei-hsiang, "Buwei renzhi de Zhang Ai-ling: Meiguo xinwenchu yishu jihua xia de Yangge yu Chidi zhi lian" [Eileen Chang—The Unknown Story: *The Rice-Sprout Song* and *the Naked Earth* under the USIS Book Translation Program], *Oumei yanjiu* [EuroAmerica: A Journal of European and American Studies] 45, no. 1 (March 2015): 92–93.

56. Quoted in Wang, "Meiyuan," 84.

57. Wang, "Meiyuan," 89–90.

58. Quoted by Wang, "Meiyuan," 88. The data cited by Wang here shows the methodical and quantitative evaluations conducted by USIS Taipei, especially the chart detailing the different types of readerships in multiple posts in Southeast Asia.

59. Quoted in Wang, "Meiyuan," 92.

60. Quoted in Wang, "Meiyuan," 89. In USIS Taipei's 1961 report to USIA, the "official" reason for the post's withdrawal of financial support was *LR*'s "failure to maintain high editorial quality" following the departure of T. A. Hsia.

61. For US campaigns to showcase American abstract expressionism and modernist art and recast modernist literature as an antidote to Communist repression of individual freedom, see Barhisel, 55–92. As related in Eric Bennett's *Workshops of Empire*, Richard McCarthy, the director of USIS Taipei around the time of the inception of *ML*, told Paul Engle, who founded the Iowa Writers Workshop, in a letter about the necessity of the writers in Free China to learn Western examples in the United States (presumably at Engle's Iowa Workshop) in order to write in "modern ways," characterizing a creative writing course taught by Yu Kwang-chung and Nie Huang-ling in Taiwan as "the blind leading the blind." See Eric Bennett, *Workshops*

of Empire: Stegner, Engle, and American Creative Writing during the Cold War (Iowa City: University of Iowa Press, 2015), 103–104.

62. Odd Arne Westad, *The Global Cold War* (Cambridge, UK: Cambridge University Press, 2005), 404.

63. Wang, "Wenxue," 10–13.

64. Christina Klein, *Cold War Orientalism: Asia in the Middlebrow Imagination, 1945–1961* (Oakland: University of California Press, 2003), 49–59.

65. It's noteworthy that T. A. Hsia's younger brother, Chih-tsing Hsia, usually known as C. T. Hsia, became a pioneering scholar of modern Chinese literature in the English-speaking world and was instrumental in identifying and giving academic endorsements of the representative contemporary Chinese writers at the time, particularly Pai Hsien-yun and Eileen Chang, from his vantage position as a Columbia University professor. Before publishing his seminal *A History of Modern Chinese Literature* in 1971, C. T. Hsia had written in Chinese a glowing review of Pai's first collection of short stories, *Taipei ren*, that was included in the 1969 edition of the volume. Having worked jointly with his older brother on a USIS Hong Kong project (see Wang, "Wenxue," 20), C. T. Hsia was no stranger to such networks of US Cold War initiatives, as he also wrote his aforementioned book on a Rockefeller Foundation grant. Not long after his relocation to the United States in 1959, T. A. Hsia passed away in 1965.

66. See Sung-sheng Yvonne Chang, *Literary*, chaps. 3 and 7.

67. Besides possibly taking cues from the American example of a relatively "hands-off" approach, the KMT's increasingly nuanced practice of social and cultural control while selectively conceding parts of its domination would eventually be extended to the political sphere and become one of the "positive cases" of what Dan Slater and Joseph Wong call the "concede-to-thrive" strategies employed by some authoritarian ruling parties. See Dan Slater and Joseph Wong, "The Strength to Concede: Ruling Parties and Democratization in Developmental Asia," in *Perspectives on Politics* 11, no. 3 (September 2013): 723–25.

68. For the general direction or overview of the program, see Richard McCarthy, interview by Jack O'Brien (Arlington, VA: The Association for Diplomatic Studies and Training Foreign Affairs Oral History Project Information Series, December 28, 1988). Books in the program that collect works by the young modernist writers, among others, include the following: Nancy Ing Chang, *New Voices: Stories and Poems by Young Chinese Writers* (Taipei: Heritage Press, 1961); Nieh Hua-ling, *Eight Stories by Chinese Women* (Taipei: Heritage Press, 1962); Lucian Wu, ed. *New Chinese Writing* (Taipei: Heritage Press, 1962); Lucy Chen, *Spirit Calling: Five Stories of Taiwan* (Taipei: Heritage Press, 1962). For the detailed account of the Taipei-based Heritage Press in the context of the USIS programs, see Wang Mei-hsiang, "Lengzhan shidai de Taiwan wenxue waiyi: Meiguo xinwenchu yishu jihua de yunzuo (1952–1962)" [Translating Taiwan Literature into Foreign Languages in the Cold War Era: The Operation of USIS Book Translation Program (1952–1962)], in *Taiwan wenxue yanjiu xuebao* [Journal of Taiwan Literary Studies], no. 19 (October 2014): 223–54.

69. Chen Ruo-xi, *Jianchi wuhui: Chen Ruo-xi qishi zishu* [Regretless Perseverance: Chen Ruo-xi's Memoir of 70 Years] (Taipei: Chiu Ko, 2008), 108. Also see Chen Chien-chung, "Meixinchu," 229–30.

70. Hou Ji-liang, *Luo Fu shishi zhi siwang ji xiangguan zhongyao pinglun* [Luo Fu's Death of a Stone Cell: The Text and Important Critical Essays] (Taipei: Han Guang Culture, 1988), 250.

71. Chen Chien-chung, "Meixinchu," 230. Chen Ruo-xi chose to go to a different creative writing program. Leo Ou-fan Lee, Joseph S. M. Lau, and Wai-lim Yip were the ones from the group who went with the scholarly path and eventually became notable scholars in their fields.

72. Shan Te-shing et al., *Chu Li-min xiansheng fangwen jilu* [Interviews with Mr. Limin Chu] (Taipei: Institute of Modern History of Academia Sinica,1996), 96–113.

73. Ibid., 122–25.

74. Ena Chao, "Guancha Meiguo: Taiwan jingying bi xia de Meiguo xingxiang yu jiaoyu jiaohuan jihua (1950–1970)" [Observing America: American Images in Taiwan Elites' Writings and the American Educational Exchange Programs (1950–1970)], *Taida lishi xuebao* [Historical Inquiry], no. 48 (December 2011): 123–24.

75. "Introduction to *Modern Literature*," trans. Robert E. Hegel, in *The Columbia Sourcebook of Literary Taiwan*, eds. Sung-sheng Yvonne Chang, Michelle Yeh, and Ming-Ju Fang (New York: Columbia University Press, 2014), loc. 4718, Kindle.

76. Margaret Hillenbrand, *Literature, Modernity, and the Practice of Resistance: Japanese and Taiwanese Fiction, 1960–1990* (Leiden, Netherlands: Brill, 2007), 12–13; 57–58.

Chapter Five

At Home in Exile

THE COLD WAR MODERNIST, THE EXPATRIATE, AND THE LITERATURE OF EXILE

The culture of US aids in Cold War Taiwan, as elaborated in the previous chapter, also aided and abetted the manifestations of the following phenomena, which could be epitomized by the textual practices and trajectories of many modernists and which would persist—albeit with varied scales and nuanced forms—into the subsequent decades. First, there was the search for, or the seizing of, an exit amidst the unabating prospect of military conflicts across the Taiwan Strait and under the stifling political and cultural climate perpetuated by the KMT regime. For those who were overwhelmed by the fear of war or burdened with a sense of alienation from most Taiwanese (as in the case of the mainlander poet Luo Fu) that was exacerbated by the insular space of Taiwan, or those simply infatuated by the assumed material affluence abroad, such an exit would mean eventual emigration out of the country—with the United States of America being the most commonplace destination. However, it could be materialized more often, particularly for those without the wherewithal to leave, by momentary flights from the monotonous and constrained reality prompted by American goods as mundane as *Reader's Digest, World Today,* or American pop songs.[1] On the front line of the US information war (which was no less propagandistic in essence, if not in approach, than its USSR counterpart), USIS Taipei's reading room nonetheless housed some publications that did offer information and perspectives otherwise inaccessible to the local readers and hence could very well represent a window into the world—although through an American lens—for those keen on looking for a way out of their insulated outlook under martial law.[2]

Second, while the search for an exit may lead to an immigration to America for a select group or type of people, the exodus wasn't necessarily booked on one-way tickets. Their experience of living in the United States did not always translate into becoming (Asian-)American or laying down (new) roots abroad, since there have continually been examples of *returnees* following shorter stays in America (e.g., students upon the completions of their studies in the United States) or longer periods of residency after establishing themselves there or even in the wake of illustrious careers in America. For those who have started families in America, or at least have obtained permanent US residencies, it's not uncommon to take on seasonal transpacific trips, like birds of passage, between Taiwan and the United States for either practical or sentimental reasons, especially since the 1980s, when air travel became handier than before. Whether their returns were calculated moves or patriotic, altruistic decisions, according to plan or because of better options, they likely were able to parley the US-aided symbolic capital to their advantage in their new endeavors in Taiwan (while the seasonable returnees could at least make the most of the spending power of the US dollar), at the same time signifying and building the coveted and valued American connections for those they had left behind. Such US-aided networks were thus expanded and strengthened by the ever-growing circles of returnees, who typically came from privileged backgrounds or were set on the fast track to elitedom through education or connections to US resources already in place.[3] In a sense, they were living their "American dream" without living in America—a localized version that was part and parcel of the culture of US aids in Taiwan, which could only be conducive to American "soft power" and influences, even if it did not yield tangible, short-term results or gains for US national interests.

Third, the culture of US aids in Taiwan, interestingly, emerged in tandem with a certain conception of "China" that bore witness to not only the seismic change of Cold War circumstances internationally but also the shifting collective identity of Taiwan. Simply put, the culture of US aids, whose material basis had first been concretized by US aids in military, monetary, and institutional terms, in turn began to lend indispensable discursive resources and symbolic capital to pivotal actors and their practices that propped up an imaginary construct of "China" surviving the withdrawal of the said concrete US aids (and since the early 1970s, the phasing out of its support of Taiwan on the diplomatic front). The transmutations of that "China imaginary" is arguably best instantiated by the writings and career paths of some of the representative modernist writers. To understand in more depth what became of modernist literature in Taiwan after its golden years in the 1960s, one needs to, I argue, critically reexamine how it wrestles with its own preoccupation with "China." In this chapter I shall elucidate the argument that the modernists appeared to go through, embody, or project their earnest quest for an exit, followed by a yearning for return, before settling for, in the end, their spiritual exile or spatial relocation—both in some cases—foregrounding an aestheticized, idealized, and borderless Chineseness, which has its Cold War origin in the appellation "Free China."

From "Free China" to Floating China

As indicated in the previous chapter, the United States made it its own business to promote the body politic run by the Nationalist government in Taiwan (Republic of China, or ROC) as "Free China" in Southeast Asia, especially during its intense anticommunist campaigns targeting the Chinese diasporic communities in the region prior to the early 1960s, effectively providing the ROC with not only the essential military and financial resources but also the international legitimacy it sorely needed in the US-led side of the postwar world order. "Free China" hence emerged as a Cold War code word for Taiwan, commonly used in the 1950s and 1960s in Taiwan as well as internationally by Taiwan's allies in the "free world," particularly the United States and those "overseas Chinese" (*huaqiao*) who identified with or chose to align with the Nationalist government. As such, "Free China" connotes the presumed legitimacy in its representation of the whole "China," implying at the same time the illegitimacy of Communist China (or "Red China") in its rule of mainland China, even though the Nationalist government controlled little more than the island of Taiwan. When they did not specifically use the term "Free China," writers and intellectuals in Cold War Taiwan tended to refer to themselves as those representing "China" *by default and spontaneously* in most cases—for instance, writing a new chapter in Chinese history, breaking new ground in the long tradition of Chinese poetry, and so on. Such an exclusivist, unrealistic claim to the ownership of "China" as a signifier, ever specious to many, roundly lost both its legitimacy and legality on the world stage when China overtook Taiwan's United Nations seat in the fall of 1971, which had been preceded by President Nixon's "pivot" in US foreign policy toward the warming of US-China ties since he took office. Shortly afterward, Nixon's historic visit to Beijing in February 1972 signaled a seismic change in the Cold War order on both international and domestic levels for Taiwan, paving the way for the eventual establishment of formal diplomatic relations between the United States and the "real China" in January 1979, at the expense of severing official ties the United States had maintained with "Free China."[4]

Bookended by the first signs of trouble around Nixon's pivotal visit and the peak of the "American betrayal" in 1979, the 1970s Taiwan saw not only the mirage of "Free China" (a name having more purchase on the transnational setting than in the confines of the island) evaporating under the weight of cold, calculated realism of international politics, but also was forced to confront the gradual yet seemingly inevitable wear and tear of an internal China imaginary that had been inculcated by the Nationalist regime and taken for granted by the mostly compliant population in Taiwan. This was largely a China trapped in pre-1949 spatial and temporal coordinates, sheltered in a Cold War "quarantine," one that fought off the validity, if not the factual existence, of the "other China" and was propped up by its sometimes anachronistic or misplaced grafting of Chinese geography onto the streetscape of Taipei—e.g., Beiping Road, Nanjing East Road.[5] Completing such wishful re-creations of the Nationalist's China was, most significantly, the pre-1949 political order frozen in time. The state of exception enabled by the declaration of martial law spelled the freezing of all elections in Communist-occupied China, which meant the elected members of the legislative branch (along with a Chinese version of electoral college that decides on the presidency) who came with the KMT could remain in their posts until after the mainland was recaptured and elections resumed. As absurd as it sounds in retrospect, this was the legal justification of the KMT's minority rule—Taiwan is but one of the thirty-five provinces of China of the past as well as the future.

Just like the Cold War "bubble" of Free China could burst anytime, the hitherto prevalent China imaginary in Taiwan also *lived on borrowed time*, as it were, before the Nationalist superimposition of the oversized space of mainland China, along with its historical baggage, onto the concurrent Taiwanese here and now could no longer avoid the blunt reality check over time. The snowballing effects of diplomatic setbacks and isolation on the international arena, aggravating the already dimly felt sense of insulation from many parts of the Cold War world order, visibly perturbed the relative stability of the US-aided KMT sociopolitical order of the 1960s, and sent intensifying shock waves of the monumental geopolitical shifts across every sector of Taiwanese society throughout the 1970s. Criticism of the authoritarian KMT rule of Taiwan as well as challenges to the Nationalist version of "China" (i.e., Free China was neither free nor representative of China) cropped up in pockets of dissidents both in and outside Taiwan, though not yet amounting to the consolidated and properly political opposition galvanized by the dramatic events since 1979.

On Taiwan's literary and cultural scene, where discontent with the status quo could be—and had been—registered in presumably more innocuous ways, the eventful 1970s' "collateral damage" to the swift ascent and predominance of modernist literature since the1960s was that most readers now had little appetite for, or had grown impatient with, the modernist "obsession with depth"[6] and/or its indulgence in formal and linguistic elements of writing after having woken up to the crude new reality that had been kept out of their Cold War bubble. The commonplace critiques of modernism's disconnect or disengagement with its immediate and surrounding realities in Taiwan, which had been audible and been levied against modernist poetry and fiction since their inceptions in postwar Taiwan, now gained significant momentum when the signs of the times prompted the collective urge to a "return to reality" (*huigui xianshi*) as a backlash against, or corrective to, the foregoing "inward turn" toward the individual psyche during modernist literature's heydays in the 1960s.[7] To be sure, the modernists in Taiwan were never concerned about any slip in their popularity among the commoners, and much like their Western predecessors, they may have relished striking a somewhat defiant posture vis-à-vis those they deemed part of the philistine crowd who now turned against them, as long as they still managed to secure a place in the literary pantheon with a cult following and strong institutional backing by elites of a certain taste.[8] Which is exactly what happened during the series of fierce debates on the 1970s literary scene coinciding with the institutionalization of modernist literature, as delineated and analyzed in chapter 4. While the new and emerging writers moved on to a largely realist episteme and produced socially conscious works, the serious challenges embodied by the Nativist and Localist advocates did not result in a clean, definitive "paradigm shift," as modernist poetry and fiction endured some "lean" years (less visible, to some extent, in mainstream outlets than before) but were further entrenched in the literary establishment before garnering a resurgence of critical interests and niche markets in the 1980s.[9]

Nonetheless, the changing tides did affect the modernists and their textual practices in discernible ways. Once proudly apolitical and reluctant to venture out of a self-delimited field of "pure literature," most modernists and their academic allies took their stand on both the series of debates on modernist poetry (*xiandaishi lunzhan*) and the 1977 debate on Nativist literature (*xiangtu wenxue lunzhan*) and decisively aligned with the official KMT positions on contested issues by publicly castigating the proponents and practitioners of *xiangtu wenxue*, with onetime modernist poet Yu Kwang-chung going as far as labeling the emerging paradigm as a "literature for workers, peasants, and red guards" (*gong nong bing wenxue*—presumably espoused in Red China) and the modernist novelist Wang Wen-hsing attempting to refute the opposing camp's underlying socialist critique of capitalist developmentalism by defending the US-led transnational economic system.[10] At this point, any trace of the fleeting antiestablishment propensities in the early-stage modernist movement were virtually gone, as the modernists appeared to knowingly make their choices when the circumstances dictated that there was very little room for neutrality, complexity, and ambiguity (which they touted as virtuous in literature and arts). They were now *the* establishment, staunchly fending off challenges to the KMT-sanctioned cultural and political hegemony, which was lending its institutional endorsement to their aestheticism by calling out those who, they suggested, were "communist sympathizers" in good old Cold War fashion. What the modernists did not yet stake their claim unequivocally to, I argue, was how to grapple with the Nationalist version of China imaginary that was rapidly losing its credibility and appeal. The KMT authorities were also struggling with what to propose in its stead amidst the fast-breaking events, before those nurtured by the modernist canon came around to a certain aestheticized "China trope" that took on "a life of its own," as Sung-sheng Chang observes, in Taiwan's mainstream literature in the 1980s.[11]

Prior to the advent of the popular 1980s iterations of "Chinese cultural nationalism" that adapted to and came to terms with the (now foregrounded) brutal realities and epochal changes of the previous decade, the transformation of the Cold War modernists' Free China imaginary to its latter-day manifestations was by no means a smooth one.[12] Aside from having to choose sides apropos of the first significant opposition to the KMT's cultural policies since *Free China Review*'s failed attempt in 1960, the modernists were also hard-pressed to confront, reflect on, and speak to their American connections. For the 1970s backlash against the modernist paradigm stemmed partly from the outbursts of anti-American sentiments galvanized by the "American betrayal" that spilled over to the cultural sphere, giving rise to a newfound hostility toward American culture in Taiwan and the critical reconsiderations of this cultural dominance by the United States among the former and current participants on the cultural scene (the cracks on the prevalent edifice of the culture of US aids did not, however, amount to a large-scale reorientation of outside influences or prevent those who left Taiwan from opting to immigrate to the United States).[13]

Coupled with the ever more glaring existential crisis facing the increasingly cornered Taiwan in the international arena, the anger, anxiety, confusion, and pent-up frustration in 1970s Taiwan combined to find their expressions most readily in the *new and nuanced forms* of nationalist reactions at this historical juncture, with each of them calling into question some of the present premises of the collective identity and the nationalism in question. Except for the non-Sinocentric outlook that centers on Taiwan, which didn't enter the permissible scope of public discourse until after the lifting of martial law in 1987, they all, I argue, emerged as alternative or competing versions of the China imaginary, or what C. T. Hsia famously encapsulates as "obsession with China."[14] The modernists, to be sure, were not overtly nationalistic in the movement phase, although Ji Xian and the soldier-poets had initially produced pieces of "combat poetry" they would rather disown. With the notable exception of Pai Hsien-yung, they were not known to dwell on China of either the past or the present in their modernist works of fiction, either. Yet all that changed in the 1970s, when there was a visible turn away from the "obsession with depth" or the individual psyche as well as stylistic virtuoso, not only among the challengers from the Nativist and Localist literature (*xiangtu wenxue*) camp, but also for most of the erstwhile modernists (albeit not as drastically),[15] whose writings in response to a new era, I contend, can be characterized as their endeavors in reconceiving "China" and "Chineseness," a process that necessarily involves certain forms of exit, return, and self-imposed exile corresponding to what I outlined in the first section of this chapter.

Cold War Exodus: From the Ex-patriot to the Expatriate

To illustrate the modernist obsession with China as well as their trajectories of exit, return, and exile that also epitomize the phenomenon of transnational movements in Cold War Taiwan, I would like to provide a reading of one of Pai Hsien-yung's short stories, collected in the celebrated volume *Taipei People* (*Taibei ren*). The story "Winter Night" revolves around the reunion of two old friends from college—a single event evoking flashbacks and reminiscences in the characters' minds in which the past would be inevitably pitted against the present and the friends compared in subtle ways. Like other "Taipei people" featured throughout the stories in the collection, the protagonist, Professor Yu Chin-lei, is a mainlander who carries with him the burdens of his pre-Taipei past intertwined with the monumental historical moments of upheaval and rupture in mainland China: the civil war that led to their relocation to Taiwan with the Nationalist government, the Sino-Japanese war, and, mostly prominently linked to the story of Professor Yu, the May Fourth Movement, whose multifaceted and contested legacies include its campaigns for modernization via Westernization that were, however, driven by its bid for national self-strengthening. Both Professor Yu and his visitor, Professor Wu Chu-kuo, an émigré scholar teaching at an American university, were among the student leaders who staged the anti-Japanese protests (as fictionalized characters in this referencing of an actual historic event) in Beijing on May 4, 1919, that marked not only the radicalization of an ongoing New Cultural movement but also the nationalist impulses and patriotic injunctions harkening back to the long-standing tradition of remonstrant intellectuals who righteously shoulder the collective fate on behalf of the rest of the nation— and this despite the participants' urge to overthrow, or at least overhaul, the Chinese tradition.

On this rainy winter night in Taipei, the delightful moods after exchanging pleasantries at the reunion became dampened as parts of their shared memories were inadvertently conjured up while the two friends recounted what had happened to each other and other members of their coterie from their college years, some of whom had died after being mired in miseries for some time. The contrast—running through all the stories in *Taipei People*—between the glorious or memorable pasts on the mainland that still haunt them and the ignominious or forgettable present in Taipei he would rather leave behind is probably brought into sharper relief when the old pals opened themselves up more candidly after not seeing each other for decades, invoking in the process their youthful idealism along with the May Fourth Movement. Formerly an English professor at the prestigious Peking University in Peking (now spelled "Beijing") in pre-1949 China, Yu now lived in a dilapidated old house among other similar structures in the faculty quarters near the university (based on the street name, though, it appears to allude to the faculty housings of National Taiwan University, the preeminent institution in Taiwan from which the modernist student-writers graduated). Matching the deterioration and disrepair of the buildings, exacerbated by the dreary weather on this drizzling winter night (the "living room floor was still covered with tatami; from years of dampness the mats gave off a musty odor of rotten straw"),[16] were the physical decay, shrinking prospects, and lost love of Yu as he emerged as a widowed, limping, bald, and aging professor whose second wife—"corpulent" and seemingly with little taste—didn't even want to miss her regular (Tuesday-Thursday-Saturday) neighborhood mahjong games to cook for and help entertain the visitor this evening, Professor Wu, whose name even came up in the local newspaper upon his arrival in Taiwan. Not only was Yu now a shell of his former self, but he also caught a glimpse—and a cruel reminder—of another component of what he had lost, thanks in part to his old friend. At one point during the reunion, Yu's son came home and passed the living room. He appeared to be such a bodily reincarnation of Professor Yu in his youth that Professor Wu, glancing "at the young man's handsome, lively face," couldn't help but point to the younger Yu and quip: "If I had seen you first when I came in, I would have thought your father had been restored to his youth!"[17]

However, the more they updated each other on the latest and refreshed their memories of the good old days, the farther they found themselves drifting away from the idealist visions, patriotic practices, and even antiestablishment sentiments (e.g., vowing not to become a government official) that forged their bonding at the height of the May Fourth Movement. This spiritual part of their losses was not lost on either of the interlocutors, who responded differently to their current situations against the backdrop of the pasts they reflected on wistfully. Yu, acutely aware of the low point he had descended to, still tried to free himself from the dispiriting paralysis of his life in Taipei by looking for an exit—a US-aided one, and he pins his dwindling hope on the visitor. As an expatriate and an absentee from the call of duty he once subscribed to, Wu would respond by planning a return—which I will elaborate on after discussing Yu's "exit strategy."

After Professor Wu lamented that he felt "ashamed" for not having contributed to the country and people he's supposed to be contributing to, while Professors Yu and Chia I-sheng, another of their cohorts from college, continued to "stick to [their] posts, educating our own young people" in spite of their "austere" lives here, Yu struggled to contain his uneasiness on this topic before looking into his friend's eyes and revealing that he "never really made any effort to 'stick to' my post; if fact, all along I've been trying to figure out a way to go abroad." To Wu's surprise, Yu added:

> I haven't just *wanted* to go abroad, either. I've jumped at every chance, at every scheme that might get me there. Every year, the minute I learned about any foreign grants to our humanities faculty, I'd be the first one to apply. Five years ago, after a great deal of trouble, I finally won a two-year Ford Foundation grant from Harvard, almost $10,000 US a year. All the formalities and travel arrangements had been taken care of.[18]

In a cruel and ironic twist of fate, a motorcycle had run into Yu right after he stepped out of the American Consulate, where he had obtained his visa, breaking one of his legs—hence his now-limping gait. Worse yet, Yu had to lie in a hospital bed for so long that he couldn't travel to the United States as scheduled. While being hospitalized, he could have, even should have, as he now recalled with remorse, informed Harvard that he was forfeiting the fellowship so that some other applicant could have it, but Yu was so desperate to go that he told Harvard otherwise. It turned out that Harvard had withdrawn the grant before Yu ended his five-month ordeal in the hospital, and the next applicant who could have gotten the fellowship was Professor Chia, whose declining health foreshadowed his death one month before Wu's visit.

The dramatic turn of events related to Yu's aborted "American dream" can hardly be typical of those who went through the same or similar routes to the US-aided exit. Nonetheless, the fictional account of the US-aided establishment of American studies in Taiwan, touched on in chapter 4 in conjunction with the US-aided literary establishment, does give us a basic sense and rather realistic picture of how this Cold War system worked and its impacts on those involved or having varying degrees of access: the reference to one of the "Big 3 foundations" (Ford, Rockefeller, and Carnegie) that have been found to be prominent actors in patently Cold War initiatives;[19] the scarcity of its resources and the ensuing competitiveness; the enormity of the monetary values in comparison with what people in Cold War Taiwan made and lived off; the life-changing potentials of such aides; and the examples and pattern that latecomers could look up to and follow. As mentioned in the previous chapter, the young modernists paved the way for other writers from Cold War Taiwan to receive scholarships to study at the International Writing Program at Iowa, but their departures had been preceded by the exit of their mentor, T. A. Hsia, who, after making a palpable difference in Taiwan's literary scene, seemed to go for permanent positions and a renewed career in the United

States, rather than the short-term stays Professor Yu in the story applied for, which enhance local scholars' credentials after their return to Taiwan. Of course, what was intended or offered as a short-term window to the American experience could very well be turned into an expatriate existence or even a "permanent residence"—if one so chose when timely opportunities presented themselves or were actively chased after. A case in point is Pai Hsien-yung, as the author of this story himself settled down in California to teach at UC Santa Barbara following the completion of his MFA at Iowa. In a broader sense, the passage quoted above also captures a widespread mentality and practice in other sectors of Taiwan society at the time that were keen on jumping at every opportunity, resorting to all schemes they could come up with, if necessary, to head for and seize US-aided exits in various forms. Notably, for Professor Yu, as for the mainlanders who relocated to Taiwan along with the Nationalist government, his first exit from the familiar environs and comfort zone in China was a forced one, possibly reinforcing his desire to look for a new one that could take him out of the present morass and be redeemed for the fresh restart that hadn't materialized after his first exit.

On the other hand, Professor Wu, who had become a world-famous authority on Chinese history (and so sought after on his lecture tours in Taiwan that Professor Yu couldn't see him until other dignitaries did), went for a US-aided exit prior to its Cold War iteration and institutionalization in Taiwan. During their reunion he told Yu that he had never taught any course on the Republican era, preferring to speak about "China's past glories" and characterize the Tang dynasty as "the most powerful and culturally the most splendid empire in the world."[20] As Yu tried to lighten the feel of the rendezvous at his house after awkward pauses by saying that he felt "comforted" that Wu was "the most successful of us all,"[21] Wu unexpectedly started to free his arm from his friend's grasp and launched into an impassioned confession: He wrote all those books on Chinese history just so he could get promoted and tenured, dismissing them as "empty talk."[22] He hasn't really been able to come to terms with the history of the Republican era he himself has helped to shape—so much so that upon hearing a conference paper read by a young American scholar about a reevaluation of the May Fourth Movement that picks apart its legitimacy, Wu simply opted to stay silent and leave the conference room:

> Just think, I've been a deserter abroad for so many years—several decades! On such an occasion how could my own pride permit me to stand up and speak for the May Fourth Movement? That's why in all my years abroad I've never wanted to talk about the history of the Republic. That time at Berkeley, I only mentioned May Fourth because I saw how excited students were by the riots

and it put me in the mood to talk about it—I just wanted to have some fun with them; it was nothing more than a joke.[23]

There are a few things worth unpacking in Professor Wu's surprisingly blunt admission. First, the self-described "deserter" status indicates that he still presumed a certain responsibility he later on abandoned, whether it be attributed to the tradition of intellectual remonstrance or, more individualistically, to his desertion of his own idealist past. The fact that he had just left for the United States to pursue his PhD the year before Beijing fell to Chinese Communist control probably added to his self-inflicted guilt for becoming an ex-patriot living an expatriate's life. Yet the taken-for-granted responsibility is arguably beyond the call of duty, since plenty of people who fled China around those chaotic years would readily chalk it up as out of necessity or a matter of survival. Second, although the reason(s) for Wu's inability or unwillingness to elaborate on the Republican era and, more pointedly, the history of the May Fourth Movement are never specified or clarified in the story, it is clear that this particular history is too overwhelming for him to address—which, in an ironic twist, is exacerbated by his profession as a historian who is "supposed to know," who should be able to tell of, account for, and gain some perspective on a period with which he is apparently familiar. Nevertheless, despite the disclaimer that he hasn't wanted to talk about May Fourth, we can make the case that, paradoxically, the historical period he is least willing or most incapable to discuss may well be the one he, deep down, most wants to talk about, based on his agitated reactions at the reunion and his impromptu retelling of his personal involvements in the movement to the UC Berkeley students who otherwise were more interested in the protests on campus and the overall anti-war unrest in the United States in the 1960s.

On a related note, Wu's mention of the student radicalism and various antiestablishment movements sweeping across America at the time appears to be more than incidental (his lecture amidst the chaos on campus notwithstanding). It emerges as a prompt in the narrative for the ensuing reminiscing, together with his college buddy, the fond memories they shared as well as rehashing the bond between them, while the historic juncture in late 1960s United States presents to Professor Wu an otherwise untimely occasion to claim some "bragging rights" about his own erstwhile heroics in front of his American students. In addition to serving as a reminder for Wu of his younger days, the juxtaposition of these two pivotal historical moments (which would call forth at once what is comparable and incommensurable—a topic not to be delved into here) in his recounting to Yu also lends us some insight into what he might think of the past and the present, respectively. Though he "just wanted to have some fun" with his UC Berkeley students by recalling a student-led demonstration in a far-away place and a distinct era, he didn't hold back his disdain for the modern-day radicals on campus: "The students are rioting all over America these days, and the UC students are the worst! They've burned down buildings, chased the Chancellor out, and beaten up professors. The way they carry on—it galls me!"[24] The careful reader may well wonder: How do these compare to the Peking University students' violent acts of setting fire to the residence of a diplomat they deemed "traitorous" and beating him up—which Wu highlighted in his class, to the thunderous applause from his American students? Does his conservative view expressed in the last quote, together with his dismissive tone, also apply to the Chinese historical event he participated in, as it does to the American instance now? The answer, ultimately, is "yes" (and the conservative orientation or traditionalist revision will be elucidated shortly), but why then does Wu call himself a "deserter," with visible regrets, if he can no longer approve of his deeds and thoughts around May Fourth and conscientiously thinks he is now in the right to jettison (or backtrack on) them?

What is at stake here, I argue, is Professor Wu's *intellectual acceptance* of what he might consider the more mature or rigorous perspective on May Fourth as a radical break with tradition, a reckoning or evolution of thought that is, however, *unacceptable in affect*. Aside from the emotional attachments reinforced by friendship and the nostalgia for youthful energies, the effect of May Fourth lies, perhaps more importantly for Wu, in its nationalist appeal—arguably a common denominator among participants of variegated backgrounds, positions, and ideological leanings. In other words, Wu isn't so much tormented by turning away from the anti-traditionalist ideas and practices likely associated with his younger self as he is by turning his back on his country, and his sense of guilt for not strengthening China, as he and May Fourth once pledged to, is magnified by his exit from China shortly before it was about to endure a colossal regime change. The limbo he finds himself in when it comes to addressing and explaining May Fourth (save for rendering another "empty talk," or "joke") is compellingly instantiated in a passage from the aforementioned conference paper that bemoans what becomes of those deeply involved in the movement:

> [L]ike a tribe of parricidal sons, they began to waver in panic; they became lost—they had overthrown Confucius, their spiritual father—carrying the heavy burden of their guilt, they set out on their spiritual self-exile. Some hurled themselves into the arms of totalitarianism; turned back and embraced the remnants of their long-since-shattered tradition; some fled abroad and became wise hermits taking refuge in their isolation. Their movement disintegrated, deteriorated.[25]

As one of the former student-activists who fit the description of their post–May Fourth trajectories quoted above, Wu appears to acquiesce to such a diagnosis without confronting head-on and as a historian the provocative invocation of both the collective past and his personal history. Rather, he walked away, which at best can be interpreted as a silent protest but is most likely an instance of him reverting to a reaction he had shown before at critical junctures of history—another exit. Yet the comfort zone the exits led to, including the material comforts of living in an affluent country as a tenured professor, has not completely sheltered him from the haunting memories of May Fourth, whose mitigated powers over him occasionally manifested themselves, not in the ideational contents that have long been debated, but in its nationalist calling—so much so that he told Yu as they're about to part ways that he would be "coming back" to the country (*"huiguo"* in the Chinese original) after his retirement one year later.[26] Interestingly, the country he's coming back to is not the China he left behind decades ago but this Cold War "Free China," where he had never before settled down (more on the destination of such returns later).

Backward Glances: The Pivots, the Returns, and the Moderationist

The postwar modernists in Taiwan, of course, are not of this May Fourth generation. However, the referencing and characterization of the May Fourth Movement in "Winter Night" can help to shed light on Taiwan's Cold War Modernist literature and its post-movement phase on multiple fronts: first, May Fourth as a historical precedence of the postwar modernization drive in addition to the Western modernism which Taiwan's young modernists modeled after; second, the remnants of nationalism that inform the modernists' renewed relation to "tradition" in response to the changing tides since 1970s; third, the modernists' trajectories—in terms of both their textual practices and career paths—of exit-return-exile, which do not necessarily adhere to the linearity and order indicated here.

Let me begin with the last category, as it pertains more clearly to the short story we have examined so far. We can infer by now that Professor Wu's desire for a return to the "China" that signified the Republican era he opted not to teach was fueled, at least in part, by the remorse and gnawing sense of guilt stemming from his fateful exit from a China in turmoil, even though this did not prompt him to embark on a return sooner. Such an abiding or rekindled nationalist sentiment, however, did not seem to preoccupy the mind of Professor Yu, as he was constantly on the lookout for a US-aided exit. Like Yu and other protagonists in *Taipei People*, the mainlanders in Cold War Taiwan, whose lives in Taipei had been precedented and foreshadowed by their own exits from mainland China, appeared to approach their exits from Taiwan, would-be or carried out, with relatively fewer qualms for some definite reasons. First and foremost, as mentioned in previous chapters, the official KMT injunction for modernization by means of US aids was one dimension of the establishment that the modernists went along with—rather than against—and took advantage of in their campaigns for the modernist paradigm of literature. Modernization via the US-aided exit after returning from the American experience therefore constituted an entirely legitimate ground for those going to the United States for advanced studies, especially through the US-aided channels that expected or mandated the recipient's return to Taiwan as the stipulated term expired. Second, some mainlanders were too consumed by their current plight and the inevitable sense of disconnect in Taiwan (e.g., due to the absence of prior family ties and emotional attachments there) that they could not care less about becoming an ex-patriot by leaving, as epitomized by the character Professor Yu.

Last but not least, the main difference between Wu's and Yu's exits from a crisis-packed China obviously lies in their distinct destinations. Unlike Wu's, Yu's first dislocation—spatial as well as spiritual—from China didn't land him in somewhere "foreign," however strange Cold War Taiwan might have been for him. It was and wasn't China—or rather, it was China in exile, as the ROC government-in-exile with which Yu migrated across the Taiwan Strait, caught up in a certain unseemly time and space, as if *in transit*, a prolonged one, to somewhere else, presumably or hopefully back to the China they were forced to exit. The acute senses of rootlessness, uncertainty, and transitoriness, in addition to the oft-cited ambiences of alienation and claustrophobia, underlie much of Taiwan's Modernist literary outputs thematically and, in works like Luo Fu's *Death of a Stone Cell* and Wang Wen-hsing's *Backed against the Sea* (*Beihai de ren*), also are instantiated in their formal and linguistic experimentations. The involuntary exile in transit here, resulting from the initial traumatic exit, is what they wish could be undone by another exit or a return. As I shall explain later in the chapter, it's not the kind of voluntary exile, in space or in spirit, many modernists come to terms with or feel at home with at the end.

It is important to note that the relocations to foreign sites often breed the urge for return as well as a nuanced brand of nationalism—a long-distance nationalism—as in the case of Professor Wu in the story. Among the postwar writers in Taiwan, the poet Yu Kwang-chung was the pioneer to study at the Iowa Writers Workshop (IWW) in 1958 and then embarked on a visiting lectureship provided by the US State Department in 1963. While Yu Kwang-chung is best known for his aestheticized China imagery and his nostalgia for a distant and inaccessible homeland (pre-1949 China), his American experience since 1958 has been noted as the watershed moment of his poetic preoccupation with the China imaginary and a visible turn toward teeming cultural nationalist sentiments.[27] Unlike the fictional Professor Yu in "Winter Night," Yu Kwang-chung, poet and professor in real life, was able to go through the US-aided exit—thrice by the end of 1969—and experienced firsthand a life in America that was not necessarily comparable to the vicarious experience of reading and learning about it. His exit to America therefore prompted in him not only the actual journeys back to his temporary comfort zone in Taiwan but also, in his writings, the longing (and mourning) for an often idealized and romanticized China that was forever lost, occasioned by what appeared to him a *primordial exit* circa 1949. There seems to be an unbridgeable gap between the "stops" Yu Kwang-chung settled for—America, Hong Kong, Taiwan, with back-and-forth moves in different periods of his long career—and the dream destination he was obsessed with, the "China" that was not even the mainland China during the Cold War, which he could not realistically reach in all those years either.[28]

Other modernist writers connected to *Modern Literature* did not leave behind as complex career paths between Taiwan and other places as Yu Kwang-chung did around the same period, and among the most well-known from the group, only Wang Wen-hsing and Wang Zhenhe went back to Taiwan to resume their writerly and/or scholarly careers upon the completion of their studies in the United States.[29] Nonetheless, whether they returned to Taiwan or settled down in America in the wake of their exits to the United States, the Cold War modernists continued to deepen and expand the indelible marks they had carved onto Taiwan's literary scene as student-writers: While those working in Taiwan wrote and spoke with the enhanced discursive power and aura associated with the newly minted US degrees they earned, those who resided abroad contributed to and participated in the unfolding development of modernist literature without missing a beat, as it were, thanks to the slower pace and mediated nature of literary practices and discourses back then. In fact, the expatriate existences of some of these writers might have helped them command a certain vantage position in terms of both their engagement with the literary and cultural scenes of Taiwan[30] and their personal reconnections with "tradition" and collective history, which probably wouldn't have taken place if they had remained in Taiwan as Westernized intellectuals without actually living among racial and cultural others in America. Most significantly, these expatriates' literary practices revolved around the literary and cultural scenes in Taiwan, in the framework of a reconceived and evolving "cultural China" seemingly irreducible to the mainland China whose presence grew increasingly real and palpable, especially from their fresh viewpoints outside Taiwan.

This leads us to another dimension of the nuanced forms of "return" following their US-aided exits: Since around the mid-1960s, the homeward glances and longing heralded by Yu Kwang-chung after his first stint in America were now being articulated through the expatriate modernists' dedicated engagements with the thriving literary landscape in Taiwan they had helped bring into being before their rather divergent responses to the eventful 1970s (more on this shortly), even though the contents of their creative writings did not focus on the immediate Cold War realities of Taiwan, as their critics decried (i.e., some aspects of the brutal reality there and then). Notably, they did not partake in the literary scenes in any part of the United States as Asian-American writers, nor did it seem that they intended to do so—their creative writings in the Chinese language basically precluded any such possibility. Those who opted to go the scholarly route instead of creative writings programs in the United States—for example, Leo Ou-fan Lee, Joseph S. M. Lau, and Wai-lim Yip—certainly engaged professionally with the American academia after obtaining their PhDs in the fields of comparative literature and/or East Asian studies in the United States and teaching in American universities, but they also made visible contributions to the institutionalization of modernist literature in Taiwan by writing—in both Chinese and English—about their college cohorts' works.[31] Regardless of their immigration statuses, personal plans, or long-term prospects of residing in the United States, their lives in America did not have ostensible bearing on their creative writings, except for the heightened nationalistic sentiments, their awakened desire to relearn the Chinese tradition, and the augmented symbolic capital of their writings on the receiving end of their homeward gaze at the height of the culture of US aids in Taiwan. As Pai Hsien-yung recalled in 1976, the "culture shock" that most new arrivals in a foreign country would feel actually spurred in him not simply a reconsideration of the American culture he presumably was disposed to embrace and learn more about but also, more importantly, a recalibration of his own relationship with his home country and culture. The newfound urge to reconnect with Chinese history and tradition got to him so acutely that he devoured piles of reading and visual materials about all aspects of the Chinese civilization at various libraries, on top of the heavy workloads he had to deal with during his studies at Iowa.[32]

Pai Hsien-yung in his post-exit stage—which comprises most years of his writerly career—is a prime example of the homeward gravitation of the modernist expatriates writing in America. Pai did not begin to write the short stories of his magnum opus *Taipei People* until 1965, the year he graduated from IWW and moved to teach at UC Santa Barbra. Featuring mainlander characters who, along with the Nationalist government, were part of the mass exodus and relocations to Taiwan circa 1949, they are "Taipei people" to the extent that they are all "stuck" in Taipei, suffering the stagnation or deterioration of their lives following the traumatic displacements; they aren't "Taipei people" only because they're essentially outsiders and newcomers to this city but also because, at different levels and in multiple senses, they are "stuck" in other spaces and times—of pre-1949 China—that seem incompatible to the here and now in Taiwan, unable or unwilling to come to terms with their reminiscences and backward glances that consume or paralyze the present. Such characters thus instantiated at least part of the homeward gaze of Pai, who moved to Taiwan with his family as a teenager (unlike most of the protagonists in *Taipei People*, who arrived there as middle-aged and old mainlanders), thereby sharing their obsession with a "lost China" while likely feeling a stronger attachment to Taiwan, where he made a name for himself. When Pai did write about stories set in the United States, as in the few stories composed within the first couple years of his arrival in America, there appear to be varying degrees of disconnect between the American locations where the actions take place and the lives of the expatriate protagonists (mostly Chinese-speaking students and new immigrants who recently settled down in the United States), which, meanwhile, are infused with the characters' recurrent invocations of being Chinese (*zhongguoren*) and the burdens of their pre-American pasts. The most extreme example among these is the story "Death in Chicago" (*zhijiage zhi si*), in which Wu Hanhun, a PhD in English from the University of Chicago, drowns himself in Lake Michigan on the day he receives his diploma. He's unwilling to return to Taipei, where his mother had recently passed away, and unable to find meanings in the works of English literary greats in which he had immersed himself for six years in Chicago or in the city slums where he led an ignominious life as a poor foreign student. In other words, whether the setting is Chicago, New York, or Taipei, what is foregrounded—against an incompatible backdrop—is always a certain enervating fixation with or gaze at a lost home that is no longer coextensive with any "China" in reality.

On a different register and in an extended sense, the return following the exit also corresponds to the retrograde trajectories and ultimately *moderationist* penchant of Cold War modernists' textual practices. Recall the traditionalist undercurrents briefly broached in previous chapters: for instance, in the inaugural editorial of *Modern Literature*, the invocations (in positive tones) of the remonstrant acts and words among "traditional Chinese intellectuals" and their show of due respect for tradition as a qualification for literary reforms.[33] Such undercurrents manifested themselves in more discernible ways in Pai Hsien-yung's and Yu Kwang-chung's post-exit writings as their attempts at reconnecting with tradition and articulating a certain Chinese cultural nationalism grew increasingly overt. In terms of the contents of their creative writings, the characters in *Taipei People* who hold on to traditionalist views or are representative of tradition and authority are often cast in more sympathetic rather than critical light, while apostrophized "China" repeatedly emerges front and center in Yu's poetry of the '60s and '70s. When it comes to Wang Wen-hsing's *Family Catastrophe*, widely regarded as the prime example of modernist iconoclasm, what tended to be overlooked in the initial outrage among conservative circles fretting over the novel's foregrounding of a family scandal and the supposedly challenged paternal order is the textually embedded and justifiable reading of the aging and emaciated father as a figure of victimhood at the hands of the abusive son rather than that of oppressive patriarchy.

With the notable exceptions of the recurring and fragmented flashbacks of a protagonist's past that resemble stream-of-consciousness rendition in "Wandering in a Garden, Waking from a Dream," most of Pai's narratives are not as edgy or experimental in form as one would expect from "modernist" fiction (though some stories can be so deceptively accessible that the casual reader may be able to find something appealing without noticing the inherent complications of the narrative points of view). In spite of Yu Kwang-chung's constant homeward glances toward the impossible home, the somewhat zigzagging trajectories of his relocations also are indicative of the pivots of his textual practices—from a romanticist keeping a critical distance from a fledgling modernist poetry movement, to his brief stints of modernist experimentation in the mid-to late 1960s, to a noticeable return to simplicity in language and a more reader-friendly aestheticization of China imagery since the 1970s that would usher in the popular "China trope" represented by the next generation of writers in mainstream literature.[34] In the longer-range view, such retrograde moves or moderations of one's foregoing emphasis on formal experimentation and the overall reformist outlook by reconnecting with tradition or adjusting one's relationship to it were more pronounced in modernist poets who resided in Taiwan in the 1970s, since they testified to a general pivot to more direct engagements with pressing issues in reality (e.g., rectifying the preceding trend of Westernization and undue dependence on the United States) beyond the venerated individual psyche, as their literary responses to the above-mentioned geopolitical challenges confronting Taiwan. The soldier-poets of the *Chungshiji* group had entered a period of recalibration around 1972, in which they touted a synthesis between the modern and the traditional, on the heels of the paradigm shift in poetry they had completed with their brand of modernist model, at one point calling for a "return to tradition" in conjunction with other means of rejuvenating the poetry scene.[35]

Without taking the US-aided exits to extended expatriate living in America,[36] as most student-writers did, the soldier-poets similarly moderated their modernist stance of the 1960s a few years later than did the expatriate modernists, partly due to the drastically changed zeitgeist that rendered earlier indulgences in individualist angst and formalist explorations inopportune and less relevant. However, they needed not range to uncharted terrains to make that self-revision, since a simpler recourse to the Chinese tradition and patriotism had been integral to their repertoire prior to their modernist turn, and their intensified foregrounding of cultural nationalist components might have been voluntary reactions to the current events in the 1970s. Just like the soldier-poets tended to walk back on or modify their spurts of excess (see chapters 2 and 3 for details), the modernist fiction writers were prone to nuanced forms of spiritual return, as elaborated above, in the wake of their exits and/or excess at the outset of their modernist pursuits. Faced with the fresh challenges to the establishment that modernist literature had become, both the poets and fiction writers fell back on or resorted to that which had been lurking under the surface or put on the back burner—the traditionalist undercurrents since the movement phase of modernism. The modernists' moderate and moderationist inclinations appear to be clearer when examined with reference to the May Fourth Movement, to which they all compared, in retrospect if not at the height of the modernist movement, their own modernist endeavors.[37] On one hand, they attempted to rectify the initial *excesses* of the historical predecessor—in terms of both the left-leaning, populist elements of the May Fourth legacies (celebrated in Communist China) and its feverish jettisoning of tradition in favor of inordinate Westernization (denounced by the Nationalist government). On the other, they upheld the practices of remonstrance demonstrated by May Fourth intellectuals (traditional intellectuals, too) that tied into the rekindled nationalist sentiments of an embattled Taiwan in the 1970s as well as the long-standing bid for national self-strengthening via modernization. Ultimately, modernist literature managed to stake out a position "between orthodox and heresy"[38]—best exemplified by Yu Kwang-chung but applicable to most other modernist practitioners—effectively and preemptively neutralized the radical potentialities of some of the modernist initiatives, if fully carried out, while subtly laying bare the inadequacy of the sanitized, reductive, and selectively distorted May Fourth narrative sanctioned by the KMT authorities—thereby burnishing its own image as a liberal-minded reformer.

THE FORKING PATHS ON THE WAY HOME: TOWARD A LITERATURE OF EXILE

It is important to note that Pai Hsien-yung's homeward glances at Taipei (the setting of most of his works of fiction) throughout his oeuvre are not exactly the same as James Joyce's insistent gaze on Dublin from afar, because the former's backward looks toward home can be cast in more than one direction.[39] Like many of his mainlander contemporaries, the displacements from

China resulted in an irreparable loss of homeland, and an insurmountable obstacle to any return owing to Cold War confrontations and bans on travels between Taiwan and China before the lifting of such restrictions around the mid-1980s. The deepest homesickness, on which their innermost basis of identification rests, it seems, would be reserved for the most original of homes for Pai and other émigré writers—the mainland China to which there was no returning. However, it wasn't always the case during the Cold War, and the destinations for homecoming still weren't as clear-cut as one might expect after most could make their personal choices beginning in the 1980s. We recall that Professor Wu in Pai's "Winter Night" took it for granted that his return to his home country (*huiguo* in Chinese) meant a postretirement life "back" in Taiwan, even though he had left China for the United States and had never lived in Taiwan before. Wu's decision may be ideological as well as practical—a historian of the Republican era of China and a career in America might not be well received in Communist China in the 1960s—although theoretically his prospect of settling down in China wouldn't be as precluded as that of his peers who relocated with the Nationalist government to Taiwan. When it comes to the Cold War modernists, Luo Fu and Ya Xian immigrated to Canada in the late 1990s, following their respective post-military careers and trips to their hometowns and other parts of China. Long before their departures, Ji Xian, much older than the young soldier-poets during the modernist movement, had moved with family to the United States in 1976. Pai and Wang Wen-hsing stayed on their separate teaching posts until retirement, having had numerous occasions of lecture tours and personal visits to various parts of mainland China, as many established writers and scholars of their generation had done since mid-1980s, although never seeming to commit to permanent residences in China. Their real-life trajectories of homecoming, I argue, reflect, to some extent, the incrementally thorny question of collective identity they have had to grapple with since the 1970s, as most people in Taiwan have. Together with their textual practices and other forms of discourse over the decades, they combine to illustrate a literature of exile that instantiates a certain poetics of exile, as Taiwan has since transitioned to a *very differently imagined community*.

There were, however, at least a couple of "roads not taken" by those canonical modernist writers mentioned above, which pointed to the divergent paths the nationalist turn in the 1970s has taken and, with them, the differing conceptions of "home" that implicate the version the Cold War modernists eventually came to terms with: In Taiwan, the 1970s debates on Nativist literature (*xiangtu wenxue*) brought to public attention earlier and much milder iterations of, on the one hand, the rivaling discourse on China predicated on realism and advocated chiefly by left-leaning intellectuals that heralded a political identification prioritizing the "real," progressively more authentic (as Cold War insulations waned) China on the mainland despite all kinds of differences; and, on the other, a fledging discourse on a collective identity centered on Taiwan, which was not to be indefinitely beholden to a government-in-exile and should be considered "home" for all living there, rather than a stopover on a prolonged transit to somewhere else. Two decades later, the second position, represented by the Localists, would evolve into a mainstream self-conception of Taiwan as a polity that is not to be tethered to mainland China or the uncertain future of "China"—however malleable the referent can be conceived—but recognizes and legitimizes, on the basis of a realist episteme, the coextension of country (*guo*) and home (*jia*). The first position, represented by the Nativists residing in Taiwan during the debates, found its expressions in the far less restrictive context of the '60s and '70s America among some members of the expatriate student-writers who, likely disillusioned by the Nationalist discourse on China after gaining some vantage viewpoint overseas, channeled their spontaneous and ardent nationalist thrusts—spurred by epochal events (e.g., Cultural Revolution and the shaken status of "Free China" on the world stage)—into actual "returns" to the true fatherland (*zuguo*) they pined for—returns that wouldn't be possible if not for the detour via the United States:[40] Chen Ruo-xi, one of the founding members of *Modern Literature*, went with her husband to China during the Cultural Revolution in 1966, lived and worked there until 1973, when she moved to Hong Kong and eventually relocated back to America. Guo Song-fen and Li Yu, a couple graduating from the same department as Chen and Pai and on track to become scholar-writers like other modernists from the *ML* group when they went together to the University of California in 1966, immersed themselves in student activism that paved the way for their forty-two-day visit to China in 1974.

The lesser-known trajectories of returns and contrasting manifestations of nationalism by fellow modernists throw into sharper relief the more excessive or radical propensities of Taiwan's Cold War modernism (its nationalist dimension in this case) that did not materialize in those of most of its moderate practitioners, who took a moderationist approach even when treating their own preoccupations with China, as with their moderationist appropriations of the May Fourth legacies. Between the Free China rendered obsolete internationally and the China imaginary undermined in Taiwan by intensifying challenges to the existing "emblematic representation of nationhood" (China trope losing ground to Taiwan imagery),[41] the moderationist writers, I argue, settled for a certain articulation of cultural nationalism as well as representations of a "cultural China" that points to alternative spaces and times and is not reducible to any single geographical materialization or political reincarnation of "China." Their shunning of mainland China before the lifting of bans very likely was to stay clear of the unwanted consequences incurred, but their circuitous paths of homecoming afterward may entail more than their moderationist penchants—that is, something besides going with the middle ground between two given options or a range of existing positions.

Before explaining further, it must be pointed out that Chen Ruo-xi, Guo Song-fen, and Li Yu all followed up their returns to China with exits leading back to expatriate living, the mode of existence in which they reflected on and wrote about their China experience in largely critical light and with visible disillusionment. Since her departure for China in 1966, Chen did not produce any work of creative writing until 1976, when she published a searing fictional account of the Cultural Revolution (which is far from being "modernist," as she had turned her back on the formal experimentation and existential angst characterizing her earliest pieces after her college years, vowing to write only works that are "understandable" to the reader).[42] Guo's and Li's practices of creative writings underwent a longer period of hibernation between the years leading up to their China visit and the first publications of their respective works circa 1983, coinciding with the considerable 1980s revival of modernist aestheticism, with its signature high seriousness, linguistic impeccability, and narrative caesura, gaps, and leaps that prove to be demanding for most readers.[43] It appears that the "really existing" China either consumed all their creative energies at the heat of the moment in their immersion in or direct experience with it or did not inspire new writerly outputs for them until after some measures of time lapse and spatial displacements. Of course, it likely dawned on them—perhaps in hindsight—that becoming a writer based in China wouldn't bode well for the latitude with which they wanted to write the works they meant to compose and eventually published. Although Chen's textual practices in the wake of her "return" to China differed significantly from those of the two "returning modernists," one commonality that stands out is the *exiles*—forced, voluntary, or self-imposed—in which their literary productions reemerged following returns that were much more direct, consequential, "real," and visceral than those undertaken by other modernists.

In other words, they reverted to the practices of expatriate writing of their fellow émigré modernists in the United States, which, in a broader sense, can be considered the comfort zone of modernist writings coming out of Cold War Taiwan, as this modernism has, since its inception, been preoccupied primarily with alternative spaces and times to the ones in which it is currently immersed. It is accustomed to maintaining—and creating, if necessary—a certain physical or imagined *distance from the immersion of the moment*—whether it be the immediate Cold War realities in Taiwan from which it sought to take flight, the destination on the other end of the US-aided exit, or even the real China with which its prominent representatives are obsessed and to which they return in nuanced forms and to varying degrees. Such actual or spiritual distance characterizes their mode of existence and the modus operandi in which they thrived, and which certainly has its Cold War origins: the divided world order and the policies of incommunicado that sheltered them in a "bubble" where the denial of the "other" or "real" China reigned supreme; the trenches of freedom in whose confines the soldier-poets were surrealistically acquiesced to roam free under the aegis of "pure literature" and their track records of loyalty; the buffer zone created by the US presence in Taiwan—and the modernists' expatriate writing from America—that aided their moderated deviance from the official line and shielded them from potential troubles.

In addition to the said modernist tendency to detach, there was also the opposite propensity to (re-)attach, which is in part instantiated in the persistent homeward glances without eventually settling on any particular locus among likely destinations of homecoming. For the poet-scholar Wai-lim Yip, who was born in southern China, migrated to Hong Kong at a young age, but attended college in Taiwan and co-founded *Modern Literature*, it's virtually impossible to rank the authenticity of, and his attachment to, any of these home sites, especially after he has made return visits, as a scholar long based in the United States, to all of them since the 1980s.[44] In Luo Fu's long poem *Driftwood* (*Piao mu*), composed and published after his immigration to Vancouver, Canada, the central and recurring metaphor of driftwood brings to the fore journeys with no prospect of return or perpetual homelessness, yet it also jostles with dogged attempts—however tenuous or doomed they appear—at returns scattered throughout the poem, including the stirring images of blood-splashing salmon swimming upstream, which is a seasonal sight at the poet's current site of self-imposed exile that evokes "home."[45] Their writings about the multiplicity of home or the forking paths of homecoming, however, are not to be conflated with the celebration of the multiplicity of identity in a multicultural, increasingly borderless postmodern globality, since there's always some nationalist undercurrent that repatriates the exilic writers to a locale, in another register, that is intertwined with but never reducible to a certain "really existing" home country (*guojia*) they still could not or would not decide on. For instance, Yip acknowledges in his preface to his 1982 book of poems—a rare output of creative writings in his decades of expatriate living in the United States—that his relative drought of poetry on landscape (which the collection features) was not due to the lack of beauty and magnificence of American landscape, but was likely related to the difference in ambience or "feel" between the surrounding sights in his life in America and the *shansui* (literally "mountain and water" in Chinese; generally speaking, landscape) his poetic explorations in this period focuses on, whose ambience or aura, in tandem with the Chinese landscape represented, to which he feels, and can claim, a sense of belonging. The difference in *jing* (concrete environs, realm; also "ambience" in Chinese) entails as much divergent mindscapes or spiritual spaces as separate geographical locations. In other words, a *shanshui* poem—and likewise, a *shansui* painting (which is a traditional genre)—on American landscape would be so incongruous, even unthinkable, that he would rather keep the form and the content apart as disparate spheres in his life. It was Yip's homeward gazes that reoriented or gravitated the meanings of the *shanshui* depicted in his poems, but he credited Taiwan's landscape, which he periodically visited over those years and which he found congenial with Chinese *shansui*, that sustained his reminiscences and imaginations stateside, thereby resuscitating his poetry writing.[46]

Significantly, it was the Chineseness of Taiwan's landscape and, presumably, the Chineseness of the people and culture there, that Yip drew on and invoked in these works, which, he realized in retrospect, revolve around two motifs—homesickness (*huai xiang*) and exile.[47] The exile takes (its) place and gains perspectives and meanings only in relation to "home," whether the latter can be specified or only vaguely, multiply conceived, and whether the exit from home is forced or by choice. The poetics of exile Yip's textual practices and other forms of discourse point to, as those of other expatriate modernists do, appear to be predicated on a cultural and long-distance nationalism that still orbits around the home left behind at the center and maintains connections with it (e.g., as seasonal returnees). What it gravitates toward and revolves around went through a series of changes over the years that also reflect the underlying logic of displacement of this poetics: The eminently untenable "Free China" had long been replaced, before the end of the Cold War, by a vaguely conceived cultural China or Greater China that could circumvent hard political choices while allowing for an idealized and culturally essentialist unity that has had little prospect of materialization in political reality. For them, the vacated center could be the pre-1949 China, Taiwan, Hong Kong, or post-1949 China at different points of their careers. However, I argue that in the end, these concrete home sites as well as their varied combination or concentric alignments seem to be displaced into a converged preoccupation with Chineseness and the expatriate writers' insistent dwelling in *the Chinese language as the home none of them ever let go* in their writerly endeavors, despite the necessity or simply the daily routine of being immersed in the English language as part of their exilic existence in English-speaking countries.

The primacy of, and the recourse to, the Chinese language and representations of Chineseness would be key to understanding (not necessarily agreeing with) the poetics of exile undergirding the literary modernism of Taiwan, which gradually transitioned to a literature of exile, especially in the wake of its movement phase, that also characterizes modernist writers residing mostly in Taiwan. Among the familiar Euro-American high modernist tenets, the belief in the redeeming powers of literary language—to shore against the inevitable loss brought about by the passing of time, the displacements in space, and all the chaos, fragmentation, and cacophony of modern life—is probably the most well received in Cold War Taiwan, taken to heart by the big-name proponents such as Wang Wen-hsing in his foregrounding of the "reawakened sensitivity toward the ideographic nature of the Chinese language"[48] and passed down to a (dwindling) number of next-generation practitioners like Li Yung-ping and, to some extent, Zhu Tian-wen. The scholarly counterpart along this line is best exemplified by Chien Cheng-chen's apology for Taiwan's modernist literature as that of exile. Invoking the Chinese tradition of intellectual remonstrance, Chien conceives of the exile in spiritual as well as spatial terms, subtly exploring how one can be shaped, intertwined, and reinforced by the other.[49] Those who did not take the route of expatriate writing could still gain the moral high ground of remonstrance, in the form of imagined distance as a result of self-imposed exile, through what Chien valorizes as the aesthetic elevation of language to a totally different realm.[50] What is at stake in this updated account of what became of Cold War modernism in Taiwan is a telling response to yet another seismic political and cultural change in contemporary Taiwan since early 2000s—the speeding up of the decentering of a Sinocentric cultural hegemony in Taiwan that had begun since the lifting of martial law in 1987. As with the varied historical predecessors of exiles Chien's book draws on, ranging from the reclusive hermitage content with the extrication from any implication by the court, to the more extreme case of intervention in Qu Yuan, who remonstrated by drowning himself, such discourses on literary redemption, which is supposed to transcend the vagaries of political realties from which modernist literature exiles itself, tends to undermine itself by uncritically falling back from time to time on one of the conceivable positions in politics at the time—railing against the decentering of Chineseness (which is not the same as its exclusion) in the reconstitution of an emerging collective identity of Taiwan. The often-unexamined oscillations between a transcendence via a seclusive garden created by literature and untouched (or not yet detected?) by the powers that be, and a transcendence by means of interventions in politics that are claimed to be apolitical, I argue, stem from the bifurcated mode of existence and modus operandi of separating the realm of the aesthetic from everything else in life while dictating such distinctions on its own terms, which date back to the Cold War conditions wherein Taiwan's postwar modernism was born and had adapted to and ultimately helped sustain their intricate workings.

NOTES

1. See Shan Te-hsing's book chapter on the magazine *World Today*, which had a larger circulation in Taiwan, and its publisher based in Hong Kong: Shan Te-hsing, *Fanyi yu mailuo* [Translations and Contexts] (Taipei: Bookman, 2009), 117–57. More historical documents and background information on *World Today* can be found on the website hklit.lib.cuhk.edu.hk. For *Reader's Digest*'s role in American Cold War campaigns in Asia, see Christina Kline, *Cold War Orientalism: Asia in the Middlebrow Imagination, 1945–1961* (Oakland: University of California Press, 2003), chap. 2.

2. See, for example, the writer Yin Di's recollections of the appeal of the reading room at USIS Taipei for young intellectuals in 1960s Taiwan, as quoted in Chen Chien-chung, "Meixinchu yu Taiwan wenxueshi zhongxie: Yi meiyuan wenyi tizhi xia de Taigang zazhi chuban wei kaocha zhongxin" ["USIS" and Rewriting the History of Taiwan Literature: A Study on the Publication of Taiwan and Hong Kong's Magazines on US Aids under the Literary & Artistic Institutions], *Guowen xuebao* [Bulletin of Chinese] 52 (December 2012), 212.

3. The once-popular saying, "Come, come to Taida—go, go to America," which is still part of the collective memory of the over-forty generation (or even younger), vividly captures the practices, mentality, set of values, or even worldview for multiple generations of Taiwanese, especially those considered elites of the population by getting into "Taida" (short for National Taiwan University, the top university in Taiwan), thereby being afforded better opportunities to go for advanced studies in the United States or to amass enough capital and resources after graduation from Taida to immigrate to the United States. Although the saying has become less well-known today, with the number of Taiwanese students going to the United States for their undergraduate and graduate degrees steadily declining in the past two decades, this particular memory, along with the catchy phrase, is still invoked from time to time. See, for instance, a very recent mention in a nonacademic book by Lin Chiao-tang, *Jiaru wo shi yi zhi haiyan: Cong rizhi dao jieyan, Taiwan xiandai wu de gushi* [If I Were a Petrel: From Japanese Colonial Period to the Lifting of Martial Law, the Story of Modern Dance in Taiwan] (Taipei: Acropolis, 2020), 156.

4. The United States had attempted to keep Taiwan, or the ROC, in the UN by proposing and unsuccessfully negotiating for a two-Chinas formula before the PRC was voted in. After Nixon's meeting with Mao Zedong, which resulted in the Shanghai Communique, the United States did not immediately agree to switching diplomatic ties to the PRC, and still maintained its defense treaty with Taiwan until it formally established diplomatic relations with China in 1979.

5. Not only is "Beiping" the old name of "Beijing," but Nanjing East Road is located to the north of Beiping Road in Taipei, while geographically Nanjing is to the south of Beijing. Cf. Joseph R. Allen, *Taipei: City of Displacements* (Seattle: University of Washington Press, 2011).

6. Sung-sheng Yvonne Chang, *Modernism and the Nativist Resistance: Contemporary Chinese Fiction from Taiwan* (Durham, NC: Duke University Press, 1993), loc. 266, Kindle.

7. The phrase "return to reality" comes from Hsiau A-chin, capturing his central argument in his book with the same title. See Hsiau A-chin, *Huigui xianshi: Taiwan yijiu qiling niandai de zhanhou shidai yu wenhua zhengzhi bianqian* [Return to Reality: Political and Cultural Change in 1970s Taiwan and the Postwar Generation] (Taipei: Institute of Sociology of Academia Sinica, 2010).

8. Wang Wen-hsing's remarks in a public speech emerged as one of the most high-profile examples of the controversies during the debate period. See Chen Chien-chung, " Meixinchu," 236.

9. This is more noticeable in the trajectories of the modernist poets. See Xie Kun-hua for the down years of *Chuanshijie* with interrupted publications in the mid-1970s: Xie Kun-hua, *Taiwan xiandaishi dianlü yu zhishi diceng de tuiyi: Yi Chuangshiji, Li shishe wei guancha hexin* [The Canonization of Taiwan Modern Poetry and the Alterations of Knowledge-scapes: The Cases of Chuangshiji and Li Poetry Society] (Taipei: Showwe Information, 2013), 36–38.

10. For Wang Wen-hsing's remarks, see Chen Chien-chung, "Meixinchu," 236; see also the following online resource on the debates: "Taiwan xiangtu wenxue lunzhan de qianhou" [An Account of the Debate on Nativist Literature], last modified April 12, 2012, https://historio.asia/1977/10/01/%E5%8F%B0%E7%81%A3%E3%80%8C%E9%84%89%E5%9C%9F%E6%96%87%E5%AD%B8%E3%80%8D%E8%AB%96%E6%88%B0%E7%9A%84%E5%89%8D%E5%89%8D%E5%BE%8C%E5%BE%8C%EF%BC%88%E6%99%82%E9%9B%A8%EF%BC%89; and Yu Kwang-chung, "Lan lai le" [The Wolf Is Here]. *Lianhe bao fukan* [Literary Supplement of the *United Daily News*], August 20, 1977, repr. in Yu Tiancong, Xiangtu wenxue taolun ji [A Collection of Discussions on Nativist Literature] (Taipei: Yuanliu, 1978), 264–67.

11. Sung-sheng Yvonne Chang, *Literary Culture in Taiwan: Martial Law to Market Law* (New York: Columbia University Press, 2004), loc. 2559, Kindle.

12. Ibid. 2518. Although the term "Chinese cultural nationalism" is a fairly generic one, it has a certain timely relevancy to the discussions about the modernists' and their detractors' nuanced versions of China imaginaries. Of course, I will have no space and occasion to elaborate on the 1980s iterations that can be traced back to the modernists.

13. Wang Zhenghe's *Rose, Rose, I Love You* is a prime example of works along this line of literary dissent and critique circa this period.

14. C. T. Hsia, "Obsession with China: The Moral Burden of Modern Chinese Literature (appendix 1)," in *A History of Modern Chinese Fiction, 1917–1957*, 2nd ed. (New Haven, CT: Yale University Press, 1971), 533–54.

15. It has to be pointed out that Wang Wen-hsing has gone against this trend toward more realistic representation of reality and less focus on form. Instead, Wang doubles down and embarks on an even more radical linguistic experimentation than *Family Catastrophe* in his fiction writings into the 1980s, as evidenced by the publication of *Backed against the Sea*.

16. Pai Hsien-yung, *Taipei People*, trans. Hsien-yung Pai and Patia Yasin, ed. George Kao (Hong Kong: The Chinese University of Hong Kong Press, 2000), 386.

17. Ibid., 414.

18. Ibid., 410; original emphasis.

19. See Inderjeet Parmar, *Foundations of the American Century: The Ford, Carnegie, and Rockefeller Foundations in the Rise of American Power* (New York: Columbia University Press, 2012).

20. Pai Hsien-yung, *Taipei People*, 404.

21. Ibid., 402.

22. Ibid., 406.

23. Ibid., 404.

24. Ibid., 396.

25. Ibid., 404.

26. Ibid., 416. The English translation I have been citing up to this point does not render the literal meaning of the Chinese word *guo* (country or nation) in the phrase *huiguo*. I also show the Chinese original because it would be relevant to my discussion here. See, too, Pai Hsien-yung, *Taipei ren* [Taipei People] (Taipei: Elite Books, 1984), 261.

27. Eliott S. T. Shie, "Yujian tazhe—Yu Guangzhong de lümei shizuo yu qi quozu rentong de xingsu" [A Brief Encounter with the Other: Yu Kwang-chung's Poems on the Journey to America and the Formation of National Identity], in *Taiwan wenxue yanjiu xuebao* [Journal of Taiwan Literary Studies], no 11 (October 2010): 113–38.

28. Chien Cheng-chen, *Fangzhu shixue: Taiwan fangzhu wenxue chutan* [The Poetics of Exile: An Inquiry into the Literature of Exile in Taiwan] (Taipei: Unitas, 2003), 34–47.

29. Wang Zhenhe, a couple of years junior to other founding members of *Modern Literature*, did not embark on his studies at the International Writing Program at Iowa until 1972. Pai Hsien-yung got his teaching job as a lecturer of Chinese at UC Santa Barbara the same year he received his MFA from Iowa and held on to this post until retirement, mirroring, in a way, what Wang Wen-hsing did with his first and only academic job at National Taiwan University, the student-writers' alma mater. Ouyang Tzu settled down in Texas following her studies at Iowa's Writer's Workshop and the University of Illinois, while Chen Ruo-xi, who went to the creative writing program at Johns Hopkins University rather than the IWW program like her cohorts did, took much more circuitous routes toward "home," as discussed later in the chapter, before finally settling back in Taiwan in the late 1990s. On the other hand, Leo Ou-fan Lee, Joseph S. M. Lau, and Wai-lim Yip all went for graduate programs of literary studies in the United States instead of those of creative writing and became scholars instrumental to the institutionalization of modernism in Taiwan.

30. See, again, Yin Di's recollections of 1960s Taiwan, quoted in Chen Chien-chung, "Meixinchu," 212.

31. These notable English-language publications include Joseph S. M. Lau, ed., *Chinese Stories from Taiwan, 1960–1970*, foreword by C. T. Hsia (New York: Columbia University Press, 1976); Yip, Wai-lim, *Modern Chinese Poetry: Twenty Poets from the Republic of China, 1955–65* (Iowa City: University of Iowa Press, 1970).

32. Pai Hsien-yung, *Jimo de shiqi sui* [Lonely Seventeen] (Taipei: Asian Culture, 2000), 335–36.

33. "Introduction to *Modern Literature*," trans. Robert E. Hegel, in *The Columbia Sourcebook of Literary Taiwan*, eds. Sung-sheng Yvonne Chang, Michelle Yeh, and Ming-Ju Fang (New York: Columbia University Press, 2014), loc. 4718, Kindle.

34. For the transformation of the "China trope" since the 1970s, see Sung-sheng Yvonne Chang, *Literary Culture*, loc. 2262–2623, Kindle.

35. Xie Kuan-hua, *Zhuanyi xiandaixing: 1960–70 niandai Taiwan xiandaishi changyu zhong de xiandaixing xiangxiang yu zhonggu* [Translating Modernity: The Imagination and Revaluation of Modernity in 1960–1970s' Taiwan Modern Poetry] (Taipei: Taiwan Student Books, 2010), 153; Xie, "Taiwan," 38–43.

36. It has to be pointed out that during the 1960s, Ya Xian, one of the founding members of *Chungshiji*, was the lone exception here, as he went to the International Writing Program at Iowa in 1966 and returned to Taiwan two years later.

37. Without directly mentioning May Fourth, the inaugural editorial of *Modern Literature* invokes Hu Shih, the central figure in the New Cultural Movement that preceded the May Fourth Movement, which was considered by many a radicalization of the former. For the student-writers' conception of their relationship to May Fourth, see Chang, *Modernism*, loc. 722. Throughout her 2004 book, Chang also elaborates on the significances and impacts of May Fourth to some key figures and developments of Taiwan's postwar literature. For similar accounts by modernist poets, see Ya Xian, *Zhongguo xinshi yanjiu* [Studies in Chinese Modern Poetry] (Taipei: Hong Fan, 1981), 3–5; Yu Kwang-chung, "Xia Wusi de banqui" [Lower the May Fourth Banner], in *Xiaoyao you* [The Untrammeled Traveler] (Taipei: Dalin, 1965), 1–4; Xie, *Taiwan*.

38. Chang, *Literary Culture*, loc. 2156.

39. For an insightful comparative inquiry into the incompatibility as well as comparability of the two works, see Margaret Hillenbrand, "Voices of Empire in Dubliners and Taibeiren: Titles, Taiwan and Comparability," in *Comparatizing Taiwan*, eds. Shu-mei Shih and Ping-hui Liao (London: Routledge, 2015), 190–216.

40. The "return" here has to be put between scare quotes because, interestingly, Chen Ruo-xi and Guo Song-feng are both Taiwanese born in Taiwan under Japanese colonial rule, had never been to China, and have no family and relatives who came from or still lived in China, as mainlanders did. Li Yu was born in China but moved to Taiwan with family when she was only five.

41. Chang, *Literary Culture*, loc. 2265.

42. Chen Ruo-xi, "Chen Ruoxi: jianchi wuhui" [Chen Ruo-xi: Regretless Perservance], interview by Su Hui-zhao in *Taiwan Panorama*, January 2011, https://www.taiwan-panorama.com/Articles/Details?Guid=3f6a39fb-2204-4771-8393-40664e9271e4.

43. Such works include Wang Wen-hsing, *Beihai de ren* [Backed against the Sea] (Taipei: Hong Fan, 1981); Li Yung-ping's short stores serialized in a major newspaper since late 1970s and collected in the 1986 volume, *Jiling Chunqiu* [Annals of Ji-ling] (Taipei: Hong Fan, 1986). Guo Song-fen had one of his major works of fiction serialized in a major newpaper in 1984, and Li Yu won her first major literary award in Taiwan in 1983. Pai Hsien-yung's *Crystal Boys*, however, is not as experimental in form as the others, though it certainly is edgy in its unprecedented treatment of

homosexuality in Chinese-language literature; see Pai Hsien-yung, Niezi [Crystal Boys] (Taipei: Vista Publishing, 1984).

44. Wai-lam Yip wrote of these forking paths of homecoming in the preface to his collection of poems published in 1982. Since the hard copy isn't retrievable to me, I consulted the web version of the preface that has been posted on the webpages at the following link, last modified November 16, 2006: http://faculty.ndhu.edu.tw/~e-poem/poemroad/ya-weilian/category/productions/.

45. Luo Fu, *Piao mu* [Driftwood] (Taipei: Unitas, 2001).

46. Yip, "Preface."

47. Ibid.

48. Chang, *Modernism*, loc. 351.

49. Chien, *Fangzhu shixue*, 8–13.

50. Ibid., 15.

Bibliography

Allen, Joseph R. *Taipei: City of Displacements*. Seattle: University of Washington Press, 2012.
Armstrong, Tim. *Modernism: A Cultural History*. Cambridge, UK: Polity, 2005.
———. *Modernism, Technology, and the Body: A Cultural Study*. Cambridge, UK: Cambridge University Press, 2004.
Arnold, A. James. *Modernism and Negritude: The Poetry and Poetics of Aimé Césaire*. Cambridge, MA: Harvard University Press, 1981.
Aubry, Timothy. "'Workshops of Empire,' by Eric Bennett." Review of *Workshops of Empire*, by Eric Bennett. *New York Times*, November 25, 2015. http://nyti.ms/1lKiPqb.
Balcom, John. Introduction to *Death of a Stone Cell*, by Lo Fu, 1–4. Monterey, CA: Taoran Press, 1993.
Barnhisel, Greg. *Cold War Modernists: Art, Literature, and American Cultural Diplomacy*. New York: Columbia University Press, 2015. Kindle.
Begam, Richard, and Michael Valdez Moses, eds. *Modernism and Colonialism: British and Irish Literature, 1899–1939*. Durham, NC: Duke University Press, 2007.
Belletto, Steven. *No Accident, Comrade: Chance and Design in Cold War American Narratives*. Oxford, UK: Oxford University Press, 2014.
Belmonte, Laura A. *Selling the American Way: U.S. Propaganda and the Cold War*. Philadelphia: University of Pennsylvania Press, 2013. Kindle.
Bennett, Eric. "How Iowa Flattened Literature." *The Chronicle of Higher Education*, February 10. 2014. https://www.chronicle.com/article/How-Iowa-Flattened-Literature/144531.
———. *Workshops of Empire: Stegner, Engle, and American Creative Writing during the Cold War*. Iowa City: University of Iowa Press, 2015.
Berry, Michael, and Chien-hsin Tsai, eds. *Chongfan xiandai: Pai Hsien-yung, xiandai wenxue, yu xiandai zhuyi* [Return to the Modern: Pai Hsien-yung, Modern Literature, and Modernism]. Taipei: Rye Field, 2016.
Biers, Katherine. *Virtual Modernism: Writing and Technology in the Progressive Era*. Minneapolis: University of Minnesota Press, 2013.

Buruma, Ian. *Occidentalism: The West in the Eyes of Its Enemies*. 2nd ed. London: Penguin Books, 2005.
Butler, Judith. *Frames of War: When Is Life Grievable*. Brooklyn, NY: Verso, 2016.
Chan, Chi-tak. "Lengzhan jushi xia de Tai Gang xiandaishi yundong: Yi Shang Qin, Luo Fu, Ya Xian, Bai Qiu yu Dai Tian, Ma Jue, Kun Nan, Tsai Yim-pui wei li" [The Modern Poetry Movement in Taiwan and Hong Kong under the Cold War: Taking Shang Qin, Luo Fu, Ya Xian, Bai Qiu and Dai Tian, Ma Jue, Kun Nan, Tsai Yim-pui as Examples]. In *Kuaguo de zhimin jiyi yu lengzhan jingyan: Taiwan wenxue de bijiao wenxue yanjiu* [Transnational Colonial Memory and Cold War Experience: A Comparative Literature Study of Taiwanese Literature], edited by Chien-chung Chen, 409–34. Hsinchu: National Tsing Hua University, 2011.
Chan, Kwok-kou Leonard. "Xianggang wu liushi niandai xiandai zhuyi yundong yu Li Ying-hao de wenxue piping" [Hong Kong Modernist Movement in the 1950s and 1960s and Li Ying-hao's Literary Criticism]. *Chung Wai Literary Monthly* 34, no. 10 (March 2006): 7–42.
Chang, Han-liang. *Bijiao wenxue yu shijian* [Comparative Literature and Practice]. Taipei: The Grand East Book, 1986.
———. "Lun Luo Fu houqi fengge de yanbian" [Comments on the development of the later stage of Luo Fu's style]. *Chung Wai Literary Monthly* 2, no. 5 (October 1973): 62–91.
Chang, Sung-sheng Yvonne. "Building a Modern Institution of Literature: The Case of Taiwan." In *A Companion to Modern Chinese Literature*, edited by Ying-jin Zhang, 116–33. Chichester, UK: Wiley Blackwell, 2016.
———. "Guo Songfen, *Yueyin*, yu ershi shiji zhongye de wenxueshi duanlie" [Guo Songfen, *Yueyin*, and the Rupture in Mid-twentieth-century Literary History]. In *Diyi jie wenhua liudong yu zhishi chuanbo guoji xueshu yentao hui lunwen ji* [Proceedings of The First International Conference on Cultural Mobility and Knowledge Dissemination], edited by Shu-ling Horng and Mei-e Huang, 63–80. Taipei: Showwe Information, 2017.
———. "Introduction: Literary Taiwan—An East Asian Contextual Perspective." In Chang, Sung-sheng, Michelle Yeh, and Ming-Ju Fan, eds. *The Columbia Sourcebook of Literary Taiwan*. Loc. 403–1340. New York: Columbia University Press, 2014.
———. *Literary Culture in Taiwan: Martial Law to Market Law*. New York: Columbia University Press, 2004. Kindle.
———. *Modernism and the Nativist Resistance: Contemporary Chinese Fiction from Taiwan*. Durham, NC: Duke University Press, 1993. Kindle.
———. "Taiwan lengzhan niandai de 'fei changtai' wenxue shengchan" [The "Abnormal" Literary Production during the Cold War in Taiwan]. In *Kuaguo de zhimin jiyi yu lengzhan jingyan: Taiwan wenxue de bijiao wenxue yanjiu* [Transnational Colonial Memory and Cold War Experience: A Comparative Literature Study of Taiwanese Literature], edited by Chien-chung Chen, 17–38. Hsinchu: National Tsing Hua University, 2011.

———. *Taiwan xiandai zhuyi wenxue chaoliu de jueqi* [The Rise of the Modernist Trend in Taiwan]. *Taiwan wenxue xuebao* [Bulletin of Taiwanese Literature] 11 (December 2007): 133–60.

Chang, Sung-sheng, Michelle Yeh, and Ming-Ju Fan, eds. *The Columbia Sourcebook of Literary Taiwan*. New York: Columbia University Press, 2014.

Chang, Su-zhen, "Wuling niandai Taiwan xinwenxue yundong" [The New Literature Movement of Taiwan in the 1950s]. In *Chung Wai Literary Monthly* 14, no. 1 (June 1985): 129–46.

Chao, Ena. "Guancha Meiguo: Taiwan jingying bi xia de Meiguo xingxiang yu jiaoyu jiaohuan jihua (1950–1970)" [Observing America: American Images in Taiwan Elites' Writings and the American Educational Exchange Programs (1950–1970)]. *Taida lishi xuebao* [Historical Inquiry], no. 48 (December 2011): 97–163.

———. "Meiguo zhengfu zai Taiwan de jiaoyu yu wenhua jiaoliu huodong (1951–1970)" [US Educational and Cultural Exchange Programs in Taiwan (1951–1970)]. *Oumei yanjiu* [EuroAmerica: A Journal of European and American Studies] 31, no. 1 (March 2001): 79–127.

Chao, Hsun-ta. *"Wenyi dazhong hua de sanxian jiuge: Taiwan zhishi fenzi de wenhua siwei ji qi jiaoli (1930–1937)"* [The Three Entanglements of "Bungei-Daishuka" in 1930s Taiwan: The Cultural Thoughts and the Contests between the Leftist, the Right and the Neo-Traditionalist]. Taipei: Yuan Liou, 2016.

Chen, Chien-chung. "'Liuwang' zai xianggang: Zhong du Zhang Ai-ling de 'Yangge' yu 'Chidi zhi lian'" ["Exile" in Hong Kong: Rereading Eileen Chang's "The Rice-Sprout Song" and "Naked Earth"]. *Taiwan wenxue yanjiu xuebao* [Journal of Taiwan Literary Studies], no. 13 (October 2011): 275–311.

———. "Meixinchu yu Taiwan wenxueshi zhongxie: Yi meiyuan wenyi tizhi xia de Taigang zazhi chuban wei kaocha zhongxin" ["USIS" and Rewriting the History of Taiwan Literature: A Study on the Publication of Taiwan and Hong Kong's Magazines on US Aids under the Literary & Artistic Institutions]. *Guowen xuebao* [Bulletin of Chinese] 52 (December 2012): 211–42.

Chen, Fang-ming. *Dianfan de zhuiqiu* [The Search for a Paradigm]. Taipei: Unitas, 1994.

———. *Houzhimin Taiwan: Wenxue shilun ji qi zhoubian* [Postcolonial Taiwan: Essays on Taiwanese Literary History and Beyond]. Taipei: Rye Field, 2007.

———. *Jingzi he yingzi* [Mirrors and Shadows]. Taipei: Zhi Wen, 1993.

———. *Shi he xianshi* [Poetry and Reality]. Taipei: Hong Fan, 1993.

———. *Taiwan xin wenxue shi* [A History of Modern Taiwanese Literature]. Taipei: Linking, 2011.

———. *Xiandai zhuyi ji qi buman* [Modernism and Its Discontents]. Taipei: Linking, 2013.

Chen, I-chih. *Shengna: Taiwan xiandai zhuyi shixue liubian* [Sonar: The Evolution of Taiwanese Modernist Poetry]. Taipei: Chiu Ko, 2006.

———. *Xiandai shiren jiegou* [Structures of Modern Poets]. Taipei: Unitas, 2010.

Chen, Kang-fen. *Shi yuyan de meixue geming: Taiwan wuling liuling niandai xinshi lunzhan yu xiandai guiji* [The Aesthetic Revolution of Poetry: Debates and

Trajectories of Modern Chinese Poetry in Taiwan from the 1950s to 1960s]. Taipei: Wanjuanlou, 2018.

Chen, Ke-hua. *Xingqiu jishi* [Notes on the Planets]. Taipei: China Times, 1987.

Chen, Li. *Qinmi shu: Chen Li shixuan (1974–1992)* [Intimate Letters: Selected Poems of Chen Li (1974–1992)]. Taipei: Bookman, 1992.

Chen, Ruo-xi. "Chen Ruoxi: jianchi wuhui" [Chen Ruo-xi: Regretless Perseverance]. Interview by Su Hui-zhao. In *Taiwan Panorama*, January 2011. https://www.taiwan-panorama.com/Articles/Details?Guid=3f6a39fb-2204-4771-8393-40664e9271e4.

Chen Ruo-xi zixuan ji [Self-Selected Works of Chen Ruo-xi]. Taipei: Linking, 1982.

———. *Jianchi wuhui: Chen Ruo-xi qishi zishu* [Regretless Perseverance: Chen Ruo-xi's Memoir of Seventy Years]. Taipei: Chiu Ko, 2008.

Chen, Xiaomei. *Occidentalism: A Theory of Counter-Discourse in Post-Mao China*. 2nd ed. Lanham, MD: Rowman & Littlefield, 2003.

Cheng, Ming-li. "Dangdai Taiwan wenyi zhengce de fazhan, yingxiang yu jiantao" [The Development, Influence and Critique of the Cultural Policies of Contemporary Taiwan]. In *Dangdai Taiwan zhengzi wenxue lun* [Politics and Literature in Contemporary Taiwan], 13–68. Taipei: China Times, 1994.

Chien, Cheng-chen. *Fangzhu shixue: Taiwan fangzhu wenxue chutan* [The Poetics of Exile: An Inquiry into the Literature of Exile in Taiwan]. Taipei: Unitas, 2003.

———. "Luo Fu zuopin de yixiang shijie" [The World of Images in Luo Fu's Works]. In *Luo Fu shishi zhi siwang ji xiangguan zhongyao pinglun* [Luo Fu's Death of a Stone Cell: The Text and Important Critical Essays], edited by Ji-liang Hou, 204–46. Taipei: Han Guang Culture, 1988.

———. *Shixin yu shixue* [The Essence of Poetry and Poetics]. Taipei: Bookman, 1999.

———. *Taiwan xiandaishi meixue* [The Aesthetics of Taiwanese Modern Poetry]. Taipei: Yang-Chih, 2004.

———. *Yuyan yu wenxue kongjian* [Languages and Literature Space]. Taipei: Han Guang Culture, 1989.

Chiu, Kuei-fen. "Cong zhanhou chuqi nüzuojia de chuangzuo tan Taiwan wenxueshi de xushu" [History Writing and Women's Literature in the Early Postwar Period]. In *Chung Wai Literary Monthly* 29, no. 2 (July 2000): 313–35.

———. "Zaidixing de shengcheng: Cong Taiwan xiandai pai xiaoshuo tan gen yu lujing de bianzheng" [Cultural Translation and the Production of Local Sensibility in Taiwan Modernist Fiction]. In *Chung Wai Literary Monthly* 34, no. 10 (May 2006): 125–54.

Chou, Wan-yao. *A New Illustrated History of Taiwan*. Translated by Carole Plackitt and Tim Casey. Taipei: SMC, 2015.

Chou, Ying-hsiung, and Joyce C. H. Liu, eds. *Shuxie Taiwan: Wenxue shi, hou zhimin yu hou xiandai* [Writing Taiwan: Literary History, Postcolonial and Postmodern]. Taipei: Rye Field, 1999.

Chu, Tien. *Hongqiao yu jiquang: Ji Xian, Qin Zi-hao, Lin Heng-tai shixue lilun zhong di xiangzheng yu xiandai* [Rainbow Bridge and Aurora: Symbol and Modernity in the Poetic Theory of Ji Xian, Qin Zi-hao, and Lin Heng-tai]. Taipei: Showwe Information, 2018.

"Chuangshiji de luxiang—dai fakan ci" [The Path Forward for The Epoch Poetry Quarterly—in Place of a Founding Statement]. *Chuangshiji* [The Epoch Poetry Quarterly] 1 (October 1954): 2–3.
Comaroff, Jean, and John L. Comaroff. *Theory from the South: Or, How Euro-America Is Evolving Toward Africa*. London: Routledge, 2016.
Dana, Robert. *A Community of Writers: Paul Engle and the Iowa Writers' Workshop*. Iowa City: University of Iowa Press, 1999.
"Editorial." *Chuangshiji* [The Epoch Poetry Quarterly] 2 (February 1955): 33.
———. *Chuangshiji* [The Epoch Poetry Quarterly] 4 (October 1955): 2.
"Fakan ci" [Introduction to *Modern Literature*]. *Xiandai wenxue* [Modern Literature] 1 (March 1960): 2.
Fang, Ming. *Dahe de duihua: Luo Fu fangtan lu* [Dialogues of the Rivers: Interviews with Luo Fu]. Taipei: Lan Tai, 2010.
Feng, De-ping. "Jingshen yu fengge de zhanxian: Wenxue zazhi de zhuanti sheji" [The Display of Spirit and Style: Thematic Design of Literary Magazines]. *Wenhsun*, no. 27 (December 1986): 94–101.
Gordimer, Nadine. *The Pickup: A Novel*. London: Bloomsbury, 2014.
Guan, Jie-ming. "Zhongguo xiandaishi de kunjing" [The Dilemma of Modern Chinese Poetry]. In *Xiandai wenxue de kaocha* [The investigation of Modern Literature], edited by Zhi-ti Zhao, translated by Jing Xiang, 137–42. Taipei: Vista Publishing, 1976.
Guo, Cheng-yi. *Shiren de zuoye* [The Tasks of Poets]. Taipei: Showwe Information, 2011.
Hillenbrand, Margaret. *Literature, Modernity, and the Practice of Resistance: Japanese and Taiwanese Fiction, 1960–1990*. Leiden: Brill, 2007.
———. "Voices of Empire in *Dubliners* and *Taibeiren*: Titles, Taiwan and Comparability." In *Comparatizing Taiwan*, edited by Shu-mei Shih and Ping-hui Liao, 190–216. London: Routledge, 2015.
Hong Kong Literature Database. Accessed March 17, 2022. https://hklit.lib.cuhk.edu.hk.
Horng, Shu-ling. "Yue hua xiandaishi zhong de zhanzheng shuxie yu lisan xushu: Jian yu Taiwan shiren Luo Fu 'Xigong shi chao' de duizhao" [War Writing and Diaspora Narrative of Modern Chinese Poetry in Vietnam: A Contrast with Taiwanese poet Luo Fu's "Saigon"]. In *Diyi jie wenhua liudong yu zhishi chuanbo guoji xueshu yentao hui lunwen ji* [Proceedings of The First International Conference on Cultural Mobility and Knowledge Dissemination], edited by Shu-ling Horng and Mei-e Huang, 423–66. Taipei: Showwe Information, 2017.
Hoskins, Janet, and Viet Thanh Nguyen, eds. *Transpacific Studies: Framing an Emerging Field*. Honolulu: University of Hawaii Press, 2014.
Hou, Ji-liang, ed. *Luo Fu shishi zhi siwang ji xiangguan zhongyao pinglun* [Luo Fu's Death of a Stone Cell: The Text and Important Critical Essays]. Taipei: Han Guang Culture, 1988.
Hou, Tzuoh-jen. *Ziyou zhuyi chuantong yu Taiwan xiandai zhuyi wenxue de jueqi* [The Search of the Relations between the Tradition of Liberalism and the Rising

of the Taiwanese Modernistic Literature]. PhD diss., Chinese Culture University, 2003.
Hsi, Mi (Michelle Yeh). *Taiwan xiandaishi lun* [Reflections on Taiwan's Modern Poetry]. Hong Kong: Cosmos Books, 2009.
Hsia, C. T. *A History of Modern Chinese Fiction, 1917–1957*. New Haven, CT: Yale University Press, 1961.
———. "Obsession with China: The Moral Burden of Modern Chinese Literature (appendix 1)." In *A History of Modern Chinese Fiction, 1917–1957*, 2nd ed., 533–54. New Haven, CT: Yale University Press, 1971.
Hsia, C. T., ed. *Twentieth-century Chinese Stories*. New York: Columbia University Press, 1971.
Hsia, Wan-yun. *Taiwan shiren de qiu yu tao: Yi Shang Qin, Su Shao-lian, Tang Juan wei li*. [Captivity and Escape of Taiwanese Poets: Shang Qin, Su Shao-lian, and Tang Juan as Examples]. Taipei: Elite Books, 2015.
Hsiao, Li-Chun. "Far-fetched Lands: The Caribbean, Taiwan and Submarine Relations." In *Comparatizing Taiwan*, edited by Shu-mei Shih and Ping-hui Liao, 145–65. London: Routledge, 2015.
———. "Piping de changshi / changshi de piping: lilun, changshi yu gaige" [Theoretical Thinking on the Fault Lines of Theory, Commonsense, and Reform]. *Chung Wai Literary Quarterly* 43, no. 1 (March 2014): 15–58.
Hsiau, A-chin. *Huigui xianshi: Taiwan yijiu qiling niandai de zhanhou shidai yu wenhua zhengzhi bianqian* [Return to Reality: Political and Cultural Change in 1970s Taiwan and the Postwar Generation]. Taipei: Institute of Sociology of Academia Sinica, 2010.
Hsu, Chun-ya. "Huishou hua dangnian (xia): lun Xia Ji-an yu *wenxue zazhi*" [Talking about the Past in Retrospect (Part Two): On Xia Ji-an and *Literary Review*]. *Huawen wenxue* [Chinese Literature] 54 (January 2003): 55–64.
Hun, Se Wook. *Xinshilun* [On New Poetry]. Taipei: Sanmin, 1998.
Ing Chang, Nancy. *New Voices: Stories and Poems by Young Chinese Writers*. Taipei: Heritage Press, 1961.
"Introduction to *Modern Literature*." In *The Columbia Sourcebook of Literary Taiwan*, edited by Sung-sheng Yvonne Chang, Michelle Yeh, and Ming-Ju Fang, translated by Robert E. Hegel, Loc. 4691–4718. New York: Columbia University Press, 2014. Kindle.
Jameson, Fredric. "Third-World Literature in the Era of Multinational Capital." *Social Text* 15 (Fall 1986): 65–88.
———. "Modernism and Imperialism." In Jameson, Fredric, Edward Said, and Terry Eagleton. *Nationalism, Colonialism, and Literature*, 43–66. Minneapolis: University of Minnesota Press, 1990.
Ji, Xian. "Bu shi ganyan" [Not a Sentimental Statement: On the Occasion of Our Journal's Sixth Anniversary]. *Xiandaishi* [Modern Poetry Quarterly] 23 (March 1959): 1.
———. "Declaration." Translated by Paul Manfredi. In *The Columbia Sourcebook of Literary Taiwan*, edited by Sung-sheng Yvonne Chang, Michelle Yeh, and Ming-Ju Fang. Loc. 4054–71. New York: Columbia University Press, 2014. Kindle.

———. "Dui 'suowei xiandai pai' yiwen zhi dafu" [A Response to the Essay "The So-called Modernist School"]. *Xiandaishi* [Modern Poetry Quarterly] 14 (April 1956): 70–73.

———. "Editorial." *Xiandaishi* [Modern Poetry Quarterly] 11 (Autumn 1955).

———. "Explicating the Tenets of the Modernist School." Translated by Paul Manfredi. In *The Columbia Sourcebook of Literary Taiwan*, edited by Sung-sheng Yvonne Chang, Michelle Yeh, and Ming-Ju Fang. Loc. 4158–96. New York: Columbia University Press, 2014. Kindle.

———. *Ji xian shi bacui* [The Essential Ji Xian]. Taipei: Chiu Ko, 2002.

———. "Xiandai pai xintiao shiyi" [Explicating the Tenets of the Modernist School]. In *Xiandaishi* [Modern Poetry Quarterly] 13 (February 1956).

———. *Yuzhou shichao* [Poetry of the Universe]. Taipei: Bookman, 2001.

———. *Zai feiyang de shidai* [In the Soaring Age]. Taipei: Baodao Wenyi, 1951.

"Jianli xin minzu shixing zhi chuyi" [A Proposal to Establish the New National Poetic Paradigm]. *Chuangshiji* [The Epoch Poetry Quarterly] 5 (March 1956): 2.

Kent, Alicia A. *African, Native, and Jewish American Literature and the Reshaping of Modernism*. Basingstoke, UK: Palgrave Macmillan, 2007.

Klein, Christina. *Cold War Orientalism: Asia in the Middlebrow Imagination, 1945–1961*. Oakland: University of California Press, 2003.

Kuo, Wen-hua. "Meiyuan xia de weisheng zhengce: 1960 niandai Taiwan jiating jihua de tantao" [Politicizing Family Planning and Medicalizing Reproductive Bodies: US Backed Population Control in 1960s Taiwan]. *Taiwan shehui yanjiu jikan* [Taiwan: A Radical Quarterly in Social Studies], no. 32 (December 1998): 39–82.

Latham, Michael E. *Modernization as Ideology: American Social Science and "Nation Building" in the Kennedy Era*. Chapel Hill: The University of North Carolina Press, 2000.

Lau, Joseph S. M., ed. *Chinese Stories from Taiwan, 1960–1970*. Foreword by C. T. Hsia. New York: Columbia University Press, 1976.

Lee, Pamela M. *Think Tank Aesthetics: Midcentury Modernism, the Cold War, and the Neoliberal Present*. Cambridge, MA: The MIT Press, 2020. Kindle.

Lepore, Jill. *If Then: How the Simulmatics Corporation Invented the Future*. 2nd ed. New York: Liveright, 2020.

Li, Min-yong. *Zhanhou Taiwan xiandaishi fengjing: Shuangchong gouzao de jingshen shi* [The Landscape of Taiwanese Postwar Modern Poetry: A Dual-Structural History of the Spirit]. Taipei: Chiu Ko, 2019.

Li, Rui-teng. *Shixin yu shishi* [Poetic Heart and History of Poetry]. Taipei: Showwe Information, 2016.

Li, Xiaobing. *The Cold War in East Asia*. 2nd ed. London: Routledge, 2017.

Li, Ying-hao. "Lun Luo Fu shishi zi siwang" [On Luo Fu's *Death of a Stone Cell*]. In *Luo Fu shishi zhi siwang ji xiangguan zhongyao pinglun* [Luo Fu's Death of a Stone Cell: The Text and Important Critical Essays], edited by Ji-liang Hou, 72–90. Taipei: Han Guang Culture, 1988.

Li, Yung-ping. *Jiling Chunqiu* [Annals of Ji-ling]. Taipei: Hong Fan, 1986.

Lin, Chiao-tang. *Jiaru wo shi yi zhi haiyan: Cong rizhi dao jieyan, Taiwan xiandai wu de gushi* [If I Were a Petrel: From Japanese Colonial Period to the Lifting of Martial Law, the Story of Modern Dance in Taiwan]. Taipei: Acropolis, 2020.

Lin, Heng-tai. "Bi 'Xiandaipai' geng 'Xiandaipai'—guanyu 'Chuangshiji'" [More Modernist than the Modernists—On Chuangshiji]. In *China Times Express*, May 31, 1992.

———. "Da sheng de xiefa" [Mahayana Mode of Writing]. In *Luo Fu shishi zhi siwang ji xiangguan zhongyao pinglun* [Luo Fu's Death of a Stone Cell: The Text and Important Critical Essays], edited by Ji-liang Hou, 92–103. Taipei: Han Guang Culture, 1988.

———. "Guanyu xiandai pai" [About the Modernist School]. *Xiandaishi* [Modern Poetry Quarterly] 17 (March 1957): 32–34.

———. *Lin Heng-tai quanji* [The Collected Works of Lin Heng-tai], edited by Heng-chhiong Li. Vol. 4. Chuanghua: Changhua County Cultural Affairs Bureau, 1998.

———. "Xinshi de zai geming" [The Second Revolution of Modern Poetry]. In *Lin Heng-tai quanji* [The Collected Works of Lin Heng-tai], edited by Heng-chhiong Li. Vol. 5. Changhua: Changhua County Cultural Affairs Bureau, 1998.

Lin, Hsiao-ting. *Accidental State: Chiang Kai-Shek, the United States, and the Making of Taiwan*. Cambridge, MA: Harvard University Press, 2016. Kindle.

Lin, Nikki Jin-li. "Lengzhan yishi xingtai yu xiandai zhuyi de wenhua xiangxiang: yi zhanhou Taiwan yu Zhongguo de xiandaishi lunshu wei guancha zhongxin" [Cold War Ideology and Modernism's Cultural Imaginations: Observations on the Discourse of Modern Chinese Poetry in Post-war Taiwan and China]. *Chung Wai Literary Quarterly* 46, no. 2 (June 2017): 119–60.

———. "Xin piping yu xiandaishi: Yi Yen Yuang-su wei jujiao" [New Criticism and Taiwan Modernist Poetry: The Case of Yen Yuang-su]. *Taiwan wenxue yanjiu jikan* [NTU Studies in Taiwan Literature], no. 15 (February 2014): 123–53.

———. "'Ziwo' yu 'dazhong' de bianzheng: Yi xiandaishi lunzhan wei guancha zhongxin" [The Dialectics between "the Self" and "the People": The Discussion on the Modern Poetry Polemic]. In *Taiwan xuezhi* [Monumenta Taiwanica], no. 6 (October 2012): 27–52.

Lin, Rui-ming. "Taiwan wenxueshi nienbiao" [Timeline of Taiwanese Literature]. In Shih-tao Yeh. *Taiwan wenxue shigang* [History of Taiwanese Literature], 181–352. Kaohsiung: Wenxue Jie Magazine, 1987.

Liou, Liang-ya. "The Ambivalence toward the Mythic and the Modern: Wu Mingyi's Short Stories." In *Tamkang Review* 39, no. 1 (December 2008): 97–124.

Liu, Joyce C. H. *Guer, Nüshen, Fumian shuxie: Wenhua fuhao de zhengzhuang shi yuedu* [Orphan, Goddess, and the Writing of the Negative: The Performance of Our Symptoms]. Taipei: New Century, 2000.

———. "The Importance of Being Perverse: China and Taiwan, 1931–1937." In *Writing Taiwan: A New Literary History*, edited by David Der-wei Wang and Carlos Rojas, loc. 93–112. Durham, NC: Duke University Press, 2007. Kindle.

———. *Xinzhi tuopu: 1895 shijian hou de lunli zhonggou* [The Topology of Psyche: The Post-1895 Reconstruction of Ethics]. Taipei: Flâneur Culture Lab, 2010.

Liu, Nai-ci. *Shehua meixue: Taiwan dangdai wenxue shengchan* [Over-Luxuriance Aesthetics: A Reproduction of Contemporary Taiwanese Literature]. Taipei: Socio, 2015.

Liu, Yi-hung. "The World Comes to Iowa in the Cold War: International Writing Program and the Translation of Mao Zedong." In *American Quarterly* 69, no. 3 (September 2017): 611–31.

Liu, Zhi-hong. *Shi-yi: Yijiu wuling liuling niandai Taiwan junlü shige kongjian shuxie* [Poems, Wars: Spatial Writing in Taiwanese Wartime Poetry in the 1950s and the 1960s]. Taipei: Showwe Information, 2017.

Liu, Zheng-zhong (Tang Juan). *Junlü shiren de yiduan xingge: Yi wuliushi niandai de Luo Fu, Shang Qin, Ya Xian weizhu* [The Poets as Soldiers and Their Heretical Inclination: Luo Fu, Shang Qin, Ya Xian in the 1950s and the 1960s]. PhD diss., National Taiwan University, 2001.

———. "Junlü shiren de shuli xintai: Yi wuliulshi niandai de Luo Fu, Shang Qin, Ya Xian weizhu" [The Sense of Alienation in the Poets as Soldiers: Luo Fu, Shang Qin, Ya Xian and Others in the 1950s and the 1960s]. In *Taiwan wenxue xuebao* [Bulletin of Taiwanese Literature] 2 (February 2001): 113–56.

———. "Zhuzhi, chao xianshi, xiandai pai yundong: Taiwan, 1956–1969" [Intellectualism, Surrealism, and the Modernist Movement: Taiwan, 1956–1969]. In *Ji Xian*, edited by Wen-wei Shiu. Vol. 9 of *Taiwan xiandangdai zuojia yanjiu ziliao huibian* [Compilation of Research Materials of Modern and Contemporary Taiwanese Writers], edited by Te-ping Feng, 135–62. Tainan: National Museum of Taiwan Literature, 2011.

Lo, Fu (Luo Fu). *Death of a Stone Cell*. Translated by John Balcom. Monterey, CA: Taoran Press, 1993.

———. *Stone Cell*. Translated by John Balcom. Brookline, MA: Zephyr Press, 2012.

Luo, Fu (Lo Fu). "Houji: Shishi zl siwang zai tansuo" [Afterword: Revisiting Death of a Stone Cell]. In *Shishi zi siwang* [Death of a Stone Cell], 118–33. Taipei: Unitas, 2016.

———. *Mo ge* [Magical Songs]. Taipei: Baksik Publishing, 2018.

———. *Piao mu* [Driftwood]. Taipei: Unitas, 2001.

———. "Qi ying" [An Abandoned Infant]. In *Chuangshiji* [The Epoch Poetry Quarterly] 5 (March 1956): 12.

———. "Shiren zi jing" [The Poet's Mirror]. In *Shishi zi siwang* [Death of a Stone Cell], 10–48. Taipei: Unitas, 2016.

———. *Shishi zi siwang* [Death of a Stone Cell]. Taipei: Unitas, 2016.

———. "Shitan chunqiu shanshi nian" [Poetry Scene of the Last Thirty Years]. In *Chung Wai Literary Monthly* 10, no. 12 (May 1982): 6–31.

———. "'Tianlangxing' lun" [A Commentary on Yu Kwang-chung's "Sirius"]. In *Xiandai Wenxue* [Modern Literature], no. 9 (July 1961): 77–92.

———. "Weilou" [Rickety Buildings]. In *Chuangshiji* [The Epoch Poetry Quarterly] 5 (March 1956): 13.

Lu, Cheng-hui. "Xiandai zhuyi zai Taiwan: Cong wenyi shehuixue de jiaodu lai kaocha" [Modernism in Taiwan: From the Perspective of Literary Sociology]. In

Taiwan shehui yenjiu jikan [Taiwan: A Radical Quarterly in Social Studies] 1, no. 4 (Winter 1988): 181–210.
Lupke, Christopher. "Xia Ji'an's (T. A. Hsia) Critical Bridge to Modernism in Taiwan." In *Journal of Modern Literature in Chinese* 4.1 (July 2000): 35–63.
Lyon, Janet. *Manifestoes: Provocations of the Modern.* Ithaca, NY: Cornell University Press, 1999.
Man, Simeon. *Soldiering through Empire: Race and the Making of the Decolonizing Pacific.* Oakland: University of California Press, 2018.
McCarthy, Richard M. Interview by Jack O'Brien. December 28, 1988. The Association for Diplomatic Studies and Training Foreign Affairs Oral History Project Information Series. Arlington, VA.
Mei, Chia-ling. "Zhandou wenyi yu shengyin zhengzhi: *Dagongbao Zhanxian* yu wuling niandai Taiwan de langsongshi" [Public Report: *Battlelines* and Recited Poetry in Taiwan in the 1950s]. In *Zhongguo wenxue xuebao* [Journal of Chinese Literature] 3 (December 2012): 39–59.
———. "*Zhongwai wenxue* yu zhongguo/taiwan wenxue yanjiu: yi xueyuan pai wenxue zazhi wei shijiao de kaocha" [*Chung Wai Literary Monthly* and the Studies of Chinese/Taiwan Literature: An Investigation from the Perspective of "Academic Literary Journals"]. In *Chung Wai Literary Monthly* 41, no. 4 (December 2012): 143–76.
Menand, Louis. *The Free World: Art and Thought in the Cold War.* New York: Farrar, Straus and Giroux, 2021. Kindle.
Nieh, Hua-ling. *Eight Stories by Chinese Women.* Taipei: Heritage Press, 1962.
Nü Jing Shih She. *Shitan xianying* [The Appearing Shadows of Poetry]. Taipei: Bookman, 1999.
Nye, Joseph S., Jr. *Soft Power: The Means to Success in World Politics.* New York: PublicAffairs, 2005. Kindle.
Osgood, Kenneth. *Total Cold War: Eisenhower's Secret Propaganda Battle at Home and Abroad.* Lawrence: University Press of Kansas, 2006.
Ouyang, Tzu. *Wangxie tangqian de yanzi: Taibeiren shangxi* [Swallows in Front of the Old Wang-Xie Buildings: An Analysis of *Taipei People*]. Taipei: Elite Books, 2008.
Oyen, Meredith. "Communism, Containment and the Chinese Overseas." In *The Cold War in Asia: The Battle for Hearts and Minds*, edited by Yangwen Zheng, Hong Liu, and Michael Szonyi, 59–93. Leiden: Brill, 2010.
Pai, Hsien-yung. *Jimo de shiqi sui* [Lonely Seventeen]. Taipei: Asian Culture, 2000.
———. *Niezi* [Crystal Boys]. Taipei: Vista Publishing, 1984.
———. *Taipei People.* Translated by Hsien-yung Pai and Patia Yasin. Edited by George Kao. Hong Kong: The Chinese University of Hong Kong Press, 2000.
———. *Taipei ren* [Taipei People]. Taipei: Elite Books, 1984.
Parmar, Inderjeet. *Foundations of the American Century: The Ford, Carnegie, and Rockefeller Foundations in the Rise of American Power.* New York: Columbia University Press, 2012.
Patke, Rajeev S. *Modernist Literature and Postcolonial Studies.* Edinburgh, UK: Edinburgh University Press, 2013.

Pavlić, Edward M. *Crossroads Modernism: Descent and Emergence in African-American Literary Culture*. Minneapolis: University of Minnesota Press, 2002.

Rancière, Jacques. *Aesthetics and Its Discontents*. Cambridge, UK: Polity, 2009.

———. *Aisthesis: Scenes from the Aesthetic Regime of Art*. Translated by Zakir Paul. London: Verso, 2013.

———. *Dissensus: On Politics and Aesthetics*. Edited and Translated by Steven Corcoran. London: Bloomsbury Academic, 2010.

———. *The Politics of Aesthetics: The Distribution of the Sensible*. Translated by Gabriel Rockhill. London: Continuum, 2004.

Saunders, Frances Stonor. *The Cultural Cold War: The CIA and the World of Arts and Letters*. London: The New Press, 1999.

Scandura, Jani, and Michael Thurston, eds. *Modernism, Inc.: Body, Memory, Capital*. New York: New York University Press, 2001.

Schedler, Christopher. *Border Modernism: Intercultural Readings in American Literary Modernism*. New York: Routledge, 2002.

Shan, Te-hsing. *Fanyi yu mailuo* [Translations and Contexts]. Taipei: Bookman, 2009.

Shan, Te-hsing, Yu-cheng Lee, Li Chang, and Shi-qing Lin. *Chu Li-min xiansheng fangwen jilu* [Interviews with Mr. Limin Chu]. Taipei: Institute of Modern History of Academia Sinica, 1996.

Shang, Qin. *Shang Qin shi quanji* [The Collected Poetry of Shang Qin]. Taipei: Ink, 2009.

Shen, Shuang. "Empire of Information: The Asia Foundation's Network and Chinese-Language Cultural Production in Hong Kong and Southeast Asia." In *American Quarterly* 69, no. 3 (September 2017): 589–610.

Shie, Eliott S. T. "Yujian tazhe—Yu Guangzhong de lümei shizuo yu qi quozu rentong de xingsu" [A Brief Encounter with the Other: Yu Kwang-chung's Poems on the Journey to America and the Formation of National Identity]. In *Taiwan wenxue yanjiu xuebao* [Journal of Taiwan Literary Studies], no 11 (October 2010): 113–38.

Shih, Shu-mei. *The Lure of the Modern: Writing Modernism in Semi-colonial China, 1917–1937*. Oakland: University of California Press, 2001.

———. *Visuality and Identity: Sinophone Articulations across the Pacific*. Oakland: University of California Press, 2007.

———. *Fan lisan: Huayu yuxi yanjiu lun* [Against Diaspora: Discourses on Sinophone Studies]. Taipei: Linking, 2017.

Taiwanese Literature], edited by Chien-chung Chen, 17–38. Hsinchu: National Tsing Hua University, 2011.

Siraganian, Lisa. *Modernism's Other Work: The Art Object's Political Life*. Oxford, UK: Oxford University Press, 2012.

Slater, Dan, and Joseph Wong. "The Strength to Concede: Ruling Parties and Democratization in Developmental Asia." In *Perspectives on Politics* 11, no. 3 (September 2013): 717–33.

Somigli, Luca. *Legitimizing the Artist: Manifesto Writing and European Modernism 1885–1915*. Toronto: University of Toronto Press, 2004.

Soto, Michael. *The Modernist Nation: Generation, Renaissance, and Twentieth-Century American Literature*. Tuscaloosa: The University of Alabama Press, 2004.

Su, Hui-chao. "No Regrets: Author Lucy Chen Reflects on an Extraordinary Life." In *Taiwan Panorama*, January 2011, https://www.taiwan-panorama.com/Articles/Details?Guid=91d948d5-2006-4877-84c3-7f1079724a8f&langId=3&CatId=7.

Suárez, Juan A. *Pop Modernism: Noise and the Reinvention of the Everyday*. Urbana: University of Illinois Press, 2007.

Suri, Jeremi. *Power and Protest: Global Revolution and the Rise of Détente*. Cambridge, MA: Harvard University Press, 2005.

Szonyi, Michael. *Cold War Island: Quemoy on the Frontline*. Cambridge, UK: Cambridge University Press, 2008.

Szonyi, Michael, and Hong Liu. "Introduction: New Approaches to the Study of the Cold War in Asia." In *The Cold War in Asia: The Battle for Hearts and Minds*, edited by Yangwen Zheng, Hong Liu, and Michael Szonyi, 1–11. Leiden, Netherlands: Brill, 2010.

"Taiwan xiangtu wenxue lunzhan de qianhou" [An Account of the Debate on Nativist Literature]. Last modified April 12, 2012. https://historio.asia/1977/10/01/%E5%8F%B0%E7%81%A3%E3%80%8C%E9%84%89%E5%9C%9F%E6%96%87%E5%AD%B8%E3%80%8D%E8%AB%96%E6%88%B0%E7%9A%84%E5%89%8D%E5%89%8D%E5%BE%8C%E5%BE%8C%EF%BC%88%E6%99%82%E9%9B%A8%EF%BC%89.

Tang, Juan (Liu Zheng-zhong). "Tianlang reng zai guangnian wai haojiao" [Sirius Is Still Howling Light-Years Away]. In *Wenhsun* 387 (January 2018): 55–58.

Tang, Wen-biao. "Jiangbi de xiandaishi" [Stiff Modern Poetry]. *Chung Wai Literary Monthly* 2, no. 3 (August 1973): 18–20.

———. "Ri zhi xi yi: 'Pingyuan ji mu' xu" [At Dusk: Foreword to "Overlook a Plain"]. *Chung Wai Literary Monthly* 2, no. 4 (September 1973): 86–99.

Tate, Allen. *Essays of Four Decades*. Wilmington, DE: Intercollegiate Studies Institute, 2001.

Ting, Wei-jen. *Zhanhou Taiwan xiandaishi shilun* [Essays on the History of Taiwanese Postwar Modern Poetry]. Taipei: Press Store, 2008.

———. *Zhanhou Taiwan xiandaishi de yanbian yu tezhi* [The Evolution Characteristics of Taiwanese Postwar Modern Poetry]. Taipei: Indepen Unique, 2012.

Trask, Michael. *Cruising Modernism: Class and Sexuality in American Lit Social Thought*. Ithaca, NY: Cornell University Press, 2003.

Tsai, Ming-yen. "Yijiu wuling niandai Taiwan xiandaishi de jige mianxiang" [On Some Facets of Taiwan Modern Poetics in the 1950s]. In *Taiwan wenxue yanjiu xuebao* [Journal of Taiwan Literary Studies], no. 11 (October 2010): 89–112.

———. "Yijiu wuling niandai Taiwan xiandaishi de yuanyuan yu fazhan" [The Origins and Development of Taiwan Modern Poetics in the 1950s]. PhD diss., National Tsing Hua University, 2008.

———. "Zhanhou chuqi Taiwan xinshi de zhonggou: Yi yinlinghui he 'chaoliu' wei kaocha" [The Reconstruction of Taiwan New Poetry in the Early Postwar Period: A Case Study of Ginreikai and "Trend"]. In *Taiwan wenxue yanjiu xuebao* [Journal of Taiwan Literary Studies], no. 20 (April 2015): 41–71.

Tsai, Pei-jun. *Shi di xinshi: Li Min-yong* [The Messenger of Poetry: Li Min-yong]. Taipei: Artco Books, 2010.

Tsai, Shih-shan Henry. *Maritime Taiwan: Historical Encounters with the East and the West*. Armonk, NY: M. E. Sharpe, 2009.

Tseng, Ping-tsang. "Meiguo de ziwei: Lengzhan qianqi Taiwan de kekoukele jinling yu xiaofei (1950–1967)" [Taste of USA: Prohibition and Consumption of Coca-Cola in Taiwan (1950–1967)]. In *Taiwan shi yanjiu* [Taiwan Historical Research] 26, no. 2 (June 2019): 113–50.

Tu, Kuo-ching. *Taiwan wenxue yu shihua wenxue* [Taiwan Literature and World Literatures of Chinese]. Taipei: National Taiwan University Press, 2015.

Végső, Roland. *The Naked Communist: Cold War Modernism and the Politics of Popular Culture*. New York: Fordham University Press, 2013.

Wagnleitner, Reinhold. *Coca-Colonization and the Cold War: The Cultural Mission of the United States and Austria After the Second World War*. 2nd ed. Chapel Hill: University of North Carolina Press, 2007.

Walhout, Mark. "The New Criticism and the Crisis of American Liberalism: The Poetics of the Cold War." In *College English* 49, no. 8 (December 1987): 861–71.

Wallerstein, Immanuel. "What Cold War in Asia: An Interpretative Essay." In *The Cold War in Asia: The Battle for Hearts and Minds*, edited by Yangwen Zheng, Hong Liu, and Michael Szonyi, 13–24. Leiden: Brill, 2010.

Wang, Chih-ming. "Lengzhan renwen zhuyi: Yan Yuan-shu ji qi piping shijian" [Cold War Humanism: Yan Yuan-shu and His Critical Practices]. In *Chung Wai Literary Quarterly* 43, no. 1 (March 2014): 121–68.

———. *Transpacific Articulations: Student Migration and the Remaking of Asian America*. Honolulu: University of Hawaii Press, 2013. Kindle.

Wang, Jing. "Taiwan Hsinag-t'u Literature: Perspectives in the Evolution of a Literary Movement." In *Chinese Fiction from Taiwan: Critical Perspectives*, edited by Jeannette L. Faurot, 43–70. Bloomington: Indiana University Press, 1980.

Wang, Mei-hsiang. "Buwei renzhi de Zhang Ai-ling: Meiguo xinwenchu yishu jihua xia de Yangge yu Chidi zhi lian" [Eileen Chang—The Unknown Story: *The Rice-Sprout Song* and *the Naked Earth* under the USIS Book Translation Program]. In *Oumei yanjiu* [EuroAmerica: A Journal of European and American Studies] 45, no. 1 (March 2015): 73–137.

———. "Lengzhan shidai de Taiwan wenxue waiyi: Meiguo xinwenchu yishu jihua de yunzuo (1952–1962)" [Translating Taiwan Literature into Foreign Languages in the Cold War Era: The Operation of USIS Book Translation Program (1952–1962)]. In *Taiwan wenxue yanjiu xuebao* [Journal of Taiwan Literary Studies], no. 19 (October 2014): 223–54.

———. "Meiyuan wenyi tizhi xia de Wenxue zazhi yu Xiandai wenxue" [*Literary Review* and *Modern Literature* under the US Aid Literary Institution]. In *Taiwan wenxue xuebao* [Bulletin of Taiwanese Literature] 25 (December 2014): 69–100.

———. "Wenxue quanli yu lengzhan shiqi Meiguo zai tai gang de wenxue xuanchuan (1950–1962)" [Literature, Power and American Propaganda in Hong Kong and Taiwan during the Cold War (1950–1962)]. *Taiwanese Journal of Sociology*, no. 57 (September 2015): 1–51.

———. "Yinbi quan li: Meiyuan wenyi tizhi xia de tai gang wenxue (1950–1962)" [Unattributed Power: Taiwan and Hong Kong Literature under the US Aid Literary Institution]. PhD diss., National Tsing Hua University, 2015.

Wang, Wen-hsing. *Family Catastrophe: A Modernist Novel*. Translated by Susan Wan Dolling. Honolulu: University of Hawaii Press, 1995.

———. *Beihai de ren* [Backed Against the Sea]. Taipei: Hong Fan, 1981.

Wen, Xin-ying. *Jingji qiji de beihou: Taiwan meiyuan jingyan de zhengjing fenxi (1951–1965)* [Behind the Economic Miracle: A Political and Economic Analysis of US Aid Experience in Taiwan (1951–1965)]. Taipei: Zili Evening News, 1990.

Westad, Odd Arne. Introduction to *Reviewing the Cold War: Approaches, Interpretations, Theory*, edited by Arne Odd Westad, 1–26. London: Frank Cass, 2000.

———. *The Cold War: A World History*. New York: Basic Books, 2017.

———. *The Global Cold War*. Cambridge: Cambridge University Press, 2005.

Winckler, Edwin A. "Cultural Policy on Postwar Taiwan." In *Cultural Change in Postwar Taiwan*, edited by Stevan Harrell and Huang Chün-chieh, 22–46. Boulder, CO: Westview Press, 1994.

Wu, Chia-rong. *Supernatural Sinophone Taiwan and Beyond*. Amherst, NY: Cambria Press, 2016.

Wu, Lucian (Lu-chin). *Didiao qiantan—xiasan huasi ji* [Low-key Recital: Miscellaneous Works]. Taipei: Chiu Ko, 2006.

———, ed. *New Chinese Writing*. Taipei: Heritage Press, 1962.

Wu, Sheng. "Meng jian Ya Xian" [Dreaming of Ya Xian]. Last modified October 22, 2014. https://okapi.books.com.tw/article/3212.

Wu, Tsong-min. "Meiyuan yu Taiwan de jingji fazhan" [US Aid and the Economic Development of Taiwan]. In *Taiwan shehui yanjiu jikan* [Taiwan: A Radical Quarterly in Social Studies] 1, no. 1 (February 1988): 145–58.

Xia, Ji-an (T. A. Hsia). "To the Reader." In *The Columbia Sourcebook of Literary Taiwan*, edited by Sung-sheng Yvonne Chang, Michelle Yeh, and Ming-Ju Fang; translated by Christopher Lupke. Loc. 4201–4219. New York: Columbia University Press, 2014. Kindle.

Xiang, Yang. "Wuling niandai Taiwan xiandaishi fengchao shilun" [On the Trends of Taiwanese Modern Poetry in the Fifties]. In *Jingyi renwen xuebao* [Journal of Humanities] 11 (July 1999): 45–61.

Xie, Kun-hua. *Taiwan xiandaishi dianlü yu zhishi diceng de tuiyi: Yi Chuangshiji, Li shishe wei guancha hexin* [The Canonization of Taiwan Modern Poetry and the Alterations of Knowledge-scapes: The Cases of *Chuangshiji* and *Li* Poetry Society]. Taipei: Showwe Information, 2013.

———. *Zhuanyi xiandaixing: 1960–70 niandai Taiwan xiandaishi changyu zhong de xiandaixing xiangxiang yu zhonggu* [Translating Modernity: The Imagination and Revaluation of Modernity in 1960–1970s' Taiwan Modern Poetry]. Taipei: Taiwan Student Books, 2010.

Ya, Xian. "Chuangshiji de piping xingge" [The Critical Natural of Genesis]. In *Chuangshiji sishi nian pinglun xuan* [The Collected Reviews of Genesis in Forty Years], edited by Ya Xian and Cheng-chen Chien, 355–60. Taipei: *Chuangshiji* magazine, 1994.

———. *Ya Xian shiji* [The Collected Poetry of Ya Xian]. Taipei: Hong Fan, 2010.

———. *Zhongguo xinshi yanjiu* [Studies in Chinese Modern Poetry]. Taipei: Hong Fan, 1981.

Yan, Yuan-shu. "Tang Wen-biao shijian" [Tang Wen-biao Incident]. In *Chung Wai Literary Monthly* 2, no. 5 (October 1973): 4–8.

———. "Xi du Luo Fu de liang shou shi" [Close Readings of Two of Luo Fu's Poems]. In *Chung Wai Literary Monthly* 1, no. 1 (June 1972): 118–34.

Yang, Chia-hsien. "Luyishi (Ji Xian) zai lunxian qi Shanghai de huodong: Yi Shi lingtu wei zhongxin de kaocha" [A Litterateur in Japanese-Occupied Shanghai: Lu Yishi (Ji Xian) and His Journal *Shilingtu*]. In *Taiwan wenxue yanjiu xuebao* [Journal of Taiwan Literary Studies], no. 11 (October 2010): 45–88.

Yang, Tsui-hua. "Meiyuan dui Taiwan de weisheng jihua yu yiliao tizhi zhi xingsu" [US Aid in the Formation of Health Planning and the Medical System in Taiwan]. In *Jindaishi yanjiusuo jikan* [Bulletin of the Institute of Modern History Academia Sinica], no. 62 (December 2018): 91–139.

Yang, Tsung-han. "Duanjie qi Taiwan xinshi shi" [The History of Taiwan Modern Poetry in the Welding Period]. In *Taiwan shixue xuekan* [Bulletin of Taiwanese Poetics] 5 (June 2005): 37–106.

———. *Taiwan xinshi pinglun: Lishi yu zhuanxing* [Criticism on Taiwanese Modern Poetry: History and Transformation]. Taipei: Independent & Unique, 2012.

———. "Wenxue zazhi yu Taiwan xiandaishi shi" [*Literary Review* and History of Modern Taiwan Poetry]. *Taiwan wenxue xuebao* [Bulletin of Taiwanese Literature] 2 (February 2001): 158–77.

———. *Yiyu: Xiandaishi yu wenxue shilun* [Heterogeneous Words: Essays on Modern Poetry and Literary History]. Taipei: Showwe Information, 2017.

———. "Zhonghua 'Xiandai': Ji Xian, xiandaishi yu xiandaixing" [Nativizing Modernity: Ji Xian, Modern Poetry and Modernity]. In *Chung Wai Literary Monthly* 30, no. 1 (June 2001): 65–83.

Ye, Shan. "Xiandaishi huigu zhuanhao" [Introduction to the Special Issue on the History of Modern Poetry]. In *Xiandai Wenxue* [Modern Literature], no. 46 (March 1972): 9.

Yeh, Michelle (Hsi Mi). "Modern Poetry in Chinese: Challenges and Contingencies." In *A Companion to Modern Chinese Literature*, edited by Yingjin Zhang, 149–66. Chichester, UK: Wiley Blackwell, 2016.

———. "'On Our Destitute Dinner Table': *Modern Poetry Quarterly* in the 1950s." In *Writing Taiwan: A New Literary History*, edited by David Der-wei Wang and Carlos Rojas. Loc. 2331–801. Durham, NC: Duke University Press, 2007. Kindle.

Yeh, Michelle, N. G. D. Malmqvist, and Xu Huizhi, eds. *Sailing to Formosa: A Poetic Companion to Taiwan*. Seattle: University of Washington Press. 2006.

Yeh, Shih-tao. *Taiwan wenxue shigang* [History of Taiwanese Literature]. Kaohsiung: *Wenxue Jie* magazine, 1987.

Ying, Feng-huang. *Huashuo 1950 niandai Taiwan wenxue* [An Illustrated History of 1950s Taiwanese Literature]. Taipei: Vista Publishing, 2017.

Yip, Wai-lim. *Modern Chinese Poetry: Twenty Poets from the Republic of China, 1955–65*. Iowa City: University of Iowa Press, 1970.

———. "Preface." Last modified November 16, 2006. http://faculty.ndhu.edu.tw/~e-poem/poemroad/ya-weilian/category/productions/.

———. "Taiwan wushi niandai mo dao qishi niandai chu liangzhong wenhua cuowei de xiandaishi" [Two Modernist Poetries in the Period between Mid-1950's and mid-1970's in Taiwan]. In *Taiwan wenxue yanjiu jikan* [NTU Studies in Taiwan Literature], no. 2 (November 2006): 129–63.

Yoneyama, Lisa. *Cold War Ruins: Transpacific Critique of American Justice and Japanese War Crimes*. Durham, NC: Duke University Press, 2016.

Yu, Kwang-chung. "Lan lai le" [The Wolf Is Here]. In *Lianhe bao fukan* [Literary Supplement of the *United Daily News*], August 20, 1977. Reprinted in Yu Tiancong, *Xiangtu wenxue taolun ji* [A Collection of Discussions on Nativist Literature], 264–67. Taipei: Yuanliu, 1978.

———. *Tianlangxing* [Sirius]. Taipei: Hong Fan, 2008.

———. "Xia Wusi de banqui" [Lower the May Fourth Banner]. In *Xiaoyao you* [The Untrammeled Traveler], 1–4. Taipei: Dalin, 1965.

———. *Zai lengzhan de niandai* [In the Cold War Era]. Taipei: Chiu Ko, 2019.

Yu, Kwang-chung, trans. *New Chinese Poetry*. Taipei: Heritage Press, 1960.

Yu, Sheng-kuan. "Zhuanxiang ji yishupai fandong de chunxenxue lun: Taiwan wenyi lianmeng luxian zhi zheng" ["Conversion" and the Reactionary Literature Viewpoint of Pure Aesthetic: A Debate between Progressive and Conservative Forces in Taiwanese Cultural Association on the Peak of Japanese Fascism in 1930s." In *Taiwan wenxue yanjiu xuebao* [Journal of Taiwan Literary Studies], no. 11 (October 2010): 257–94.

Zhang, Muo. "Bianjiren shouji" [Editor's Notes]. In *Chuangshiji* [The Epoch Poetry Quarterly] 11 (April 1959): 36.

———. "Cong 'Ling he' dao 'Mo ge' (zhai lu)" [From "Spiritual River" to "Magical Song" (extract)]. In *Luo Fu shishi zhi siwang ji xiangguan zhongyao pinglun* [Luo Fu's Death of a Stone Cell: The Text and Important Critical Essays], edited by Ji-liang Hou, 162–68. Taipei: Han Guang Culture, 1988.

Zhu, Shuang-yi. "Youguan Taiwan xiandai zhuyi wenxue de chengyin he pingjia de zhuzhong shuofa bianxi" [An Analysis of Different Accounts of the Genesis and

Evaluation of miTaiwanese Modernist Literature]. In *Diyi jie wenhua liudong yu zhishi chuanbo guoji xueshu yentao hui lunwen ji* [Proceedings of The First International Conference on Cultural Mobility and Knowledge Dissemination], edited by Shu-ling Horng and Mei-e Huang, 81–126. Taipei: Showwe Information, 2017.

Index

American dream, 11, 122, 129
"An Abandoned Infant" (Luo Fu), 45
Anticommunism, xiii, 10, 19–23, 29, 41, 43, 46, 47, 53, 73, 75, 102–04. *See also* patriotism
Armstrong, Tim, xiii
art for art's sake, 22, 41, 50, 94, 99
autonomy, artistic, 41, 43–44, 46, 53, 95, 97–99, 100, 103–04, 109

Backed against the Sea (*Beihai de jen*) (Wang Wen-hsing), 134
Barnhisel, Greg, 1–2, 4–5, 12, 19–21
Baudelaire, Charles, xi, 47
Bennet, Eric, 2, 12
Breton, André, 46

Camus, Albert, 92
Chan, K. K. Leonard, 71
Chang, Eileen, 110
Chang, Han-liang, 68, 69, 77
Chang, Sung-sheng Yvonne, 4, 50, 96, 109, 126
Chen, Chien-chung, 11, 93
Chen, Fang-ming, 72, 74
Chen, Ruo-xi, 113n2, 141, 142, 148n29, 149n40
Chen, Yi-chih, 51
Chiang, Ching-kuo, 55n9

Chiang, Kai-shek, 17, 21, 22, 72, 79, 84n38, 96, 98, 112. *See also* Nationalist government
Chien, Cheng-chen, 13, 145
China imaginary, 13, 122–26, 135, 141
Chinese Civil War, xiii, 3, 20, 41, 65, 127
Chinese Communist Party, 41, 102
Chu, Hsi-ning, 78, 79
Chu, Limin, 110–11
Chuangshiji (The Epoch Poetry Journal), 36n39, 39–53, 62, 64, 78, 89, 138; "A Proposal to Establish the New National Poetic Paradigm," 42–43, 48
Chung Wai Literary Monthly, 68
chunwenxue (pure literature), 50, 51, 53, 72, 73, 98, 109, 143
classical Chinese poetry, 24–26, 27
Cold War, xiii–xiv, 8–9, 29–30, 102; paradoxes of, 1, 23, 30–31
Cold War modernism in Taiwan, xii–xiii, 2–3, 10–11, 18–23, 53, 61–62, 89–90; antiestablishment character of, 4, 10, 11, 23–27, 52–53, 72–75, 77, 89, 91, 112–13; and appropriation, 45–48; beginnings of, 17–31; bifurcation in, 10, 23, 40, 44, 47–48, 69–70, 78, 145; conformism

of, 23–24; contexts of, 4–6, 20, 29–30, 40–41, 65–66, 69–71, 76, 111–12, 142–43; and elitism, 26, 39, 77, 95, 100, 106; as escapism, 72–73; and exile, 8–9, 13–14, 121–23, 133, 134, 139–45; experimentation of, 24, 40, 44, 46–47, 52–53, 66, 76, 94; institutionalization of, 4–6, 11, 13–14, 74–81, 125, 136; and interiority, 64, 66–69, 70–74, 125; and mobilization, 29–31, 52–53; and modernization, 28–29, 47, 49, 51, 53; moderation of, 27–28, 40, 43–44, 48, 53, 64, 75, 93, 95, 97–98, 112–13, 137, 139, 141; and nationalism, 40, 42–44, 126, 133, 136, 141–42, 143–44; paradoxes of, 27, 40, 70; and poetic purity, 41, 43–44, 49, 65; professionalism of, 26, 68, 95; and propaganda, 28, 41, 49, 53, 95, 96; reformism of, 12, 13, 138; and traditionalism, 5, 13, 94, 137, 139
combat literature (*zhandou wenyi*), 10, 21, 27, 40, 43, 46, 53, 78, 93, 96, 97; combat poet (*zhandou shiren*), 42; combat poetry (*zhandou shi*), 41, 44, 51, 78, 126
Confucianism, 43
Crescent Moon School (*Xinyueh pai*), 25, 35n39
Crystal Boys (*Niezi*) (Pai Hsien-yung), 91, 150n43
Cultural Revolution, 141, 142
culture of US aids, 5, 9, 11–13, 105–13, 121–23

Dadaism, xi
Dai, Tien, 113n2
"Death in Chicago" (Pai Hsien-yung), 137
Death of a Stone Cell (*Shishi zhi siwang*) (Luo Fu), 7, 10, 45–46, 52, 61–77, 134; difficulty of, 62–63, 64–65, 71; radicality of, 76–77; and referentiality, 63–65, 71, 76; and war, 71
debates (*lunzhan*): on Modern Poetry (*xiandaishi lunzhan*), 77, 125; on Nativist literature (*xiangtu wenxue lunzhan*), 77, 125; on New Poetry (*xinshi lunzhan*), 48–49
Department of Foreign Languages and Literature (*waiwenxi*), 6, 12
Department of Foreign Languages and Literature at National Taiwan University (*Taida waiwenxi*), 6, 7, 11, 12, 68, 91, 99, 110
diaspora, Chinese, 102, 107, 112
Driftwood (*Piao mu*) (Luo Fu), 143
Duan, Cai-hua, 78, 79

Engle, Paul, 110
existentialism, 46, 63, 64–65, 67, 70

Family Catastrophe (Wang Wen-hsing), 91, 109, 138
February 28 Incident, 20
Foucault, Michel, 79
Free China, 42, 105, 113, 123–27, 133
Free China Review (*Ziyou Zongguo*), 53, 57n42, 84n38, 96–99, 103, 110, 112, 126
freedom, artistic, xiv, 8, 10, 62, 75, 143

Guo, Song-fen, 141, 142, 149n40

Hillenbrand, Margaret, 112–13
Hsi, Mi, 40, 46. *See also* Yeh, Michelle
Hsia, C. T., 118n65, 126
Hsia, T. A. (Xia Ji-an), 92–95, 99–105, 106, 108–09, 129
Hu, Shih, 96, 110
Huang, He-sheng, 32n7, 49, 57n37

International Writing Program at the University of Iowa (IWPI), 9, 12, 99, 110, 129
IWPI. *See* International Writing Program at the University of Iowa

IWW. *See* University of Iowa's Writers' Workshop

James, Henry, 92
Ji Xian, xii, xiii, 8, 9, 18, 22, 23, 24, 26–27, 28–29, 39, 41, 47, 48, 49, 50, 51, 78, 91, 93, 126, 140; "Explicating the Tenets of the Modernist School," 19, 22, 28–29; manifesto on modern poetry, xi–xiii, 9–10, 17–22, 24, 26–27, 28, 30, 48
Joyce, James, 139

KMT. *See* Nationalist government
Korean War, 17, 21, 96
Kuomintang government. *See* Nationalist government

Lanxing (Blue Star) Society, 35n39, 44, 48, 94
Lau, Joseph S. M., 113n2, 119n71, 136, 148n29
Laughlin, James, 21
Lee, Leo Ou-fan, 113n2, 119n71, 136, 148n29
Lei, Zheng, 84n38, 96
Li, Ying-hao, 65, 67, 69, 71
Li, Yu, 141, 142, 149n40
Li, Yung-ping, 145, 149n43
liberalism, 53, 95–99
Lin, Heng-tai, 32n11, 50, 51, 66, 72, 74, 76
Lin, Zong-yuan, 57n37
Literary Review (*Wenxue zazhi*), 92–109; "To The Reader," 93; and realism, 93–94; and traditionalism, 94
Literary Star (*Wenxing*), 53
literary supplementary pages (*fukan*), 49, 59n59
Literature and Art in the Military (*Junzhong wenyi*), 41
Liu, Zheng-zhong, 22, 23, 50
Luo, Fu (Lo Fu), 7, 10, 40, 41, 43, 44, 45, 46, 52, 61–81, 110, 121, 134, 140, 143; poetry as revenge against reality, 10, 65, 74

Magical Songs (*Mo ge*) (Luo Fu), 68
Mao, Zedong, 146n4
martial law, xii, 3, 21, 79, 121, 124, 126, 145
May Fourth Movement, xii, 25, 92, 127, 133, 139, 141
McCarthy, Richard, 100, 109–10
modern Chinese (*baihuawen*), 24–26
modernist school (*xiandai pai*), 17, 39–40
modernism: afterlife of, 18; characteristics of, 2, 3, 19, 95; contextualization of, xii; Euro-American, 5, 7, 9, 18, 19, 26, 29, 44, 47, 64, 90, 91, 94, 144; origin of, xi–xii; transnational, 18; utopian impulses of, xii, xiii
Modern Literature (*Xiandai wenxue*), 4, 6, 7, 11, 90–91, 92, 99, 103, 105–10, 115, 135, 141, 143
Modern Poetry (*xiandaishi*), 40
Modern Poetry Quarterly (*Xiandai shi*), 18–19, 22, 23, 24–25, 40, 49, 50, 51

Nationalist government, xii, xiii, 3, 8, 17, 20–23, 30, 32n13, 41, 48, 49–50, 61, 73, 79, 93, 95, 97–113, 121, 123–25, 134; censorship in, 20, 21, 29, 53, 98–99, 104; cultural policies of, 21–22
Nativist literature (*xiangtu wenxue*), 69, 72, 77, 125, 126, 140
New Chinese Poetry, 110
New Criticism, 6, 7, 67–68, 71, 73, 75, 76, 94, 108
New Poetry (*xinshi*), 24, 40
New Poetry Weekly, 22
new regulated verse (*xin gelushi*), 25
Nie, Hua-ling, 110
Nixon, Richard, 123
nostalgia, 21, 23

Ouyang, Tzu, 92, 110, 113n2, 148n29

Pai, Hsien-yung, 7, 13, 79, 90, 92, 110, 113n2, 126, 127, 130, 136, 137, 139–40, 141, 148n29
patriotism, xiii, 10, 19, 20–23, 41, 43, 46, 50, 112, 139. *See also* anticommunism
Perspectives USA, 21
"The Poet's Mirror" (Luo Fu), 52, 64
PRC. *See* Chinese Communist Party
proletariat literature (*gong nong bing wenxue*), 77, 125

Qin, Zhihao, 35n39, 48, 49, 57n38
Qu, Yuan, 145
Quemoy (Jinmen), 8, 17, 20, 63–64, 65, 70

Rancière, Jacques, xiv
Republic of China. *See* Nationalist government
"Rickety Buildings" (Luo Fu), 45
ROC. *See* Nationalist government

sentimentalism, 25, 26, 92
Shang, Qin, 40, 44, 52, 78
Shui, Yin-ping (Yang Chi-chiang), 58n45
Sima, Zhong-yuan, 78
Sino-Japanese War, 127
soldier-poets, 9–10, 39–53, 64, 69–70, 73–75, 78, 126, 138, 143
soldier-writers, 2, 4, 7–8, 10–11, 41, 78–81; covert power structure of, 79–81. *See also* soldier-poets
Soupault, Philippe, 51
Student Review (*Xuesheng yingwen zazhi*), 101
Su, Xue-lin, 57n38
surrealism, xi, 41, 42–53, 63, 64, 67, 75, 77

Taipei People (*Taibei ren*) (Pai Hsien-yung), 13, 127, 133, 136–37; "Wandering in a Garden, Waking from a Dream," 138; "Winter Night," 13, 127–33, 135, 140
Taoism, 43
Tsai, Ming-yen, 64, 66, 94

United Daily (*Lianhe bao*), 79
United Nations, 123
United States Information Agency (USIA), 9, 11, 100, 101, 102
United States Information Service (USIS) in Taipei, 9, 11, 12, 99–111, 121
University of Iowa's Writers' Workshop (IWW), 12, 99, 108, 110, 134
US aids (*meiyuan*), 5, 9, 11–13, 17, 21, 50, 98–113, 134; and literary establishment (*wenyitizhi*), 11–12, 92–93, 99–105, 108, 111–12, 129–30
USIA. *See* United States Information Agency
USIS. *See* United States Information Service

Végső, Roland, 2
Vietnam War, 65

Wang, Mei-hsiang, 99, 105
Wang, Wen-hsing, 90, 91, 109, 110, 113n2, 125, 134, 135, 138, 140, 145, 148n29
Wang, Zhenhe, 135, 147n13, 148n29
Woolf, Virginia, xi
World War II, 3
Wu, Lu-qin (Lucian), 100, 101, 108
Wu, Sheng, 87n55

Xie, Kun-hua, 30, 51, 75
Xu, Zhimo, 25

Ya, Xian, 40, 44, 46, 52, 59n59, 78, 79, 140, 149n36
Yan, Yuan-shu, 68, 72, 77, 79; "Close Readings of Two of Luo Fu's Poems," 68

Ye, Shan (Yang Mu), 83n26
Yeh, Michelle, 23, 24, 26. *See also* Hsi, Mi
Yin, Di, 146n2
Yin, Hai-Kuang, 84n38
Yip, Wai-lim, 113n7, 114n7, 119n71, 136, 143, 144, 148n29
Youth Literary (*Youshi wenyi*), 79
Youth Warrior Daily (*Qingnian zhanshi bau*), 41
Yu, Kwang-chung, 49, 77, 94, 110, 125, 134–39

Zhang, Muo, 40, 41, 56n28, 58n49, 78, 85n47
Zhu, Tian-wen, 145

About the Author

Dr. Li-Chun Hsiao studied comparative literature at the University at Buffalo (State University of New York), specializing in postcolonial studies, literary and cultural theories, Taiwan literature and culture, and anglophone Caribbean literatures. Having taught at National Taiwan University, Hsiao is currently a professor at Waseda University in Tokyo, teaching at its School of International Liberal Studies, as well as its Graduate School of International Culture and Communication Studies. Previously, he was editor in chief of *Chung Wai Literary Quarterly*, served on the editorial board of *Concentric: Literary and Cultural Studies*, and he has been a visiting scholar at Hitotsubashi University in Tokyo and at UCLA. Hsiao is the author of the monograph *The Indivisible Globe, the Indissoluble Nation: Universality, Postcoloniality, and Nationalism in the Age of Globalization* (ibidem Press, 2021). He edited, introduced, and contributed a chapter for *"This Shipwreck of Fragments": Historical Memory, Imaginary Identities, and Postcolonial Geography in Caribbean Culture and Literature* (Cambridge Scholars Publishing, 2009), and he has book chapters collected in the edited volumes *Representing Humanity in an Age of Terror* (Purdue UP, 2010), *Comparatizing Taiwan* (Routledge, 2015), and *Keywords of Taiwan Theory* (Unitas 2019). Among other journals, his papers have been published by *Critical Arts* (2020), *Chungwai Literary Quarterly* (2014), *Concentric: Literary and Cultural Studies* (2010), *CLCWeb: Comparative Literature and Culture* (2009), and *M/MLA Journal* (2008).

www.ingramcontent.com/pod-product-compliance
Lightning Source LLC
Chambersburg PA
CBHW020122010526
44115CB00008B/935